49.95

INDUSTRIAL AND ORGANIZATIONAL PSYCHOLOGY SERIES

Editors

Cary L. Cooper

Neil Schmitt

The Union and Its Members

A Psychological Approach

Julian Barling

Clive Fullagar

E. Kevin Kelloway

New York   Oxford
OXFORD UNIVERSITY PRESS
1992

Oxford University Press

Oxford   New York   Toronto
Delhi   Bombay   Calcutta   Madras   Karachi
Singapore   Hong Kong   Tokyo
Nairobi   Dar es Salaam   Cape Town
Melbourne   Auckland

and associated companies in
Berlin   Ibadan

Copyright © 1992 by Oxford University Press, Inc.

Published by Oxford University Press, Inc.
200 Madison Avenue, New York, New York 10016

Oxford is a registered trademark of Oxford University Press

Library of Congress Cataloging-in-Publication Data
Barling, Julian.
The union and its members: a psychological approach/
Julian Barling, Clive Fullagar, E. Kevin Kelloway.
p. cm.—(Industrial and organizational psychology series)
Includes bibliographical references and index.
ISBN 0-19-507336-3
1. Trade-unions—Psychological aspects.
2. Psychology, Industrial.
3. Organizational behavior.
I. Fullagar, Clive.
II. Kelloway, E. Kevin.
III. Title.
IV. Series.
HD6490.P78B37   1992
158.7—dc20
91-25183

2 4 6 8 9 7 5 3 1

Typeset by Thomson Press (India) Ltd., New Delhi, India
Printed in the United States of America
on acid-free paper

Preface

The writing of this book has grown out of, and has helped us to refine, several shared convictions about organizational psychology, about unions, and about the need to combine the two. First, we share a mutual concern that organizational psychology, as it is currently taught and practiced, effectively ignores the role of unions in shaping organizational behavior. In perpetuating this situation, the risk of developing and disseminating a truncated body of knowledge about organizational psychology looms large. Second, we believe that unions in themselves are fascinating organizations to study. The very nature of unions as democratic organizations that operate in the economic marketplace provides a unique setting in which to evaluate theoretical propositions of organizational psychology. Moreover, union membership gives rise to a unique set of attitudes and behaviors that are worthy of study. Third, we are convinced that the study of unions from the standpoint of organizational psychology offers considerable benefits to both parties. In this sense, the theories and methods of organizational psychology may assist labor organizations in achieving their goals. Similarly, the study of unions has the potential to advance theorizing in organizational psychology.

Developing and refining these convictions has lead us to the belief that the relationship between the union and its members is a logical focus for behavioral investigations. A primary aim in writing this book is to apply the knowledge base of organizational psychology to an understanding of the unionization process. We employ the term "unionization process" advisedly. While "unionization" is commonly used to described the decision to vote for, or join the union, we explicitly reject this limited definition. Rather, we hold that unionization is a *process* that begins well before a certification campaign (e.g., through early family socialization) and continues long after an individual has joined the union. In this view, the development of general and specific union attitudes and commitment to the union, the decision to participate in union activities, and, ultimately, the decision to retain or discontinue union membership (whether through the collective act of decertifying the union or individually resigning from the union) are all vital components of the unionization process. Of equal importance is the decision by some members to assume a formal leadership position within the union, and the effects of their leadership behavior on the attitudes and behaviors of other rank-and-file members.

For too long, both unions and organizational psychology have been ill served by the ongoing relationship of mutual neglect. Neither the study of organizational psychology nor unions can afford to ignore each other any longer. The knowledge base of organizational psychology is well suited to furthering our understanding of unions. Likewise, with their unique characteristics of democracy, conflict, and voluntary participation, unions provide an ideal setting for theory testing for organizational psychology. Thus, substantial benefits to both parties will accrue from a more informed and equitable exchange. It is our hope that this book advances the understanding of the unionization process in its broadest context, and contributes to the developing interaction between unions and organized psychology.

Acknowledgments

One of the lessons learned in writing a book of this nature is the extent to which the completion of our tasks and projects depends on those around us. This book is no exception, and we acknowledge the diverse contributions that others have made. First, the financial support of the Social Sciences and Humanities Research Council of Canada (to Julian Barling and E. Kevin Kelloway) is gratefully acknowledged. Second, in their different ways, Valerie Angus, Steve Bluen, Julie Chatterton, and Karyl MacEwen helped us to see the project through to completion. Third, we would like to acknowledge the influence of Michael E. Gordon. More than any other person, his courage, and, yes, commitment in legitimizing unions as a valid focus for organizational psychology and his intellectual contributions made it that much easier for us to approach this topic. Lastly, we acknowledge the support of our wives, Janice, Dorothy, and Debra, and our children, Seth, Monique, Megan, James, and Thomas.

Kingston, Ont.   J. B.
Manhattan, Kan.   C. F.
Guelph, Ont.   E. K. K.

Contents

The Union and its Members

1

Organizational Psychology and Unions

Unions are fascinating organizations and contrary to what the prophets of doom would have us believe, they will not vanish in the near future. (Klandermans, 1986, p. 199)

In this statement Klandermans (1986) articulates two critical assumptions for anyone interested in organizational functioning and unions. First, Klandermans reminds us that in and of themselves, unions are interesting, if not intriguing organizations. Second, despite pessimistic predictions to the contrary, Klandermans asserts that unions will be with us for a long time. We accept that Klandermans is correct on both accounts, and this raises an intriguing paradox for anyone studying organizational behavior, industrial relations, or both: Simply stated, organizational psychology has treated unions as both uninteresting and unimportant. At the same time, scholars of industrial relations have not looked to organizational psychology to further their understanding. As Strauss (1979, pp. 391–392) noted so cogently over a decade ago:

> IR scholars have almost actively rejected psychological contributions; psychologists (with a few distinguished exceptions) have displayed little understanding of the institutional peculiarities of IR. Thus the institutional naivete of most psychological studies is matched only by the psychological naivete of IR analysis. Put another way, IR scholars too often view industrial relations as a unique institution regarding which lessons from other spheres of life are almost irrelevant; by contrast, psychologists tend to view industrial relations as mostly interpersonal relations, ignoring its institutional setting.

This argument is easy to sustain. Social scientists who have chosen to comment on the relationship between organizational psychology and unions invariably describe this relationship as one of indifference at best, and neglect or animosity at worst (Fullagar, 1984; Gordon & Burt, 1981; Huszczo, Wiggins, & Currie, 1984; Rosen & Stagner, 1981; Shostak, 1964). During the 1980s, there was some awareness that these two disciplines could learn from and contribute to an understanding of each other. For example, several major journals devoted

3

special sections (*American Psychologist*, 1984; *Journal of Occupational Psychology*, 1986) or special editions (*International Review of Applied Psychology*, 1981) to the interdependence of organizational psychology and industrial relations or unions. However, while some rapprochement may be emerging between organizational psychology and unions, considerable distance still needs to be covered. The general aim of this book is to show how a knowledge of organizational behavior and unions can be strengthened by an understanding of both.

Some Effects of Unions

If union membership was (1) infrequent and (2) exerted no effects on organizational functioning, the neglect of unions in the study of organizational functioning would be of no conceptual or practical consequence. We argue, however, that union membership certainly does make a difference. The extent to which this is true can be gauged from both the extent and the effects of union membership. Let us focus first on the extent of union membership. While it is certainly true that the proportion of unionized employees in the private sector in the United States has decreased virtually every year since 1980, public sector unionism has increased, and the absolute number of unionized employees is substantial: Even at its lowest level, close to 17 million employees in the United States were unionized (Kumar, Coates, & Arrowsmith, 1987). During the same period, other countries such as Canada witnessed a growth in union membership (see Table 1.1). While the absolute number of union members in Canada and the European countries is certainly lower than that in the United States, the proportion of their workforce that is unionized remains significant. Moreover, it is the aim of most labor organizations to continually increase the extent of their coverage.

Of course, focusing only on the *extent* of union membership could provide a misleading picture: For example, union membership status could be unrelated, or even negatively related to organizational functioning. It is thus important

TABLE 1.1   Union Membership of Labor Organizations in Selected Countries as a Percentage of Total Wage and Salary Earners[a]

Country	1961	1971	1981	1983	1984	1985	1986
Australia	59	53	57	58	57	57	55
Canada	30	32	36	38	38	37	38
Japan	34	34	31	30	29	29	28
Sweden	68	76	91	94	95	89	89
United Kingdom	43	50	56	54	53	52	50
United States	30	30	23	21	19	18	17
West Germany	31	37	42	43	42	43	43

[a]All data taken from Coates, Arrowsmith, and Courchene (1989).

also to ask about the effects of union membership on various aspects of organizational functioning. We will analyze this issue extensively elsewhere (see Chapter 8). Suffice it to note that several factors point to the importance of union membership status for an understanding of organizational functioning, and extensive reviews exist examining this issue. In their classic text *What Do Unions Do?*, Freeman and Medoff (1984) show that differences exist between union members and nonmembers on critical macro-level variables such as wages, fringe benefits, and turnover. Throughout this text we will demonstrate how attitudinal and behavioral variables of some significance to organizational functioning are influenced by union membership status (see Chapter 8), union commitment (see Chapter 4), and union participation (see Chapter 5).

One visible way of illustrating the effects of union memebership is by analyzing the workdays lost through work stoppages. As can be seen from Table 1.2, while there is wide variation between countries, the number of workdays lost per thousand employees is substantial. Also, the decreasing proportion of unionized employees is not an accurate indicator of the meaning of union membership for organizations. Note that while the proportion of unionized workers in the United States is substantially lower than that of the United Kingdom (see Table 1.2), the number of workdays lost per thousand employees in some years (e.g., 1983, 1986) is higher in the United States than in the United Kingdom. (This is also true for other between-country comparisons.)

Clearly, unions are important and are perceived to be important by government and business. As one example of this, Margaret Thatcher's government in the United Kingdom during the 1980s (Towers, 1989) devoted extensive resources to reducing the power of unions. Also, as will become apparent in Chapters 3 and 7, organizations expend considerable financial and human resources in attempts to ensure union-free environments. Thus, the argument that unions do exert a substantial influence on organizational and

TABLE 1.2   Workdays Lost per Thousand Employees[a]

Country	Average		1981	1982	1983	1984	1985	1986
	1960–70	1971–81						
Australia	259	674	797	377	318	246	230	na[b]
Canada	547	912	908	615	469	400	319	554
France	176	200	88	136	85	79	51	60
Germany	14	49	3	<1	2	264	2	1
Italy	1,185	1,189	635	1,148	881	539	234	334
Japan	144	104	14	13	12	8	6	6
Sweden	20	147	55	1	10	8	90	178
United Kingdom	187	549	198	252	182	1,303[c]	304	88
United States	591	274	172	102	195	91	74	121

[a]Data taken from Arrowsmith and Courchene (1989).
[b]Data not available.
[c]Elevated levels for 1984 were a function of the nationwide strike by the National Union of Mineworkers (Barling, 1988).

social functioning can be easily sustained, and will be examined in more depth in Chapter 8.

The Neglect of Unions by Organizational Psychology

Because unions affect organizational functioning, it is simply impossible to obtain a comprehensive understanding of organizational behavior while simultaneously ignoring the role of unions (Barling, 1988; Fullagar, 1984). Yet organizational psychology has certainly been guilty of neglecting unions. The reason for examining the extent of this neglect is not pedantic; nor is the rationale for such an examination by organizational psychologists a prelude to placing the blame for this situation on the shoulders of other disciplines. Rather, as Gordon and Burt (1981) remind us, "those unfamiliar with the past are condemned to relive it" (p. 151).

Arguably, we study and teach organizational psychology as though unions do not exist, or have no substantial impact on organizational functioning (Barling, 1988). The truth of this becomes evident with an examination of the content and conduct of organizational psychology research. From a content perspective, issues relating to collective bargaining and the nature and effects of union membership are largely ignored in organizational psychology. For example, Campbell, Daft, and Hulin (1982) studied the content of five major organizational psychology journals (*Journal of Applied Psychology, Personnel Psychology, Organizational Behavior and Human Performance, Academy of Management Journal*, and *Administrative Science Quarterly*) during 1977 and 1979. Their analysis showed that of the 464 articles that appeared during these two years, only *six* articles dealt with issues related to collective bargaining or union membership! Clearly, organizational psychologists have not chosen to address issues related to the nature or effects of unions. At the same time, organizational psychologists have not chosen to study topics that would be of greatest relevance to unions and their members. For example, while workers and unionists frequently emphasize their interest in occupational health and safety issues, this is again a topic that organizational psychologists have largely ignored (Campbell et al., 1982).

The way in which organizational psychologists conduct their research also indicates a neglect of unions. To illustrate this issue, Barling (1988) subjected all articles published in four leading organizational psychology journals (*Journal of Applied Psychology, Journal of Occupational Psychology, Academy of Management Journal*, and *Organizational Behavior and Human Performance*) between 1980 and 1986 to a content analysis. These journals were deliberately selected because they cover a variety of issues relevant to organizational psychology. The specific question of interest was whether the authors mentioned if their subjects were unionized or not. This is critical, because union membership status exerts a significant impact on organizational functioning (see Freeman & Medoff, 1984; and Chapter 8 of this book). Not identifying whether the subjects under investigation are unionized or not limits the amount of knowledge that can be gained. The results of this analysis showed the extent to which unions are ignored: On average, the union membership status of the subjects studied was mentioned in 6.3% of the articles in the *Journal of Occupational Psychology*, 4.1% in the *Journal of Applied Psychology*, 3.8% in *Organizational Behavior and Human Performance*, and 5.9% in the *Academy of Management Journal*. This is a conservative estimate of the number of studies identifying subjects' union membership status, because some studies were conducted with people who were not unionized (e.g., students, CEO's, military personnel; Barling, 1988). Nonetheless, it is obvious that union issues are studied infrequently; and most studies on organizational psychology do not even report the union membership status of their subjects, further impeding our knowledge of both organizational psychology and unions.

A compelling argument can also be made to support the assertion that the effects of unions are invariably ignored when organizational psychology is taught. First, this practice can be illustrated by examining the extent to which frequently used undergraduate organizational psychology textbooks consider the nature and effects of unions. To address this question, the subject index of a nonrandom sample of North American texts was inspected, and the total number of pages devoted to issues relevant to unions (manifested by subject index terms such as collective bargaining, negotiation, certification, union, trade union, labor union, labour relations, grievance, strikes) as a proportion of the total number of pages was calculated (see Appendix). The results of this analysis lead to only one inference—that organizational psychology is taught as if unions fulfill no meaningful role in organizational functioning. These findings replicate similar analyses conducted earlier (Barling, 1988; Fullagar, 1984). Whether deliberate or not, the consequences of this neglect are important, because students gain much of their knowledge of organizational psychology from such textbooks. Hence, if undergraduate books fail to consider unions and industrial relations, or at best devote minimal attention to them, we may be producing generations of students emerging from undergraduate courses who are unaware that employees' union membership status and activity are critical for a comprehensive understanding of organizational functioning, or that unions have any impact on the behavior and attitudes of workers.

Another source of evidence exists documenting the neglect of unions by organizational psychologists. Barling (1988) conducted a survey in Canada in which questionnaires were distributed asking professors responsible for undergraduate courses in organizational psychology about the extent to which they considered issues related to unions. Ten of the eighteen undergraduate courses and three of the four graduate courses did not deal with unions in any way. The possibility that numerous students complete courses in organizational psychology unaware of the effects of unions on behavior in organizations, therefore, is clearly supported. As we will note in more detail later in this chapter, a major aim of this text is to redress this imbalance. As Ross Stagner (1981) has noted, "the facts of life would indicate that a very large proportion of the area called 'industrial psychology' involves unions of employees as major determinants of perception and behavior" (p. 135).

Why the Neglect?

Just why this neglect, indifference, or antagonism between organizational psychology and unions has emerged, and has endured so persistently, would provide a fascinating topic of study in and of itself. It is not the intent of this chapter to dwell on this topic; numerous excellent reviews devoted to an understanding of this issue already exist (Fullagar, 1984; Gordon & Burt, 1981; Gordon & Nurick, 1981; Hartley & Kelly, 1986; Huszczo et al., 1984; Rosen & Stagner, 1981). Many of the reasons for this neglect are ideological. First, organizational psychologists are often closely affiliated with management; their methods have been used to aid in union avoidance or union busting, and research by organizational psychologists has invariably been sponsored by management. Unions do not enjoy the financial resources that management does, and hence do not support as much research (the "sponsorship effect"; Fullagar, 1984). Second, management and psychology have always subscribed to the simplistic "unitary perspective" of industrial conflict, which interprets any conflict as the result of factors that could be easily prevented or treated (e.g., poor communication). This ignores more realistic perspectives of conflict typically accepted by unionists, namely, the pluralistic or radical perspectives, which emphasize the systemic or structural causes of conflict (Bluen, 1986; Hartley & Kelly, 1986). Third, research psychologists' traditional focus on "objectivity" and "scientific rigor" makes the study of value-laden issues such as industrial relations, unions, and conflict somewhat difficult. As Rosen and Stagner (1981) note, however, unionists must share in the blame for the continuing neglect. For example, because of the adversarial role between union and management, any outsiders, no matter how well intentioned, are treated with suspicion by unionists. As a result, organizational psychologists may be denied access to the union during times of conflict (e.g., strikes), thereby inhibiting investigation of critical phenomena.

Plan of the Book

On a general level, it is clear that some rapprochement is long overdue between the disciplines of management and industrial relations. This book intends to provide a psychological understanding of what is referred to as the "unionization" process. Whereas the unionization process has previously been viewed as synonymous with voting in certification elections, we argue that this reflects neither the first nor the final phase of the complete unionization process. Instead, as will become apparent throughout, the unionization process begins long before the certification campaign commences. In particular, the effects of early family socialization on the development of general union attitudes is critical, and influences all stages of the unionization process, which includes initially voting for or against the union, commitment to and participation in the union, and the decision whether to retain or decertify one's bargaining unit.

We focus first on the structure of unions (see Chapter 2), and consider in some detail structural issues that might plausibly influence employees' decisions whether to seek and retain membership of the union (e.g., the bureaucracy vs. efficiency debate). Chapter 3 analyzes the reasons why individuals choose to vote for, or join, a union. After individuals become members of the unions (and in many cases they may do so involuntarily), the issue of their commitment to (see Chapter 4) and participation in (Chapter 5) the union emerges. One critical factor that may further bind individuals to the union is the behavior of union stewards and leaders. Although there is considerable recognition of the role of leadership in organizational behavior in general, the influence of union stewards and union leaders has received considerably less attention (see Gordon et al., 1980), and we focus on the role of union leadrship, and its effects on rank-and-file members in Chapter 6. Perhaps the final stage of the unionization process occurs when disenchanted union members try to decertify the bargaining unit, or exercise their individual right to exit, and this will be discussed in Chapter 7.

The psychological process of unionization, therefore, is described in Chapters 3 through 7. This process is akin to the development of the psychological contract between the union and its members (Schein, 1980). For this contract to endure, it is critical that union members continue to see their expectations fulfilled. This is reflected in the extent to which union membership effects positive consequences for the individual. Accordingly, we will consider the effects of unions on individual level psychological functioning in Chapter 8. In the final chapter, conceptual, research, and practical challenges and implications for organizational psychology and for unions will be examine. In sum, this book represents an attempt to correct the neglect of unions by organizational psychology, and document how a knowledge of psychological principles and research findings can enhance our understanding of both organizational functioning and the behavior of individuals in unions.

2

The Structure of Labor Organizations

As noted in the previous chapter, this book is about the process of attachment between individuals and labor organizations, and the contribution organizational psychology can make to an understanding of this process. If the purpose of organizational psychology is to understand individual behavior in organizational settings, then its focus must include both the individual and the organization as well as their interaction. Such interactive models consider the attitudes and behaviors of the individual to be determined by an interaction between individual and organizational characteristics. Examples of such integrating models include Katz and Kahn's (1978) open-systems approach and Bennis' (1969) organic-adaptive model for organizational functioning.

In this chapter, we first consider a framework for understanding structural characteristics of trade unions as organizations. This analysis builds on the strengths of organizational psychology, which has targeted its focus primarily at the individual level, and other social sciences that have concentrated primarily on group or macro-level factors. Thereafter, we discuss how the structural characteristics of labor organizations impinge on two broad functional objectives of unions, namely, the democratic or representative function, and the collective bargaining or administrative function. Finally, we will consider the impact of a union's structure on the attitudes and behaviors of its members.

The Structure of Organizations

Consistent with the widespread belief that individual behavior is at least partially a function of environmental characteristics and constraints, the effects of organizational structure on employee attitudes and behaviors have been the subject of much debate; and extensive reviews of the findings of research on this topic have accumulated (e.g., Berger & Cummings, 1979; Dalton, Todor, Spendolini, Fielding, & Porter, 1980; James & Jones, 1976; Porter & Lawler, 1965). Significant relationships have been found between organizational structure and communication networks (Bacharach & Aiken, 1977), leadership style (Jago & Vroom, 1977), job satisfaction and work motivation (Adams, Laker, &

Hulin, 1977), differential compensation (Mahoney, 1979), and perceptions of conflict and satisfaction (Dewar & Werbel, 1979). More pertinent to the purpose of this book, structural characteristics have been found to affect individual attachments to and participation in organizations (Mowday, Porter, & Steers, 1982). For example, Morris and Steers (1980) found that employees whose organizations emphasized formality of written rules and procedures, greater decentralization, and greater dependence on the work of others felt stronger commitment to the organization than those employees whose organizations emphasized these structural characteristics to a lesser extent.

Although industrial/organizational psychologists have only recently acknowledged the importance of structural determinants of work-related attitudes and behaviors, the social scientific study of labor organizations has a conspicuous tradition of focusing on environmental and structural determinants of industrial relations. However, this focus on macro-level characteristics has taken place at the expense of the psychological concerns of the human actors involved (Hyman, 1975). For example, systems approaches such as Dunlop's (1958) have ignored individual attitudes, stressors, perceptions, expectations, and motivations (Bain & Clegg, 1974; Jackson, 1977).

The division of labor between organizational psychologists and other social scientists in research on organizations is mimicked in the study of labor organizations. When psychologists have studied unions, they have usually investigated their microcosmic functions at the individual and small group level. In sharp contrast, sociologists, economists, and political scientists have concentrated on the macrocosmic characteristics of organizations, such as the dimensions and effects of large organizational subsystems and total organizations. We argue that neither approach in isolation is sufficient, and will result in a limited body of knowledge. The emphasis on micro-levels of analysis ignores structural determinants of behavior and attitudes; focusing primarily on macro issues neglects the effects individuals have on organizations (Porter & Lawler, 1965; Prien & Ronan, 1971). Both the macro and micro aspects of labor organizations must be investigated if labor researchers and behavioral scientists are to understand the complex relationships between labor organization settings and individual behavior and attitudes.

The Dimensions of Organization Structure

A considerable amount of effort within contemporary organization theory has been expended in conceptualizing and measuring the structural dimensions of organizations. Various reviews of this literature have distilled the structural characteristics of organizations into several primary dimensions (Berger & Cummings, 1979; Dalton et al., 1980; James & Jones, 1976; Porter & Lawler, 1965; Pugh, Hickson, Hinings, & Turner, 1968). Perhaps the most influential of these typologies, with respect to an understanding of the structure of labor organizations, has been that of Pugh et al. (1968). In a survey of fortysix randomly selected organizations (stratified by size and product or purpose), these researchers empirically derived five primary dimensions of structure:

TABLE 2.1 Dimensions of Organization Structure

Structural Dimensions	Definition
Specialization	The division of labor and distribution of duties and responsibilities within the organization. Specifically, this refers to the degree of role specialization.
Standardization	The extent to which the organization specifies procedures for dealing with such aspects of the work situation as the task, personnel selection, advancement, and so on.
Formalization	The degree of documentation of rules, procedures, instructions and communications. This can be broken down into formalization of role definition, information channels, and recording of performance.
Centralization	The extent to which the authority to make decisions and take action is located in the upper levels of the organizational hierarchy.
Configuration	The overall shape of the role structure. This consists of the vertical span of control (number of hierarchical levels) as well as the horizontal span of control (ratio of subordinates to managers).

specialization, standardization, formalization, centralization, and configuration. These dimensions are briefly defined in Table 2.1. The main purpose of Pugh et al.'s (1968) research was to develop a conceptual and methodological means for analyzing and comparing diverse organizations (e.g., military, academic, church, labor, and commercial organizations) to see if generalizations are possible. The five dimensions of structure they identified are still regarded as crucial components of organizational structure (Hall, 1987; James & Jones, 1976).

The Conceptualization and Measurement of Union Structure

Many industrial relations theorists have acknowledged the importance of structural characteristics (Barbash, 1969; Dunlop, 1958; Shirom, 1985). Systems frameworks for analyzing industrial relations have speculated on the central role for union structural characteristics in influencing several different collective bargaining (and other) outcomes. For example, union structure is suggested to influence wage negotiations (Anderson, 1979b; Fiorito & Hendricks, 1987a), workers' individual decisions to unionize (Walker & Lawler, 1979), the outcome of union certification and decertification elections (Maranto & Fiorito, 1987), the propensity of the union to strike (Roomkin, 1976), and overall union effectiveness (Kochan, 1980).

Despite the recognition of a theoretical role, the research on union characteristics and structure is still both scarce and largely reliant on either anecdotal, impressionistic, and qualitative description, or the use of such limited operationalizations of structural characteristics as percentage of workers unionized, or the number of unions in the industry (e.g., Feuille, Hendricks, & Kahn, 1981; Kochan & Block, 1977; Kochan & Wheeler, 1975). Although the empirical association between organizational attitudes, behavior, and effectiveness has been relatively well established, research in industrial relations has tended to ignore the structural characteristics of unions and how they impinge on membership behavior, union strategy, democracy, and bargaining effectiveness. More than ten years ago, Anderson (1979a) noted the complete absence of empirical research investigating the impact of union structural characteristics on union effectiveness in obtaining improved wages and favorable working conditions for their members.

The Dimensions of Union Structure

As with organizational structure, a great deal of the research on union structure has concentrated on establishing the dimensions along which the structure of labor organizations should be measured. One question that has been posed (Child et al., 1975; Warner, 1975) is whether the same criteria for investigating the structural characteristics of traditional organizations (i.e., commercial, military, not-for-profit organizations) can be used when studying labor organizations. This is an important consideration given that a great deal of the research on union structure looks to the literature on organizational structure for conceptual and operational direction.

Trade unions share many similarities with commercial organizations, but also differ from them in fundamental respects. Trade unions are different because of their historical development, the predominantly voluntary nature of their membership (even where membership is compulsory, participation is not), the sources of power they use (unions are egalitarian in that, at least initially, leadership is responsible and accountable to an undifferentiated membership), their objectives (which have as their ultimate reference the interests of their membership), and overall social and political position (Warner, 1975). Nevertheless, commercial organizations and unions still share many structural features of complex organizations. In most industrialized nations, unions as labor organizations have developed from small, voluntary associations, to larger, more formal bureaucracies. With the formation and expansion of large scale industrial unions, the structure of labor organizations has shifted from that of informal communities of workers to more centralized, hierarchical, and rational bureaucracies.

In theory, unions are constitutional democracies ruled from the bottom up. In reality, as Robert Michels (1959) described them, unions have largely tended to be bureaucratic oligarchies, ruled from the top down by an administrative team dominated by national officers. As such, they share the same structural characteristics as other bureaucratic and complex organizations. For example, at a national level, unions have an administrative structure very similar to that of management and other traditional or commercial organizations. This may be due to a functional similarity, in that the union also provides a direct livelihood for its administrative staff, engages in the specialization of functions and a division of labor, coordinates activities through the use of authority, and relies on a complex communicative network. Relationships are necessarily formalized and routinized, with operating codes and rules of conduct. Unions then are bureaucratic in that they administer their functions to achieve defined goals by means of structural arrangements, formal rules of conduct, and a variety of impartial mechanisms that allocate responsibilities and resources.

It is not surprising, therefore, that research which has attempted to outline the structural characteristics of unions has derived much of its theoretical and methodological impetus from the literature on bureaucratic, organizational structure. Several studies have utilized the primary dimensions developed from studies of organization structure to ascertain whether the characteristics of business organizations are generalizable to labor unions (Child, 1973; Warner, 1975). In one attempt to establish their structural similarity, Warner (1975) investigated the administrative characteristics of trade unions and professional associations using the dimensions of bureaucratic structure outlined by Pugh et al. (1968). Specifically, Warner measured the five dimensions outlined in Table 2.1, namely, specialization, standardization, formalization, centralization, and configuration.

The results of Warner's (1975) study suggest that labor organizations share many bureaucratic features of complex business firms. The development of these features in trade unions may be due to the large size of organizations. Perhaps more important for our purposes though is the indication that similar criteria used to measure the structural characteristics of complex organizations may also be used to understand trade unions.

The evidence also suggests a considerable overlap among many of the structural characteristics that define organizations. Research on large samples of organizations (including labor organizations) has found that whereas specialization, standardization, formalization, centralization, and vertical span have been conceptualized as theoretically distinct, empirically they tend to form two clusters (Child, 1973). The first cluster, labeled Structuring of Activities, consists of formalization, specialization, standardization, and vertical span, and is differentiated from Centralization, the second cluster. As Fiorito and Hendricks (1987a) point out, the Structuring of Activities is essentially a bureaucratization dimension and is very similar to Barbash's (1969) concept of rationalization, which emphasizes decision making through rules, formal organization, and reliance on expertise. Consequently, the Structuring of Activities can be defined as the degree to which (1) union activities are specialized via a division of labor, and (2) the application of procedures and documentation are formalized and standardized. These defining characteristics conform closely to Max Weber's and modern organizational theorists' descriptions of complex bureaucratic structures.

The other underlying structural factor identified by Warner (1975) is the Centralization of Decision Making: that is, the extent to which decision making is confined to the higher levels of the union structure. In an empirical analysis of centralization, Fiorito and Hendricks (1987a) factor analyzed the construct using data from fifty national unions and found three underlying dimensions. The first pertained to centralized control by the national union of the content of bargaining and local contracts or agreements. The second factor dealt mainly with the process or conduct of negotiations. Specifically, it reflected the amount of centralization (or "nationalness") of negotiating personnel, decision to strike, ratification of the contract, and bargaining level. The third factor identified by Fiorito and Hendricks (1987a) was a "checks and balances" dimension that again indicated national and local control in various dimensions of centralization. The checks and balances dimension was the most ambiguously conceptualized of the three factors. Nevertheless, this research suggests that even though centralization has been treated as unidimensional in the literature, it would appear to be multidimensional in nature.

One other structural characteristic included in the literature on organizational structure is size. Unions, both national and local, vary in size, from those with memberships of less than twenty to those whose memberships approach two million. Although the number of members is the most obvious indicator of union size, other proxy variables exist. Fiorito and Hendricks (1987a) suggest such alternatives as the union's assets, revenues, and the number and size of union locals. However, size of union membership is perhaps the best indicator of financial resources, political power, and size of staff. In a study that investigated fiftynine national U.S. unions, Fiorito and Hendricks (1987a) factor analyzed six variables relating to the size of the union, including the number of union members, union locals, members per local, full-time employees of the national union, and the total assets and receipts of the national union. While much of the literature relies on the size of staff as an indicator of size, Fiorito and Hendricks (1987a) found this variable to be strongly associated with size of national union membership and the number of union locals. The two primary and independent dimensions of size derived from this research were the size of the national union (measured by number of full-time employees, national union members, locals, and amount of assets and receipts) and the size of the local union (indicated by the number of local members).

Size has been positively associated with other structural dimensions such as bureaucratic characteristics (Lipset et al., 1956), rationalization (Barbash, 1969), and structuring of activities (Warner, 1975; Donaldson & Warner, 1974). Centralization of decision making is negatively related to size. This is understandable in that the larger the union the more difficult it is to maintain centralized control over operational matters (Donaldson & Warner, 1974). Having illustrated the dimensions of the union's structure, we now turn our attention to a more important issue from the perspective of this book, namely, a consideration of the correlates of the union's structure.

Correlates and Consequences of Union Structural Characteristics

There is general agreement in the literature as to the internal and external reasons for bureaucratization in labor organizations. These reasons include such environmental pressures as the expansion of markets and the development of economies of scale, the growth in the size of employers' organizations, the corresponding tendency toward more centralized decision making within management, and the increase in the complexity of bargaining issues (Barbash,

1969, Clegg, 1976; Kochan, 1980). Other scholars (Lester, 1958; Lipset, Trow, & Coleman, 1956) have argued that the tendency toward greater bureaucratization in unions can be explained by their increase in size, and Michel's "Iron Law of Oligarchy." The iron law posits that all organizations inevitably become controlled by a small group of people who use the organization to further their own ends. Following this line of reasoning, it is argued that the passage of time leads to increasing centralization of power and control and a greater effort among the powerful to maintain control. Consequently, there is a decrease in the amount of effective political constraint on the union leadership and a tendency to minimize the ideological objectives of unions.

Another environmental characteristic associated with the structural features of the union (Child et al., 1973) is the degree of variability in environmental conditions. The more the environment changes, the greater the necessity for flexible organizational structure and less structuring of activities. Several organizational theorists (e.g., Etzioni, 1961; Perrow, 1972) have arrived at the same broad conclusion: Under conditions of environmental uncertainty, organizational roles and functions have to be frequently redefined and integrated. Child et al. (1973) point to a potential conflict here between the union's representative and administrative functions. Unions need to have relatively clearly defined work roles to maintain accountability to members' representatives. However, this may produce administrative problems in terms of flexibility under conditions of change. Kochan (1980) has noted that "If a union is to effectively pursue its goals in collective bargaining, it must adapt its organizational structure to meet the requirements of this process" (p. 150).

Although researchers have paid scant attention to the causes of union structure, there is a large body of literature on the consequences of the union's structure. The structural characteristics of labor organizations and their effectiveness cannot be separated: The primary objective of unions is to build an organizational structure that facilitates effective performance in collective bargaining. However, the effectiveness of unions should not merely be determined in terms of the quality and quantity of bargaining outcomes. As Kochan (1980) points out, the correspondence between bargaining outcomes and the needs and expectations of the union membership must be taken into account. The extent of correspondence between the two can be interpreted as an indication of the degree of representativeness or internal democracy in the union. Indeed, Kochan (1980) views the achievement of internal union democracy as an integral dimension in assessing overall union effectiveness. Consequently, we will now consider the impact that union structural characteristics have on (1) union democracy, and (2) collective bargaining outcomes.

Union Democracy

Despite the "Golden Age" of research and discussion on union democracy in the 1950s, and the resurgence of interest in the 1970s, there still remains little consensus in the literature on how to define union democracy, let alone how to measure it. One common thread in the cloth of diversity is that democracy is a process inextricably bound up with union government and decision making. More than three decades ago, Seidman, London, Karsh, and Tagliacozzo (1958) emphasized the problem with defining union democracy and proposed a tentative solution when they stated:

> Democracy in the trade union context may be defined in a variety of ways. If it is defined to mean active participation by the members in forming policy, there is relatively little democracy in the labor movement. If the test is responsiveness of the leaders to the desires of the members, an opposite conclusion is reached: most unions are democratic, at both the national and local levels. In our view, however, democracy requires more than this; the essential factor is the ability of the rank and file to affect decisions, replace leaders, and to change policies (p. 185).

Perhaps at its simplest level, democracy may be defined as "control by the governed, whether in a participatory or representative form" (Hochner, Koziara, & Schmidt, 1980, p. 15). In other words, union democracy is a system in which union members actively participate directly, or indirectly through their representatives, in decision making, policy implementation, and selection of officials, at all levels of the union organization. Involvement in all levels of union decision making would include participation in contract negotiation and administration, service to members, administration of the union, and involvement in external political and community activity.

Even though there is little agreement in the literature on the definition of union democracy, the very fact that unions should be democractic is widely suggested. Hochner et al. (1980) have outlined six basic functions of union democracy: Union democracy (1) fosters industrial democracy by encouraging worker participation in workplace decisions; (2) protects individual rights by preventing manipulation and exploitation of the worker by the union; (3) enhances union effectiveness by facilitating the selection of representative leaders, increasing union power by enhancing union commitment and solidarity through participation, and making unions more responsive to the needs of their members; (4) fosters the democratic ideal in societies that espouse democracy as an essential value; (5) enables unions to provide a training ground for citizens to participate in the larger democratic society; and finally (6) enhances unions' role in the class struggle as potential forums empowering workers in a capitalist society.

Regardless of how union democracy is defined, most theorists accept that it is multidimensional in nature, and research has tended to measure democracy using a variety of criteria to capture its complexities. These include participation of members, accountability of officials, legitimacy of opposition, closeness of elections, leadership turnover, breadth of electoral base, number of candidates, the existence of a two-party system, and constitutional protection of individual rights.

To facilitate our understanding of the effects of union structure, we have collapsed the outcomes of union structure into three primary dimensions: membership influence, participation, and opposition.

A certain amount of influence and control can be exercised over union leadership by rank-and-file members in terms of the perceived legitimacy of, commitment to, and acceptability of the decisions made by the union leadership. The influence of union members may be indirect in that both the formulation and implementation of leaders' decisions may be controlled by their perceptions of how acceptable their decisions would be to the union membership. If a decision by the union leadership is perceived as unacceptable by the union's members, then the union leadership will be aware that such a decision will probably not be enacted, or enacted against the wishes of the rank-and-file. This type of influence does not require the union members' active participation in decision making, but is reliant on union leaders' perceptions of membership commitment to, and acceptance of, leaders' decisions. Nicholson et al. (1981) term this "negative control" and point out that although little empirical research exists on the construct of negative control, any divergence between membership sentiment and leadership policies often forces change in leadership-directed policies. Strauss (1977a) referred to this aspect of democracy as a test of responsiveness, in that it is an indication of how responsive union officers are to the values and suggestions of their members.

The terms democracy and participation are often used interchangeably. Because participation can be investigated with behavioral measures such as member participation in unions, voting in elections, and officer turnover, this outcome of structure has received some attention in the empirical literature, especially by organizational behaviorists. Nevertheless, there are relatively few attempts to develop participatory theories of democracy, despite the acknowledgement that participation is a crucial means for transforming social institutions and restraining union oligarchy and bureaucrats. One reason for the scarcity of participatory theories of democracy may be the difficulty in precisely conceptualizing participation (see Chapter 5). In his attempt to understand participation, Ramaswamy (1977) adopts a very broad definition that encompasses a wide variety of behaviors: "any interaction between members or between them and their leaders over (work-related) issues is participation in union affairs" (p. 470). Such a definition is too broad to be of much use. We address the issues of conceptualization and operationalization of union participation in far greater detail in Chapter 5.

For several theorists (e.g., Edelstein & Warner, 1975; Lipset et al., 1956), the concept of democracy is associated with the extent to which the system is capable of generating opposition to those who hold power. These same theorists measure democracy in terms of how close the outcome of union elections are and the degree to which the union system generates representatives of near equal strength for elections. Strauss (1977a) referred to this concept as "legal democracy," in that it is conceptualized and measured in terms of union constitutions, honest elections, regularity of meetings, and, generally, the extent to which a viable opposition can develop.

Although in extreme cases, achievement of the different outcomes of democracy may be mutually exclusive, they all share an important goal. Each exerts pressure on leadership decision making either directly or indirectly (through the representative structure) to restrain oligarchical control and increase the democratic function of the union. Consequently research on democracy should focus on all the factors that promote internal union democracy as well as the possible impacts these factors have on union objectives, membership behaviors and attitudes, and the union environment.

Strauss (1977a) has suggested two alternative approaches to studying union democracy; (1) an informal approach, which focuses on the existence of an occupational community a member can identify with, and a "middlemass" of active members independent of union leadership; and (2) a structural approach, which focuses on such features as formal arrangements that encourage the formation of power bases independent of the union leadership. Strauss sees the structural approach as more valuable at the national level or in large subunits. However, he viewed the two approaches as consistent in that they both require a "middlemass," or intermediate and independent power base, but at different levels of the labor organization. For this power base to develop, Strauss believed that the structure of the union should be consistent with the goals of collective bargaining and the expression of members' occupational interests.

Several studies have attempted to ascertain the extent of the democratic nature of unions by comparing it with the level of oligarchy one might expect to find, consistent with Michels' (1958) iron law of oligarchy. The earliest empirical attempt was Lipset et al.'s (1956) study of the American International Typographical Union. They found that although far more variation in the internal organization of unions existed than the iron law of oligarchy would imply, there was still a high level of oligarchical control in the labor organization studied. This was indicated by the lack of viable political opposition to the union's leadership. Lipset et al. (1956) argued that more centralized unions are less capable of maintaining internal democratic procedures and decision-making processes. Leadership in centralized unions loses touch with the needs and expectations of the rank-and-file membership. As a result, union democracy declines and the union's effectiveness as a collective bargaining agent atrophies. Subsequent research has drawn a far less pessimistic picture of union democracy and indicated that democratic ideology and practice still survive in modern trade unionism (Donaldson & Warner, 1974; Lahne, 1970; Roomkin, 1976).

Perhaps more relevant for our purposes, however, is how union democracy is related to the structural characteristics of trade unions, rather than just the extent to which democracy exists in labor organizations. Cook (1963) considered a clear definition of the powers and responsibilities of leaders and a decentralization of collective bargaining to be fundamental to union democracy. Two of the most extensive (and recent) studies that have addressed this issue are those of Edelstein and Warner (1976) and Anderson (1978).

Edelstein and Warner (1976) researched democracy and oligarchy in thirty-one British and fifty-one American national unions. Their criteria for democracy were the effectiveness of opposition in elections for top-level union posts and the existence of an electoral machinery to ensure effective electoral opposition. These criteria were measured by looking at the closeness of the outcome of union elections, frequency of defeat of incumbents, and existence of competing factions. Edelstein and Warner (1976) regard the absence of such electoral machinery as an indication of oligarchy, that is, "control over the organization by a limited number of individuals on a noncompetitive basis" (p. 33). Findings from this study indicated that structural characteristics, such as greater size, centralization, and number of hierarchical levels (i.e., greater structural complexity), produced less balanced election outcomes, longer terms of office among incumbents, and fewer competitors in elections—all indications of a decrease in union democracy.

Anderson (1978) examined the environmental, structural, and internal determinants of union democracy. Democracy was more extensively measured than in the Edelstein and Warner study, in that the extent of membership participation in union activities and the amount of influence members exerted were analyzed in addition to the closeness of the outcome of union elections. In a survey of ninety-five local Canadian unions representing manual workers, clerical employees, and firefighters, Anderson (1978) found that structural characteristics were important predictors of participation in union meetings and membership influence. Specifically, Anderson noted that the increased complexity of the union (measured by the degree of specialization, and horizontal and vertical differentiation) and union bureaucracy (assessed by the extent of centralization of decision making, standardization of procedures, and formalization of rules) were associated with lower levels of participation in union meetings. Furthermore, union bureaucracy, structural complexity of the union, and closely fought elections were all associated with limits on members' influence.

Both these empirical studies demonstrated that the more bureaucratic and complex the union's structure, the less the membership participates in, and influences, union decision making. However, the structural complexity of the union was found to be positively associated with other dimensions of democracy, such as the number of candidates in union elections and the closeness of these elections. Complexity (where complex structures have several intermediate steps between the local and national bodies) has also been associated with local union autonomy and internal democracy. Intermediate bodies have been proposed to increase the bargaining autonomy of union locals by protecting them from national power (Cook, 1963) and also to facilitate internal democracy by broadening the election base (Gamm, 1979) and providing a greater challenge to the existing leadership (Strauss, 1977a).

Some research, such as that by Olson (1982) and Roomkin (1976), although not directly investigating democracy, has found correlations between measures of the formal structural characteristics of national unions and various indicators of the internal distribution of control such as frequency of national conventions, provisions for national approval of local contracts, and local ratification (all of which may be considered proxy measures of democracy).

The above research again underlines the necessity of regarding union democracy as a multidimensional concept. Different dimensions (and definitions) of democracy have different relationships with different structural characteristics. As Kochan (1980) notes, "the growth of large union bureaucracies and complex structures may have different effects on different dimensions of union democracy and on the vitality of the internal political process" (p. 157). One factor that influences the relationship between aspects of democracy and union structural characteristics is the collective bargaining and organizing environment. For example, contrary to expectations, Rogow (1967) found that high levels of union participation were associated with strong, centralized leadership in a union confronting political and economic problems. To deal with financial pressures, the union encouraged members to perform union functions the union could no longer afford to fulfill.

One finding that consistently emerges from this research is that the various dimensions of union democracy are inextricably interrelated with such structural characteristics as size, centralization, bureaucratization and rationalization. However, even though there is an acknowledgment that structural and democratic characteristics are related, the precise causal nature of these relationships is not understood. For example, all the research cited above has relied on cross-sectional, correlational analysis and therefore gives little indication of the causal direction of the effects.

One final issue concerning union democracy deserves attention. A distinction is frequently drawn in the literature between construing democracy as a means or as an end. Theorists such as Barbash (1969) and Bok and Dunlop (1970) have pointed to the need for unions to rationalize their structure to increase their effectiveness. This would require internal democracy to be sacrificed on the altar of functional efficiency. The horns of this dilemma were already apparent to Webb and Webb (1897) in the nineteenth century, who wrote about the quandry concerning administrative efficiency versus popular control. Not much later, Cole (1920) referred to this as the dilemma between union functions versus purposes. More recently, the same quandry has been referred to as existing between administration versus representation (Fox, 1971); and administrative versus representative rationalities (Child et al., 1973). In both the popular and social scientific literature, these separate functions or goals are seen as conflicting with each other. As Nicholson et al. (1981) point out, it is difficult to solve this dilemma without examining the goals of unionism, which in itself is a controversial area touching on social and political ideology. We will not attempt to resolve this dilemma here, as this would require social and political analysis that would distract us from the primary aim of this book, which is a psychological understanding of the attitudes and behaviors associated with union attachment and the unionization process in general. However, having examined one goal of unions (namely, union democracy), we will now turn our attention to another goal of labor organizations, and that is collective bargaining effectiveness.

Collective Bargaining Effectiveness

A second major objective of labor organizations is to improve the conditions and terms of employment of their members. The most widely used mechanism for realizing this objective is collective bargaining. Kochan (1980) describes one structural dilemma of modern trade unions as the conflict between increasing centralization to cope with the complexities of the collective bargaining process and a deterioration in internal democracy that facilitates a decline in political vitality and an increase in oligarchy, corruption, dissent, and factionalism.

> The essence of the dilemma therefore, is that while centralization may be needed to perform effectively in bargaining ... at any given point in time, the longer centralization is maintained in the absence of an effective political process, the more union effectiveness is likely to decline (Kochan, 1980, pp. 157–158).

Although Kochan (1980) appreciated that union democracy and bargaining effectiveness are interrelated, other scholars have raised the question of whether internal union democracy is necessary for an effective union. Bok and Dunlop (1970) argued that union governance and effective administration are more important than union democracy, and that researchers have accorded too much importance to the concept of democracy. Bok and Dunlop contend that union members "have doubtless suffered far more from inefficient and unimaginative administration than they have ever lost through corruption and undemocratic practices" (1970, p. 90). In a similar vein, Lipset (1960) suggested that even dictatorial unions are better than ineffective ones. (Bok and Dunlop (1970) and Lipset's (1960) arguments are well illustrated by a situation that emerges when considering certification of a bargaining unit: It is argued that union members will often vote for a corrupt union if it is effective in meeting the needs of its members; see Chapter 3). The main thrust of Barbash's (1969) argument is that because democracy entails decentralization of decision making, it conflicts with the process of rationalization and an increase in bargaining effectiveness. Barbash did concede, however, that democracy and rationalization are not necessarily incompatible. As noted above, Warner's (1975) research suggests that centralization and democratic functioning are positively correlated. Recent research by Fiorito and Hendricks (1987b) suggests that union democracy may detract from wage-related outcomes, but appears to enhance nonwage-related outcomes, such as issues concerning equity, job security, fringe benefits, and pay supplements.

Although the provision of a democratic system is a debated goal of trade unions if they are to fulfill their representative function, an equally important aspect of union functioning is their influence through collective bargaining. The structure of the union is not only important in determining internal union democracy and the distribution of power and decision making, it also affects the outcomes of collective bargaining. For example, Bok and Dunlop (1970) criticized highly bureaucratic union structures for producing ineffective communication systems, selection, training, and motivation processes, and generally inefficient administration to fulfill the goals of labor organizations. Paradoxically, some labor theorists see the improvement of unions' administrative function as lying in increasing the complexity of the union structure and a further centralization of union decision making, specialization of staff, and planning of procedures. Nevertheless, the administrative performance of unions is an extremely important function in terms of union effectiveness.

What the outcomes of the collective bargaining process should be has also been the topic of considerable debate. This debate ranges from those who prefer to see unions maintain their focus on "bread-and-butter" issues such as wages, hours, and working conditions (e.g., Gomberg, 1973) to those who would like the bargaining agenda broadened to reflect the needs and interests of the changing workforce and focus increasingly on quality of worklife issues (i.e., the psychological needs of workers for more significant, meaningful, and varied jobs, and for making the job a source of personal growth and development; Garson, 1981; Work in America, 1972). Sometimes, this is extended to include collective bargaining goals that address community and public issues such as illiteracy, discrimination, poverty, pollution, substance abuse, child care, and other public and social interests (Konvitz, 1970). A more extremist position favors the inclusion of radical political change as part of the collective bargaining agenda; witness, for example, the role of many black unions' opposition to apartheid in South Africa (Middleton, 1990).

Previous research on the effects of unions on bargaining outcomes has tended to focus on wage-related issues. More recently this focus has broadened to include a variety of nonwage outcomes such as fringe benefits, worker attachment to firms, hiring standards, and nonwage contractual terms (Freeman, 1980; Kochan & Block, 1977; Medoff, 1979). Most of this research has focused on the effects of economic, legal, and political environmental characteristics on the wage determination process (Anderson, 1979). Very few empirical studies have researched the association between the structural characteristics of unions and different bargaining outcomes.

Roomkin (1976) investigated the relationship between the internal structure of unions and their collective bargaining behavior, which he argues is the most important function of the trade union as an organization. Specifically, Roomkin (1976) investigated the association between the extent to which the union's collective bargaining function is centralized at a national level and the collective bargaining and strike activity of local and intermediate bodies. Even though Roomkin's study was methodologically restricted because a limited number of proxy variables were used to assess union structure and behavior, the results do indicate that centralization of the national union reduces the likelihood that local units will be involved in a strike. This is important if strike activity is viewed as a necessary means for achieving collective bargaining aims. Thus, Roomkin's results emphasize the conflict between the centralization of industrial relations and the capacity of unions to represent the interests of their members. In the interests of democracy it has been suggested that unions modify their internal structures to engage in less centralized decision making and become more representative of the rank-and-file membership. Roomkin's (1976) research suggests that such changes in union structure may be accompanied by an increase in strike activity and therefore bargaining effectiveness.

Fiorito and Hendricks (1987b) have conducted perhaps the most comprehensive study on the effects of union structural characteristics on bargaining outcomes. These researchers included two structural characteristics of unions in their study, namely, size and centralization of the union. Size was measured in terms of the number of members and the average size of locals in the union.

Centralization was assessed by measuring the extent of national union control over both the content and process of bargaining (Fiorito & Hendricks, 1987b). Bargaining outcomes were divided into wages (i.e., wages per hour) and nonwage-related outcomes (i.e., issues concerning equity, job security, work rules, pay supplements, and fringe benefits). Data were collected from several sources of union statistics including over 3000 union wage contracts negotiated in the manufacturing industry between 1971 and 1981, and the nonwage provisions of 700 manufacturing and 500 nonmanufacturing contracts.

The results of this research suggest that the size of the union, as indicated by the number of members, has a consistent *negative* impact on both wage and nonwage outcomes, with the effect being stronger for nonwage outcomes. In other words, smaller unions achieve greater wage and nonwage benefits for their members. However, a different criterion of size, namely, the average size of locals within the union, produces a different result: Size of the local union was found to be *positively* associated with better outcomes. Fiorito and Hendricks (1987b) interpret their findings with respect to size as follows:

> These results suggest that the most efficient unions have a smaller number of large locals in several industries. This finding may indicate economies of scope. Thus, the results also suggest that union mergers can have a favorable influence on bargaining—especially if they lead to a rationalization of local units (p. 581).

The effects of centralization were less consistent. With the exception of job security, national control of the bargaining process was found to have a negative impact on wage and nonwage bargaining outcomes. Furthermore, centralized control of the decision to strike was positively, although weakly, associated with desired outcomes. Fiorito and Hendrick's (1987b) study indicated that the structural characteristics of unions are significantly associated with bargaining outcomes and bargaining effectiveness. However, Fiorito and Hendricks (1987b) themselves note that drawing conclusions from these results is problematic. Because the data are correlational, it is difficult to ascertain conclusively whether union characteristics determine bargaining outcomes or vice versa, and whether differences in bargaining outcomes are due to differences in union characteristics or bargaining goals. Indeed, considerable conflict may exist between bargaining goals and bargaining effectiveness when there is centralized control of bargaining by the national union, especially if the bargaining goals of the national and local officials do not coincide.

So far we have focused on bargaining *outcomes*. Fiorito, Gramm, and Hendricks (1990) also investigated the impact of union structural characteristics (specifically, centralization) on various bargaining *strategies* unions can adopt to improve bargaining outcomes (i.e., the working conditions of their members). Fiorito et al. (1990) distinguish between three types of bargaining strategy, each necessitating a different degree of centralization in the union to be effective. First, there is the Monopoly-Strategy Model, whereby the union improves the compensation and working conditions of its members by monopolizing the market, either by controlling the supply of labor by forming exclusive craft unions, or by using the threat of industry-wide strikes by forming an industrial union. The effectiveness of such a strategy depends on centralization of the bargaining function.

Second, Fiorito et al. (1990) describe the Efficiency-Strategy Model. Here the union improves the terms and working conditions of its members by improving the employing firm's efficiency, and consequently the profitability of the firm and the well-being of its workers. This is a central premise of the Exit-Voice-Loyalty model (see Hirschman, 1970), which suggests dissatisfied workers have two main alternatives to redress their dissatisfaction: One is to exit or leave the job, the other is to express their grievance/s through the collective voice of the union. As Fiorito et al. (1990) point out, this model assumes that using the union "voice" can improve efficiency by (1) providing management with representative information to enable them to design compensation and employment terms that satisfy worker's needs, (2) improving communication and thereby facilitating the development of more efficient contracts, and (3) enhancing worker morale and union-management cooperation which, in turn, can lead to increased productivity. Obviously, the efficiency- strategy model is most effective when collective bargaining takes place at the level of the plant or firm, and where there is the greatest understanding of the needs of both the workers and the enterprise. Consequently, a decentralized governance structure is most appropriate for this form of collective bargaining strategy (Fiorito et al., 1990).

Third, Fiorito et al. (1990) identify a Monitoring-Strategy Model, which is essentially a hybrid model whereby the national union provides expertise, assistance, and information to increase the efficiency of collective bargaining in local situations. Consequently, some aspects of the collective bargaining process are centralized to facilitate decentralized local bargaining.

Fiorito et al. (1990) outline several issues that warrant further investigation concerning the relationship between union structural characteristics, bargaining strategies, and bargaining outcomes. Specifically, there is a need to explicate the relationship between union structural characteristics and the effectiveness of labor organizations:

> Our monopoly strategy/model of centralization may result in a lower dispersion of wages and labor costs in the union's jurisdiction. Our monitoring/information model, on the other hand, suggests that in certain circumstances centralization of control over the bargaining process may give negotiators access to better and more complete information, which in turn may influence both bargaining power and strike activity. A more thorough investigation of these issues would provide useful information to both labor leaders and policy-makers, as well as enhance our general understanding of the determinants of organizational effectiveness (pp. 30–31).

Another indicator of a labor organization's efficiency is the extent and impact of their political activity. Union political lobbyists have an important influence on legislation affecting organized labor. There is considerable variation across unions in terms of the amount of time, money, and energy expended on political activity and the kinds of strategies adopted by unions to achieve their political goals. Delaney, Fiorito, and Masters (1988) have shown that structural characteristics of unions explain differences in union political involvement and political preferences. Specifically, union size was found to have a curvilinear relationship with political action (measured by PAC contributions, lobbying staff size, and political action costs). Smaller unions may not have access to the financial resources necessary to engage in political action. In contrast, as union resources increase there is a tendency to spend more on political action. However, it would appear that larger unions may perceive diminishing returns for extra political action once a certain level of political activity is reached; also, after a union reaches a certain size there are decreasing benefits associated with additional lobbyists or PAC contributions. The amount of dues collected from union members affects resources available for lobbying and PAC fund raising and administration, and consequently affects the extent of union political involvement. Delaney et al. (1988) also found that the composition of a union's membership and the breadth of its constituency, especially the proportion of female members, affects its PAC contributions and political expenditures.

Several implications are derived by Delaney et al. (1988) from the results of their study. First, they suggest that unions may have to confront the dilemma of choosing between organizing activity and political activity. With a political and economic climate that is anti-union, it becomes difficult for unions to allocate sufficient resources to both activities. Second, the more heterogenous the union membership (with respect to occupation, gender, and industry), the smaller the PAC contributions per member are. Delaney et al. (1988) suggest several reasons for this decrease in political activity, including reduced solidarity among the rank-and-file as well as greater difficulty for union leaders in representing membership interests and formulating a common political agenda. Third, unlike other indices of union effectiveness, union political activity was found to be positively associated with union democracy; the most autocratic unions were the least politically active.

Finally, the success of the union in organizing workers (i.e., getting them to join a union) is yet another indicator of union efficiency. Organizing new units increases the union's power base, political influence, and revenues (Voos, 1983). Research attention to the organizing process has shown that election outcomes are strongly influenced by employees' job satisfaction, the industry and technology of the employer, the election process, and the economic environment (see Chapter 3). Using archival data, Heneman and Sandver (1989) investigated the effects of several union characteristics on the organizing success of more than fifty national unions. The only structural characteristic having an impact on organizing success was the average unit size (see Chapter 3), or the average number of employees eligible to vote in the union's elections. This was found to have a negative relationship with the percentage of elections won by the union, and the average percentage of pro-union votes cast. Paradoxically, this research found that many structural characteristics implemented by unions to facilitate organizing efforts (such as functional specialization amongst organizing staff, the number of organizers per election, and the total number of organizing staff) did not have their hypothesized effect on organizing success. Heneman and Sandver (1989) suggest that some degree of caution be exercised in interpreting these results, because they may be a function of measurement problems associated with the data and the assessment of organizing activity.

Union Structure and Member Attitudes and Behavior

The dimensions of organizational structure have long been known to have a major impact on the attitudes and behavior of the individuals who constitute those organizations. Several structural theorists (e.g., Argyris, 1964; Blake & Mouton, 1968; Likert, 1967; McGregor, 1960; Taylor, 1911; Weber, 1964) have viewed the structural characteristics of organizations as important determinants of human characteristics. At the beginning of this chapter, we referenced some of the research that has established a relationship between organizational structural characteristics and organizational attitudes and behaviors. We now consider the link between unions' structure and the attitudes and behaviors of their members.

So far, we have focused on describing and distinguishing unions strictly in terms of their structural characteristics. Fiorito and Hendricks (1987a) have outlined additional characteristics used in the literature to understand national unions. For example, some structural characteristics that can be distinguished from bureaucracy, rationalization, centralization, and size are union type (e.g., craft versus industrial unions), and occupational and industrial scope (i.e., the range of occupations and industries the union represents). The results obtained from existing research are contradictory. Although Warner (1975) found that the craft-industrial distinction made little contribution to understanding unions as organizations, Strauss (1977a) has shown that the sense of occupational community is stronger in craft-based unions and consequently union democracy is greater than in industrial unions. Further research certainly needs to be undertaken to ascertain the relationship between these additional characteristics and the other structural dimensions of unions, and their implications for union democracy and bargaining effectiveness.

Complexity has also been associated with local union autonomy and internal democracy. Intermediate bodies have been proposed to increase the bargaining autonomy of union locals by protecting them from national power (Cook, 1963) and also to facilitate internal democracy by broadening the election base (Gamm, 1979) and providing a greater challenge to the existent leadership (Strauss, 1977a). Further research certainly needs to be undertaken to ascertain the relationship between these additional characteristics and the other structural dimensions of unions and their implications for union democracy and bargaining effectiveness.

Even though ideology cannot strictly be regarded as a structural characteristic of unions, Fiorito and Hendricks (1987a) suggest that it is inextricably enmeshed with union structure. They attribute the lack of attention devoted to union ideology in the United States to American unions' nonideological character, or alternatively to the monolithic adoption of "business unionism" as the dominant form of U.S. unionism.

Nontheless, subtle ideological distinctions do exist between unions, for example, in terms of their emphasis on political action and concern with social issues. Hoxie (1921) was one of the first researchers to outline certain ideological typologies when he distinguished between business, friendly, uplift, revolutionary, and predatory unions. Walker and Lawler (1979) have classified unions into aggressive versus protective unions, which differ with respect to their emphasis on political versus economic objectives, the character of the collective bargaining relationship (distributive versus integrative), and the nature of their membership. Aggressive unions draw their membership from "alienated employees who are relatively deprived and seek to establish greater group control" (Walker & Lawler, 1979, p. 3). By contrast, protective unions consist of "employees who are relatively privileged and seek to protect their control in the face of actual or potential threats" (p. 3). Recent research (Fullagar, Barling, & Christie, 1991) has shown that the ideological character of the union has a significant effect on individuals' attitudes both toward their union and their employing company. Specifically, it was found that members of a protective union were more likely to develop dual allegiance to both the union and the company. In contrast, individuals who belong to an aggressive labor organization are more likely to develop a unilateral attachment to the union.

In addition to affecting union attitudes, Fiorito and Hendricks (1987a) have suggested that union ideology influences union structure, dues levels and schedules, membership solidarity, and union political and organizing activities. Nevertheless, the definition and measurement of union ideology are both varied and vague. There are no operationalizations that enable systematic differentiation between unions. Perhaps the clearest indicator of union ideology is bargaining strategy. For example, the extent to which the union utilizes militant actions, such as strike activity, or resorts to political persuasion to achieve favored bargaining outcomes is a clear proxy of ideological position (Anderson, 1979). Fiorito and Hendricks (1987b) have investigated the relationship between militancy and bargaining outcomes. Their results indicated that energies devoted to organizing activities have a negative impact on bargaining outcomes in that they detract from the enhancement of outcomes. However, it must be said that unions with better organizing facilities have greater penetration in the industries they are representing, and this has a positive effect on bargaining outcomes. Fiorito and Hendricks (1987b) also found the propensity to strike improved union bargaining outcomes, in that militancy in bargaining is positively associated with desired outcomes. In summarizing their findings, Fiorito and Hendricks conclude that militancy in bargaining may have a beneficial impact on the union, but too much attention to organizing or political activities may detract from effectiveness at the bargaining table.

Conclusion

It should be apparent that the understanding of union functioning and the attitudes and behavior of union members requires a substantial increase in the effort provided by organizational psychologists. Still more research must be undertaken to explicate fully the total impact of union structural characteristics. From the research available thus far, several conclusions are in order. First, increases in the centralization of decision making, standardization of procedures, and formalization of rules decrease levels of membership participation in union meetings and influence on union decision making (Anderson, 1978). Second, greater centralization of the union collective bargaining function reduces the strike activity of local branches (Roomkin, 1976). Third, the larger the union the more negative the impact on both wage and nonwage outcomes (Fiorito & Hendricks, 1987b). If bargaining outcomes have any effect on union commitment, one would also expect structural characteristics to be associated with commitment to the union.

The studies on union structure and its effects, although constrained by several limitations including small samples, variables, and measures, do provide a basis for the development of integrating models. A more complete development of such models requires larger samples, more variables, longitudinal designs, multivariate analysis, and greater financial and human resources. For example, additional research is required to ascertain the extent to which structural characteristics and the various dimensions of democracy and bargaining outcomes are generalizable across jurisdictions and time.

Having considered structural characteristics of unions and their effects, we now turn our attention in the next five chapters to the "unionization" process: Just why individuals would choose to vote to certify a union, offer their commitment and participation in the union, and follow/obey union leaders. As the final stage, we will also consider what happens when the unionization process breaks down and union members are faced with the choice of decertifying or exiting from their bargaining unit.

3

The Unionization Process

Just why employees vote for or against union representation in certification elections has captured the attention of researchers and practitioners alike for many decades. Most of the research on unionization has been conducted in the United States, where its extent in the private sector has decreased from 35.7% in 1953 to only 17.8% in 1983 (Troy, 1986). (Union membership in the public sector increased from 11.6% to 34.4% during the same period.) The decline in American union membership is in sharp contrast with increases in unionism in most other Western countries, including Canada (see Table 1.1). Several reasons have been posited for this decline: The shift in employment away from traditionally heavily unionized industries in the manufacturing sector toward less unionized, service industries; the population and employment swing away from heavily unionized Northeastern and North Central regions to the less unionized South; the effects of foreign competition from countries that have undercut American labor costs; and the influx of nontraditional workers into the labor force, such as professional women. The trend is also reflected in the significant decline in the number of workers organized through the National Labor Relations Board (NLRB) representation elections. Freeman (1985) reports that the success rate of unions in NLRB elections has dropped from 60% in the mid-1950s and 1960s, to 45% in the early 1980s. He attributes this to increased management opposition, reduced organizing efforts on behalf of unions, and economic structural changes such as the ones we have outlined above.

However, our interest in the process of unionization is not solely motivated by the crisis confronting American labor organizations. The act of joining a union, or voting for a union in a representation election, is the first behavioral gesture in the process of attachment to a labor organization. Once the individual has become a member of a union, then he or she starts to develop attitudes of commitment or disillusionment, and to participate in, or ignore, union activities. Numerous reviews already exist of the unionization process (e.g., Fiorito, Gallagher, & Greer, 1986; Heneman & Sandver, 1983). However, our approach within this and subsequent chapters differs substantively from these major reviews. Without exception, these previous reviews regard the certification election and the unionization process as one and the same. In contrast, we argue that these two processes are not synonymous, and that the certification of the union in no way implies its permanent right to represent members of the bargaining unit. Instead, individuals have the right to decertify their union under specified conditions. Any consideration of the certification phase alone, therefore, would provide a truncated perspective of the entire unionization process. Hence we consider certification in this chapter and decertification campaigns in Chapter 7. Moreover, we do not view the union vote itself as necessarily the only phase of the unionization process. Long before any certification process is undertaken, individuals develop attitudes toward unions that are of critical importance in determining the outcome of the campaign itself (Barling, Kelloway, & Bremermann, 1991). Nor is the vote to certify the union the last phase in the unionization process. After a union has been certified, socialization into, and commitment to, the union commences (see Chapter 4). Thereafter, individual union members are faced with the choice of whether to participate in union activities, and which activities to engage in (see Chapter 5). Thus, to provide a complete perspective of the comprehensive unionization process, attitudes to the union, socialization, commitment to, and participation in the union are discussed in the ensuing chapters, after which we consider decertification.

Before we examine the predictors of individual voting in certification elections, several issues should be clarified. First, most representation elections are hard fought and often described using words with warlike connotations: The literature on unionization is replete with metaphors such as victory and defeat (rather than such terms as win and lose) to describe the outcome of certification elections. Second, management and unions commit considerable financial and human resources to these elections. Third, not only are certification elections hard fought between management and labor, they are invariably closely contested as well. For example, Roomkin and Block (1981) estimate that when unions are successful, the margin of victory is around eight votes. In situations where management is successful in defeating the union's attempt to certify, the margin is even closer! The closeness of union certification elections has critical implications for research: While there is a considerable body of data available on macro-level predictors (e.g., region, race, inflation) of election outcomes (e.g., proportion of pro-union votes, number of union or management successes), this focus is insufficient, because votes from each and every employee could well constitute the deciding factor in a labor or management victory. Thus, a focus on macro-level factors *together* with an in-depth knowledge of the reasons why *specific* individuals choose to vote for or against a union in a particular certification election is of critical importance. Fourth, it is worth noting that the desire to understand the predictors of union certification is not a recent phenomenon. Even DeCotiis and LeLouarn's (1981, p. 105) oft-cited belief that "empirical studies of union phenomena are of fairly recent interest to the social scientist, the first study (Uphoff & Dunnette) being reported in 1956" ignores research that was conducted well beforehand (e.g., Bakke, 1945; Chamberlain, 1935; Whyte, 1944). In the interest of historical integrity and a spirit of intellectual humility, we will attempt to refer to earlier work throughout our consideration of the predictors of union certification.

In considering these predictors we have divided them into four categories: (a) demographic predictors, (b) personality factors and beliefs about work, (c) macro-level predictors, and (d) micro-level predictors. Because a primary aim of this chapter is to understand individual voting behavior, we will focus extensively on this latter aspect, assessing the roles of work experiences, union-related experiences, and nonwork experiences on union voting behavior.

Demographic Predictors of Certification Elections

In their review, Fiorito et al. (1986) pointed out that demographers must surely be concerned and irritated by the way in which the term *demography* is used so frequently and so imprecisely. Often included within this category are personal characteristics such as age, personality characteristics such as the Protestant work ethic, and even workplace variables such as part-time or full-time employment status. In an attempt to lessen the ambiguity and misuse of the term demographic, we include in the present discussion only those aspects specific to the employee that are of a stable nature. Personality characteristics (e.g., the Protestant work ethic) and workplace variables (e.g., job satisfaction) will be discussed in other sections. The reasons for this differentiation are not solely semantic. As will become apparent, the potential consequences of demographic and workplace predictors of union voting differ. Also, of all the predictors of union voting behavior, demographic factors (e.g., age, race) are not amenable to modification by the union or the organization.

There are several reasons for positing totally different effects of age on the likelihood of pro-union voting. On the one hand, because one of the primary concerns of organized labor has been to enshrine the seniority system, which accords priority to protecting the rights of workers on the basis of job tenure, older workers might be more favorably disposed toward unions. On the other hand, because younger workers are supposedly more militant than their older counterparts, it could be argued that they would be more likely to vote in favor of a union. A number of studies have investigated this relationship empirically, but there is very little consistency in the findings. Some studies have shown that age is inversely related to union voting preference (e.g., Bigoness, 1978; DeCotiis & LeLouarn, 1981), voting intentions prior to assuming full-time employment (Barling, Kelloway, & Bremermann, 1991) and attitudes to unionization (Allen & Keaveny, 1981); others have demonstrated that younger workers are more likely to vote for a union (Brett, 1980). Other studies have found no significant relationship between age and union voting preferences (Bornheimer, 1985; Deshpande & Fiorito, 1989; Kochan, 1979) or attitudes to unionism (Bass & Mitchell, 1976; Gordon & Long, 1981).

Perhaps more important than the direction of the relationship, however, are additional findings from Bigoness' (1978) and DeCotiis and LeLouarn's (1981) studies. Both studies showed that when the influence of work-related factors are acknowledged, any effects of age on pro-union voting are not longer statistically significant. This highlights the importance of focusing on the *relative* importance of demographic variables, and suggests that no demographic variables influence voting preferences in isolation. As will become evident, this particular method-ological issue permeates an evaluation of the effects of any demographic factors on pro-union voting, and we will explore this issue in more detail toward the end of this chapter.

Closely related to the relationship between age and union voting preferences is the relationship between seniority and union voting. Competing hypotheses for the effects of seniority could also be offered. Individuals with less tenure and seniority may look to union representation for job security. In contrast, because unions continue to honor the concept of seniority, individuals with more seniority may be more positively disposed toward union representation. Again, the data on this issue are not conclusive. While some studies show that individuals with less tenure and seniority are more favorably disposed toward unionization (Allen & Keaveny, 1981; Bass & Mitchell, 1976; Feuille & Blandin, 1974), others found no significant associations (Bornheimer, 1985). Also, understanding the unique effects of tenure and seniority on union attitudes and voting preferences is difficult because they are highly associated with other demographic characteristics, such as age and salary, and themselves are so highly intercorrelated. It is also important to note that when the effects of salary, job attitudes, and experiences are controlled, job tenure no longer predicts interest in unionization (Allen & Keaveny, 1981).

The question of whether employees' level of education predicts their union voting preferences has also attracted some attention. The pattern of results parallels those from the link between age and union voting inclination. Specifically, positive relationships have emerged (e.g., Bornheimer, 1985), as have negative relationships (Bass & Mitchell, 1975; Deshpande & Fiorito, 1989), and null relationships (DeCotiis & LeLouarn, 1981; Hills, 1985). In some studies, this relationship is no longer significant when work-related experiences are controlled statistically (e.g., Bass & Mitchell, 1975); in others, the relationship remains significant (e.g., Deshpande & Fiorito, 1989).

In addition to these inconclusive findings, isolating the unique effects of education is again difficult because education is associated with other demog-raphic characteristics such as salary and job level. Also, even when demog-raphic variables such as education are associated with union voting preferences, the magnitude of such relationships is invariably modest at best. We will return to both these issues throughout this chapter.

Several trends with respect to the relationship between gender and unioni-zation have been noted. Women certainly are underrepresented in terms of union membership. Yet two studies have shown that there are no gender differences in terms of the propensity (Kochan, 1979) or intent (Youngblood, DeNisi, Molleston, & Mobley, 1984) to join a union. In studies that did show pro-union voting intentions to be greater among females, these differences were not significant after controlling for work-related factors (Deshpande & Fiorito, 1989; Youngblood et al. 1984).

Thus, two points should be underscored. First, the results are dependent to some extent on the nature of the criterion variable under consideration. When union *membership* is the focus, gender differences do appear. However, such differences are more likely a function of the unequal distribution of males and females within different jobs in the workplace, and the considerable challenges in organizing part-time, temporary "female" jobs. In addition, females might be less likely to seek union representation because union membership and union participation require involvement in activities beyond work time that would conflict with family responsibilities (Barling, 1990; Roby & Uttal, 1988). In contrast, when individual voting *intentions* are considered, no gender differences emerge. As noted at the beginning of this chapter, understanding individual behaviors is of greater conceptual and pragmatic consequence than understanding membership patterns. Second, any effects of gender tend to dissipate when viewed together with work-related variables. The importance of considering the predictors of unionization together rather than in isolation is again supported.

One of the primary factors that have sustained the hypothesis that minorities are more likely to vote for union representation than whites is their greater experience of discrimination in the workplace. Under conditions of racial discrimination, the presence of unions might realistically be viewed as a voice mechanism and a safeguard against discrimination. Somewhat unlike other demographic characteristics, the data do suggest that minorities in the United States manifest more positive union attitudes (Hills, 1985) and a greater likelihood to vote in favor of union representation (Deshpande & Fiorito, 1989; Kochan, 1979). This finding is significant because, unlike other demographic characteristics, this race effect remains significant even when work-related experiences are controlled. In understanding the meaning of this finding, it is critical to note, as we have argued elsewhere (Fullager & Barling, 1989), that such findings in no way imply any kind of racial bias. Instead, they speak to the strength and persistence of racial discrimination in the workplace, and to concerted attempts over time by workers to overcome discriminatory practices.

The idea that differences exist between urban and rural individuals in the extent to which they seek unionization is by no means new. In his early observational study, Whyte (1944) noted with respect to voluntary union organizers that "not one grew up on a farm" (p. 227). This is consistent with the view that rural workers are more individualistic than their urban counterparts. Nonetheless, more recent research suggests that rural versus urban differences do not exert a major influence on union attitudes or union voting decisions. Although it is true that rural workers are less likely to belong to unions, this may be more a function of the unavailability of unions in rural areas rather than individual decisions not to join unions. Unions would experience practical difficulties in organizing and servicing rural routes (for example, due to the geographical distances involved). Also, the likelihood that bargaining units in rural areas will be comparatively small and relatively underpaid may make it less likely they will be organized. Certainly, the data do not suggest that rural workers are against unions (Fiorito et al., 1986; Hills, 1985). Thus, the limited data available suggest that there are no urban/rural differences in the extent to which employees would be prepared to vote for union representation, even though rural workers are indeed less likely to be union members. This again points to the importance of considering the nature of the criterion variable.

Because it would be difficult for married workers and/or those with dependents simply to leave an organization when they are dissatisfied with their jobs, it is sometimes hypothesized that such workers would seek a voice mechanism, and therefore be more favorably disposed to unionization. Alternatively, such workers might be concerned that any move toward unionization would be met with reprisals by employees, lessening the likelihood that they would seek union representation (Fiorito et al., 1986). Although there is no evidence to support the hypothesis that married workers are more likely to favor unions (Hills, 1985), the number of child dependents is associated with favorable attitudes toward collective bargaining (Feuille & Blandin, 1974).

Given the increasing tendency toward part-time employment, one further variable of some interest is employment status (part-time vs. full-time). However, findings from initial research suggest that there are no differences in union attitudes (Hills, 1985) or voting preferences between part-time and full-time employees (Keaveny, Rosse & Fossum, 1988).

The demographic characteristics considered above lead to several conclusions. First and foremost, with the exception of race, little support exists for the notion that demographic characteristics predict union attitudes or voting preferences. Even race *per se* is probably not responsible for union attitudes or voting. Rather, race is probably a proxy for the experience of discrimination that minorities continue to confront in organizations that makes it more likely they will turn to unionization to redress racial inequities.

Second, even where significant associations do emerge between demographic characteristics and union attitudes or pro-union intent, the magnitude of these associations is modest at best (Heneman & Sandver, 1983; Hills, 1985). The importance of this will become more apparent later in this discussion, when the extent to which other work-related variables predict union voting behavior is explored. This also points to the need to investigate the role of demographic characteristics together with, and relative to, other predictors of unionization. As already noted, when such a comparative approach is followed, any influence of demographic characteristics is minimized even further. Third, even if no differences emerge in the *level* of unionization between different demographic groups, this certainly does not exclude the possibility that the *processes* leading to an interest in unionization differs across demographic groups. For example, although Keaveny et al. (1988) show that there are no differences between full-time and part-time workers with respect to the intent to vote for a union, their results suggest that the process of unionization differs for part-time and full-time workers.

One final explanation of the findings of the above research is that perhaps demographic characteristics really do predict pro-union dispositions and preferences, but researchers have yet to isolate these specific demographic characteristics. The sheer volume of research on this topic conducted over more than three decades, together with the range of demographic attributes studied, mitigates against the plausibility of this hypothesis. Thus, researchers have been led to a more likely conclusion, namely, that there is no "union profile," in that it is not possible to depict the stereotypical pro-union employee on the basis of demographic attributes (DeCotiis & LeLouarn, 1981; Gordon & Long, 1981; Kochan, 1979). Some implications follow from this conclusion. For example, over and above being ethically questionable, management attempts to ensure a union-free environment by excluding specific demographic groups would most likely be misguided. Also, as Gordon and Long (1981) note, it is both unnecessary and unwise for union organizers to target unionization campaigns for specific demographic groups.

Personality Characteristics and Beliefs about Work as Predictors of Certification Elections

If we cannot characterize the typical union supporter in terms of demographic characteristics, it is still possible that pro-union employees share similar personality attributes or beliefs. A limited amount of research has focused on this question, and several different personality variables have been investigated.

One personality variable that has received some empirical attention is individuals' perceptions of control. Based on Rotter's (1966) distinction between perceptions of internal and external control of reinforcement, it has been hypothesized that individuals who perceive their global and work environments as being under the control of powerful external forces are more likely to be positively disposed toward unions (Beutell & Biggs, 1984; Bigoness, 1978). The results from these two studies are mixed. Beutell and Biggs (1984) found no significant association between perceived locus of control and union voting intentions. In contrast, Bigoness (1978) showed that externals were more favorably disposed toward collective bargaining. However, the magnitude of the relationship in Bigoness' (1978) study was moderate at best, suggesting that perceptions of control do not exert a meaningful effect on union attitudes or union voting behavior.

Another personality attribute that might predict pro-union propensity is the extent to which individuals are accepting of change. Elsewhere, we have noted that change is one of the central elements of the industrial relations process (Bluen & Barling, 1988): When workplaces undergo elections and a bargaining unit is subsequently certified, the work environment changes. As a result, individuals who would normally choose to avoid change may be less likely to vote for unions. Presumably such individuals would be more concerned with maintaining the status quo. One study explicitly investigated this issue. Operationalizing the fear of change with Wilson's (1973) "psychological conservatism" construct, Barling, Laliberte, Fullagar, and Kelloway (1990) showed that any effects of psychological conservatism on pro-union voting intentions were indirect, and mediated by their direct effect on union attitudes. Specifically, psychological conservatism had no direct effect on union voting. However, psychological conservatism predicted attitudes to unions, which in turn predicted union voting intentions.

Fundamental beliefs about the nature of work have also been investigated as predictors of union attitudes and union voting intentions. The hypothesis that work beliefs predict the unionization decision can be justified as follows. First, it might be argued that work beliefs are more proximal to the voting decision than are personality characteristics, which are presumably independent of the work context. Second, work beliefs clarify, simplify, and help to organize perceptions of the world of work, thereby placing boundaries on behavior (Buchholz, 1978). Several work beliefs that could influence union attitudes and voting have been investigated.

As Buchholz (1978) writes, the Marxist work belief asserts that workers are alienated from and exploited within the workforce. To change this, workers must exert greater control over the workplace. Because unions represent one means of exerting such control, employees manifesting strong Marxist work beliefs would be likely to favor unions. The humanistic work belief asserts that individual growth is more important than productivity; hence workplaces should be redesigned to be meaningful and facilitate personal growth. With respect to these two work beliefs, Buchholz (1978) showed that union officials and union members revealed stronger Marxist and humanist beliefs than their non-unionized counterparts. Also, union officials manifested stronger Marxist work beliefs and humanistic work beliefs than rank-and-file members.

Two studies investigating work beliefs have been conducted on non-unionized individuals. Barling, Kelloway, and Bremermann (1991) investigated how Marxist and humanistic work beliefs predicted the union attitudes and voting intentions of a group of young (average age = 18.8 years), pre-employed university students. Focusing on pre-employed subjects is important, because their beliefs can be assumed to be independent of work or organizational experience. Both Marxist and humanistic work beliefs exerted *indirect* influences on pro-union voting intentions through their direct effect on union attitudes. Neither of the two work beliefs exerted a direct influence on pro-union voting intentions. In another study, Barling, Laliberte, Fullagar, and Kelloway (1990) investigated the role of Marxist work beliefs among non-unionized Canadian and American faculty members. Their results again showed that any effects of Marxist work beliefs on po-union voting intentions were indirect, and mediated by their direct effects on attitudes to unions in general.

In conclusion, several observations are justified concerning possible links between personality characteristics and work beliefs and union voting. First, there is very little research relating personality factors to union voting behavior. Second, the little research that has been conducted suggests that work beliefs and personality characteristics, while significant, exert indirect effects on union voting intentions.

Macro-level Predictors of Voting Behavior
in Certification Elections

So far, we have considered demographic and personality/work belief pre-dictors of the decision to unionize. Demographic predictors reflected stable characteristics of the individual (e.g., age, gender, race); work beliefs and personality attributes refer to characteristics specific to the individual that are theoretically amenable to change, and whose development is largely independent of current work experiences. Similarly, macro-level predictors are not static. Some authors refer to such variables as "structural" characteristics (e.g., Robinson & McIlwee, 1989). However, this term fails to capture critical predictors such as the effects of company and union campaigns on individual voting during certification elections, to which we will devote considerable attention. Other authors favor terms such as "economic" and "non-economic" predictors (Lewin & Feuille, 1983). Arguably, however, these two terms are too broad to be illustrative. In discussing what we call "macro-level" influences, Fiorito et al. (1986) include "worker orientation." Because they use the term macro-level predictors to reflect predictors such as unit size, its descriptive value is also questionable. At the risk of defining macro-level variables in terms of what is not covered within this category (namely, demographic, personality, and employee workplace experiences), we choose to use the generic term macro-level predictors. As will become evident, some macro-level predictors have been the focus of very few studies (e.g., studies investigating whether the day on which elections are held influences voting); others have attracted considerable attention (e.g., the effects of company campaigns on pro-union voting).

Several hypotheses concerning the effects of macro-level predictors on certification elections have been posited, subjected to varying degrees of empirical scrutiny, and rejected. For example, it has been suggested that the day of the week on which the certification election occurs has a bearing on the outcome of the election. The logic underlying this proposition is that employers are more likely to win elections on Friday because of their greater access to employees during the week (and hence their increased ability to communicate and influence employees' decisions). Along similar lines, it is argued that unions are more likely to win elections that are held on Mondays because of their greater access to employees over the weekend. Although significant zero-order correlations emerged with respect to voting on a Tuesday and pro-union voting (Hindman, 1988), the magnitude of these correlations is so trivial ($r \leqslant 0.08$) as to render them substantively meaningless. More important, Hindman (1988) found no support for this hypothesis when he used multivariate statistical techniques and considered the influence of the weekday relative to other predictors. Thus, although appealing, this hypothesis has not received any strong empirical support.

Another hypothesis that is conceptually appealing but, unlike the day of the week hypothesis, has received considerable empirical attention is that union election victories are far more likely in jurisdictions that are more hospitable to unions with respect to public policy and labor legislation. On the basis of this assumption, it is frequently suggested that union victories are more likely in non-Southern states in the United States. The rationale for this hypothesis is based on the preponderance of "right-to-work" states in southern regions of the United States and their lower levels of union density. The different states within the United States can be dichotomized according to whether their state legislation allows or prohibits closed-shop agreements. In right-to-work states, the political environment is hostile to unions, and closed shop agreements are prohibited. It is assumed that such legislation is a proxy for prevailing attitudes to unions. Hence, community attitudes to unions in right-to-work states would be generally unfavorable. These unfavorable attitudes would be compounded, because workers would derive fewer benefits if unions are viewed unfavorably (Cooke, 1983). In general, there is precious little support for this "regional" hypothesis (e.g., Brett, 1980; Heneman & Sandver, 1983; Lewin & Feuille, 1983; Robinson & McIlwee, 1989; Sandver, 1982). Even when some support has emerged for this hypothesis (e.g., Cooke, 1983), the results are mixed, with an equal number of findings from the same study showing no effect for region at all. Possible reasons for such findings will be explored in more detail in Chapter 7 when discussing the predictors of decertification outcomes.

As will become apparent later in this chapter, financial pressures or strain are frequently assumed to be associated with the desire for union representation. Some of these financial factors will be discussed later, as they really reflect micro-level factors (e.g., wages, salary). However, the possible effects of inflation will be considered here. In general, it is assumed that inflation encourages unionization, inasmuch as inflation brings about a loss in earning power. Individual employees may well look to unions as a means of income protection during times of inflation, especially given the extent to which COLA's (i.e., cost of living allowances) form a central part of any bargaining agenda. Although there is some support for this hypothesis (Fiorito et al., 1986), Lawler and Walker's (1984) findings suggest that the nature of the outcome must be considered carefully. Their results reveal that while the probability of a union victory is unrelated to inflation, certification elections are *less* likely during periods of inflation. In addition, employees may be more concerned with job security during such periods.

Varying hypotheses exist about the effects of unemployment rates on certification outcomes. First, employee fear of reprisals from management when unemployment is high and jobs are scarce is believed to be positively associated with an interest in unionization (Fiorito et al., 1986). Second, the reduced opportunities for alternative employment during such periods are posited to stimulate pro-union voting because of the need for union protection (Cooke, 1983), or discourage pro-union voting because of the fear of management reprisals (Fiorito et al., 1986). The data support the former hypothesis more strongly: Cooke (1983) estimates that for every 1% increase in unemployment, the percentage of employees voting pro-union increases 1.3%, and the likelihood of a union victory increases 2.5%. Worker expectations about future unemployment can also significantly affect their current behavior. Using changes in unemployment rate as a proxy for worker expectations, Cooke (1983) showed that there was some (albeit limited) support for the notion that expectations concerning future unemployment predict current support for a union.

Consistent with the central role long accorded to sociopolitical and social psychological factors in the unionization process (Hoxie, 1919) are suggestions that the extent to which a particular jurisdiction or industry is organized will influence the outcome of certification elections. This is frequently referred to as the *saturation effect*, and asserts that diminishing returns exist for unions based on current saturation levels. Interestingly, though, researchers investigating the saturation hypothesis differ as to whether they predict a negative or positive effect of saturation. Cooke (1983), for example, suggests that the extent to which any state or jurisdiction is unionized reflects general attitudes to unions. Hence, the likelihood of union victories in certification elections would correlate positively with union saturation. A contrasting hypothesis is that units that are relatively easier to organize are more likely to be organized first (Fiorito et al., 1986). As union saturation increases, therefore, organizing would become more difficult. Empirical support exists for a positive saturation effect. Both Cooke (1983) and Hindman (1988) showed that as saturation levels increase, so does the likelihood of union certification victories. However, Cooke's (1983) findings place some limits on this phenomenon. He found that the saturation effect no longer applied after the extent to which a union has penetrated a particular industry exceeds 35%. Two caveats are necessary. First, even though Walker and Lawler (1984) found a modest relationship suggesting that election *victories* become more difficult as saturation increases, the likelihood of a certification election taking place (irrespective of the outcome) was positively correlated with saturation level. Second, the 35% penetration level shown by Cooke (1983) is industry and jurisdiction specific. Cooke's research was conducted in an industry in which the average penetration rate was substantially less than 35%. In some jurisdictions, the baseline level is greater than 35% and the ceiling level might be substantially greater.

Of all the macro-level factors, the size of the bargaining unit has attracted perhaps the most empirical attention. One plausible reason is the ready availability of this information (Fiorito et al., 1986; Heneman & Sandver, 1983). A more important reason for considering the effects of the size of the bargaining unit derives from the hypothesis that unit size serves as a proxy for group cohesion. Thus, election victories would be predicted in smaller units where within-group cohesion is more likely than in larger units. However, an opposite hypothesis has also been advanced to account for the effects of size on union victories. Because scale economies are more favorable in larger units (Fiorito et al., 1986), and human and financial resources more readily available, election victories might be more likely in larger bargaining units.

With perhaps only one exception (Hindman, 1988), most studies show a negative effect of size. Other than pointing to the fact that the relationship in this study, while statistically significant, was so small as to be virtually meaningless, Hindman offers no further explanations for this finding. Other studies show that size is negatively associated with union election outcomes (e.g., Heneman & Sandver, 1983; Kochan, McKersie, & Chalykoff, 1986; Lawler, 1984; Messick, 1974). However, two studies point to the fact that the influence of size of the bargaining unit on certification election outcomes is not necessarily linear. Brett (1980) showed that employees in small (less than 10) and large (more than 1000) organizations are less interested in unionization than those in medium-sized organizations. Cooke's (1983) findings refine those of Brett (1980), showing that the likelihood of winning a certification election is positively related to the size of the bargaining unit but falls abruptly when the bargaining unit comprises approximately sixty-five members; thereafter, size is not associated with election outcomes. These two findings question the hypothesis suggesting that economies of scale underlie the relationship between size of the unit and election outcome: If this hypothesis were to be supported, election victories would increase in a linear fashion with the size of the unit. Instead, the group cohesion hypothesis receives more support (Cooke, 1983; Fiorito et al., 1986), because cohesion is far less likely in larger units. Nonetheless, the fact that election victories are unlikely in very small units (< 10 members; Brett, 1980) suggests that a certain economy of scale may be a necessary precondition for a union victory.

A number of studies have investigated whether voter turnout has any bearing on the outcome of certification elections. These studies show that voter turnout is associated negatively with union victories (Becker & Miller, 1981; Hindman, 1988; Sandver, 1980). Voter turnout in certification elections is also negatively associated with the margin of victory, regardless of who wins (Block & Roomkin, 1982). However, the meaning of these findings is limited. First, their statistical magnitude is sufficiently low to raise doubt about the inferences that can be drawn. For example, Hindman's (1988) significant zero-order correlations are small, and when multivariate statistics are computed, they only reach significance in one out of three cases. Block and Roomkin's (1982) correlations between voter turnout and margin of victory are also modest at best ($r \leqslant .10$). Second, even if these findings achieved greater levels of statistical significance, implications for both labor and management would be dubious: Given organized labor's democratic ethos, encouraging and facilitating participation in elections should be a primary objective, even if it makes victories more difficult to achieve (Becker & Miller, 1981; Hindman, 1988). From a managerial perspective, trying to restrict voter turnout in an election would contradict the democratic spirit.

Campaigns for and Against Union Representation

One of the most controversial, if not the single most frequently researched, macro-level predictor of union voting behavior is the effect of the company campaign against union representation during the certification election. Underlying the interest in these campaigns are two paradoxes: First, the well-known study by Getman et al. (1976) focusing on thirty-one representation elections concluded that "the campaign does not influence many employees to vote contrary to their predispositions, because employees do not pay close attention to the campaign" (Getman et al., 1976, p. 143). Yet their conclusion contradicts the rationale underlying most company campaigns during certification elections. Some estimates suggest that over 70% of companys hire outside consultants to direct their efforts to remain union free (Hindman, 1988). Given the costs of such consultant services, it would seem obvious that management does not subscribe to the belief that the company campaign against union representation is of no consequence.

Second, in the United States, the National Labor Relations Act specifically assumes that individual workers are free to choose whether to seek and opt for union representation. To ensure this, the National Labor Relations Board has designed "elaborate rules to govern campaign tactics with much higher standards of conduct being required in Board elections than in elections for presidents, congressional representatives and the like" (Strauss, 1977b, p. 833). Yet while the number of representation elections have only doubled in the past thirty-five years, unfair (i.e., illegal) labor practices may have increased five to sixfold during the same period (Chalykoff & Cappelli, 1986; Lawler, 1986), and continue unabated. The extent of unfair labor practices is at least partly a result of insufficient penalties being levied for committing unfair labor practices to ensure that the "laboratory conditions" required by the National Labor Relations Board do indeed prevail (Walker, 1984).

Another more pragmatic factor underlies interest in the possible effects of company campaigns on union voting behavior. Because the results of union certification elections are invariably close (Roomkin & Block, 1981), both management and labor have an obvious interest in understanding, as well as in controlling, the process and outcome of certification elections.

At the heart of any campaign orchestrated by management to defeat any attempt to unionize the workforce is an attempt to communicate with employees. It is not surprising, therefore, that some research has been conducted on the effectiveness of the various communication methods used. In this discussion, we exclude the books written about and seminars devoted to what is euphemistically referred to as "preventive labor relations" (Lawler, 1986), as these are directed at management. Instead, in this discussion, we focus on management attempts to communicate with employees.

Written communication would appear to be the activity used most frequently by management in their attempts to communicate with employees. Small group meetings with employees and large meetings with a "captive audience" of employees (i.e., large groups of employees for whom attendance could be mandatory; Lawler, 1986) are also used frequently (Lawler & West, 1985). The data focusing on the effects of these communicative techniques are somewhat mixed. While Lawler and West (1985) suggest that the distribution of written literature is ineffective, Dickens (1983) suggests that meetings held early in the campaign, combined with written communication later in the certification campaign, are probably effective. Lawler (1986) suggests that films portraying an anti-union message may also be effective. However, there would not appear to be any research testing this specific suggestion. Likewise, while personal contact with individual employees may be important (Martin, 1985), more research is clearly needed on the effectiveness of different communication methods. After all, the different tactics used by management are all based on some form of communication.

The range of management tactics varies widely between "subtle" and "blatant" attempts to defeat attempts to organize the workforce. On the one hand are the "subtle" strategies. For example, to conduct a successful certification campaign, the union would need access to all employees. To obtain such access, unions would require comprehensive lists of all employees, which are presumably only obtainable from the employer. The National Labor Relations Board requires that the union be given such a list after the petition is filed. Although illegal, employers can choose to provide inaccurate or incomplete lists. Lawler and West (1985) demonstrate that this practice is relatively infrequent, but their data also show that failure by the union to obtain a comprehensive list had the most negative effect on union voting behavior of all the company practices they studied. Indeed, providing an inaccurate list of names and addresses was shown to reduce the likelihood of a union victory by 13%.

Another subtle procedural strategy that management can use is to deliberately delay the certification campaign (Lawler, 1986). The reasons for attempting to delay certification elections include increasing the size of the bargaining unit (which would lessen the likelihood of union victory; Brett, 1980; Cooke, 1983; Lawler, 1984), signalling management's opposition to unions, and draining the union's limited financial resources (Cooke, 1983). With few exceptions (Hindman, 1988), studies show that pro-union voting is negatively associated with procedural delays (Lawler, 1988). Cooke (1983) estimates that for every month the election is delayed, the percentage of workers voting pro-union decreases .5%, and the likelihood of a union victory is reduced by approximately 1%. Given that the average margin of victory is so low, delays of several months could exert substantial effects. Nonetheless, studies using multivariate techniques again show that the *relative* effect of such delays compared to other company campaign tactics is limited (Lawler, 1988; Lawler & West, 1985). Also, as Heneman and Sandver (1983) argue, we cannot necessarily attribute all election delays to deliberate management resistance. Legitimate problems such as specifying the appropriate bargaining unit, or the inefficiency of the National Labor Relations Board, could also delay certification elections.

To defeat attempts to organize the workforce, another subtle strategy management can use is to portray an image of enlightened management philosophy and practice. One practical way of doing this is to provide supervisory training when faced with the possibility of union organizing, thereby suggesting that management is concerned about employees' well-being. Lawler and West (1985) have shown that as a deliberate strategy, supervisory training is used in about 38% of elections. However, their results also show that whether or not supervisory training is used has no effect whatsoever on the outcome of representation elections.

At a higher level within the organizational hierarchy, innovative managerial strategies and policies that are perceived to benefit employees can also be used to portray an enlightened image. There are data to suggest that unionization is less likely in such companies. Kochan, McKersie, and Chalykoff (1986) estimate that for each workplace innovation introduced in a non-unionized company, the number of workers ultimately represented by a union was reduced. However, the extent to which management would be able to implement such policies or to arrange supervisory training in the face of an imminent effort to organize the workforce is questionable. Such strategies and practices would probably be difficult to organize and implement when confronted unexpectedly by an organizing campaign. There could also be legal challenges to any changes implemented by management once the election campaign has commenced.

A more blatant way in which management can signal their opposition, if not antagonism, to a unionized workforce is by hiring outside experts to assist them in defeating any organizing campaigns. Management consultants are reportedly used in only 20% of elections supervised by the National Labor Relations Board (Lawler & West, 1985), but consultants and/or attorneys are used in 80% of all elections (Lawler, 1986). There is some research on the effects of outside consultants on the outcome of certification elections. In one study, Lawler and West (1985) showed that the presence of consultants does decrease the likelihood of a union victory. In understanding the meaning of this finding, it must be noted that the presence of a consultant does more than signal employer sentiments; presumably, outside consultants would also bring with them greater expertise and experience in union-avoidance strategies. In another study, Lawler (1984) showed that the effect of a consultant was most marked (1) in small organizations in the service sector that were unlikely to have sufficient resources to fight a union organizing campaign themselves, and (2) in closely fought elections. Both these factors contribute to the overall effect of consultants in the outcome of an organizing drive and certification election. First, union efforts at organizing are most difficult in small firms in the service sector, and, second, most representation elections are decided by a few votes. As a result, the presence of a consultant would often be sufficient to influence the course of a representation election (Lawler, 1984). This conclusion is reinforced by Hindman's (1988) finding that the effects of a consultant are statistically significant even after controlling for other predictors of unionization. However, one counterintuitive finding should be borne in mind. The simultaneous presence of a consultant and an attorney *increases* the likelihood of a *union* victory. One possible explanation for this is that conflicting strategies may result if the two parties do not actively cooperate in the campaign (Lawler & West, 1985). Another possible explanation is the "backfire" effect, which will be discussed shortly.

Another tactic on the part of management is the willingness to expend resources to defeat and avoid unions. If the hiring of a consultant can be taken as a proxy for anti-union sentiment by management, so too can management's willingness to commit financial resources to defeat an organizing campaign. Although there are no data as to whether the extent of resources expended is related to the outcome of the election, it is clear that considerable amounts of money are dedicated to defeating union organizing attempts (Lawler, 1984). Clearly, research is needed to assess whether the resources allocated for this purpose achieve their goal (Heneman & Sandver, 1983), particularly in those situations where public funds are used to fight the presence of a union.

Another tactic that indicates managements' outlook to unionization is the presence of "consent elections," that is, where the employer agrees on the composition of the bargaining unit. In such situations, the employer provides little indication of concern over the possibility of union representation. Certainly, where consent is not achieved (i.e., where management opposition is manifest) the likelihood of a union victory is decreased (Cooke, 1983; Hindman,

1988). Similarly, pre-election procedural challenges concerning the composition of the bargaining unit decreases the chances of union victory by 14% (Lawler, 1986).

At the other end of the spectrum of management resistance to unionization lie the most blatant tactics, which include intimidation, harassment, and actual firing of union activists. Despite stringent rules that render such actions illegal, their practice is both widespread and increasing (e.g., Harris, Reichman, & Jacobs, 1983; Lawler, 1986). In eight of the thirty-one elections studied by Getman et al. (1976), union supporters were fired. Despite Getman et al.'s (1976) suggestions that such illegal practices exert minimal effects because of the critical role of prior union attitudes and their stability throughout the certification process, re-analyses of their data suggest otherwise. For example, in his re-analysis of the Getman et al. (1976) data, Dickens (1983) showed that implied and actual actions against union activists did indeed deter employees from supporting the union. Moreover, despite the difficulties associated with investigating the effects of such employer practices (presumably, if they are successful, employees would also be disinclined to report their occurrence), Lawler and West (1985) showed that alleged discrimination against union supporters is associated with an 11% decrease in support for collective bargaining. Likewise, Cooke (1985) has shown that firing union activists decreases the likelihood of a union victory by between 17% and 23%. Clearly, therefore, earlier suggestions that company campaigns exert no effect on the outcome of certification elections (Getman et al. 1976) are not consistent with the data (e.g., Dickens, 1983; Martin, 1985).

Can the effects of company campaigns aimed at avoiding unions be quantified? A number of empirical analyses allow us to begin to answer this question, and the indications are that the effects of company campaigns should not be underestimated. For example, it has been estimated that although unions were successful in 36% of the elections studied by Getman et al. (1976), had management not campaigned against unionization at all, the union success rate would have been 66%. At the same time, a powerful campaign by management in all instances would have reduced the union success rate to 5% (Dickens, 1983). Other estimates suggest that union victories are reduced by between 17% and 50% by management resistance (Cooke, 1985; Freeman & Medoff, 1984). There is a further reason for suggesting that employer resistance has a substantial effect on the outcome of certification elections. Although the impact of each strategy alone may be modest (with one exception still to be discussed, namely, the joint effect of consultants and attorneys), the various strategies used exert additive effects on the likelihood of union victories (Lawler & West, 1985).

Other non-empirical arguments can be advanced for the effectiveness of company campaigns. First, the effects of forceful, possibly illegal management tactics on employees might be subtle and difficult to detect empirically. Some authors have written that the effect of such strategies is to "chill" pro-union sentiment and voting, presumably because it is fear-provoking to employees (see Youngblood et al., 1984). It seems reasonable to assume that the more employees are affected by such strategies, the less likely they are to report their incidence in research programs. Second, it has been argued that company campaigns against unionization may be least effective closer to the actual election, yet that is precisely when most of the research on company campaigns has been conducted (Montgomery, 1989). Two implications follow. First, the effects of company campaigns may be underestimated by this data. Second, to some extent this may explain Getman et al.'s (1976) conclusion that company campaigns exert no influence on voting in certification elections: They interviewed employees within three weeks of the election or immediately afterwards. Yet the company campaign really begins long before that (i.e., when the union organizing drive is launched). This may be when company campaigns are most effective.

It must be noted that negative effects of company campaigns on union victories are by no means inevitable. As already indicated, there are data showing that employer efforts to resist unions can result in an *increase* in pro-union voting (Lawler, 1984). This has been referred to as a "backfire" effect, where employer overreactions to attempts to organize creates a favorable atmosphere for union success. For example, when employers use both consultants and lawyers in an effort to defeat the union, the likelihood of union success increased (Lawler & West, 1985). One potential reason for this could be, as Brett (1980, p. 54) notes, that "pro-union employees may view threatening employer behavior simply as confirmation ... that they need a union." Another possible explanation for the "backfire" effect exists. Employers who decide to increase pay and/or benefits in an attempt to prevent organizing campaigns may inadvertently provide some signal to employees of the benefits of unionization, thereby enhancing attitudes toward collective bargaining or pro-union voting. As noted earlier, it is also possible that the failure to coordinate the activities of the two outside parties results in some conflict that is counterproductive. Lastly, it is likely that management is more likely to hire consultants *and* lawyers when it perceives a real threat of unionization. Thus, the increased prospect of a union victory occurring when both lawyers and consultants are used in the same campaign could simply reflect the union's prior strength relative to management.

Any consideration of the effects of company tactics on union organizing campaigns and certification elections would be both incomplete and biased without some attention to the question of how unions try to organize workers in the first instance, or counteract the effects of management tactics. One widespread stereotype is that unions use "outside agitators" who convince employees that they are dissatisfied and that they need union representation to redress their grievances. Such arguments have been discredited for some time (Whyte, 1944). Nonetheless, adherence to this stereotype continues, possibly because it serves a self-protective function to those who do not want to accept why employees might seek union representation in the first instance. Brett's (1980) observation that the "boss" remains the best union organizer (inasmuch as he or she exerts substantial control over the work environment) is certainly instructive here. At a broader level, Thompson (1987), by no means a supporter of union representation, notes that "organizations invite unions by poor management" (p. 32).

There does not appear to be any empirical research on the effects of union campaigns (see Lawler, 1986). When the surfeit of research on the effects of company campaigns on the outcome of representation elections is contrasted with the scarcity of similar research on union campaigns, it is clear that more research is obviously required on union campaigns (Cooke, 1983). In addition, research should also focus on just why company campaigns are successful.

With respect to counteracting the effects of company tactics, just as management organizes meetings and attempts to establish personal contact with employees, so do union leaders (Brett, 1980; Lawler, 1986). However, management may be more successful for several reasons. First, while management can make meeting attendance mandatory, attendance at union meetings is invariably voluntary and usually extremely low (Brett, 1980; Gordon et al., 1980). Second, although management has access to all employees during work for some form of personal contact, they can deny or make difficult similar opportunities for union organizers to contact all employees. In addition, by providing incomplete or inaccurate lists of employees' addresses, management can further frustrate the efforts of union organizers to meet with employees outside the work context.

Contact with individual employees is only one method for counteracting the effects of a company campaign against unionization. Lawler (1986) observes that unions are now more willing to engage in a wider range of activities to neutralize management tactics. One example of this is to pressure companies by influencing public perception of their company's image. This can extend to the implementation of consumer boycotts against the company. As one illustration, in an attempt to influence the use of pesticides that affect workers' health and safety, the boycott of grapes organized by Cesar Chavez of the United Farm Workers now extends beyond the United States. Because union avoidance must be seen as a deliberate company policy (Kochan et al. 1986), unions have also purchased shares in companies in an attempt to exert direct influence over company policy through attendance, voicing concerns, and voting at annual meetings of shareholders (see Lawler, 1986).

In concluding this section on the effects of macro-level predictors of unionization, several issues deserve comment. First, most of the studies discussed focus on the *outcome* of certification elections, whether as a dichotomous win vs. lose variable, or a proportion of votes cast for and against the union. As noted at the beginning of this chapter, however, the closeness of the typical certification election directs us also to concentrate on the individual employee's voting decision, given that a mere handful of votes can make the difference between winning or losing a certification election. Nonetheless, some information can be gleaned from these studies to guide an understanding of the effects of individual level factors on union voting, because many of these macro-level variables serve as proxies for individual level factors. For example, studies on regional differences in voting patterns are meant to serve as a proxy for attitudes toward unions (Cooke, 1983); studies on whether the day on which the election is held reflects the relative power of labor and management to influence individual employees. Nonetheless, it is appropriate now to turn our attention to studies that have investigated specifically whether micro-level factors predict voting decisions in union certification elections.

Micro-level Predictors of Union Voting Behavior

So far, we have focused our attention on demographic, personality/work beliefs, and macro-level predictors of certification elections. As we argued at the outset of this chapter, however, if our ultimate goal is to predict how individuals will vote in certification elections, the most appropriate level of analysis is the individual. Brief and Rude (1981, p. 261) summarize this argument most cogently when they note that "The results of the election are a function of the individual votes cast by the employees; therefore, voting in union certification elections can be appropriately studied at the individual level of analysis."

In moving to an individual level of analysis, several substantive changes from the preceding discussions will be apparent. First, whereas previous discussions focused mainly on the likelihood of certification elections taking place or the outcome of the election, we now concentrate on individuals' union attitudes, union voting intentions, or union voting behavior. Second, whereas the studies we have considered thus far invariably used proxy measures as the predictor variables, our attention will now be directed toward individual experiences. For purposes of clarity and parsimony, we will separate this discussion into three sections. In the first section, we consider work-related experiences (e.g., job dissatisfaction) as predictors of voting; thereafter, union-related experiences (e.g., general union attitudes) will be presented; and finally, nonwork experiences (e.g., the role of family socialization) will be investigated.

Work Experiences

More than any other work experience, job dissatisfaction has attracted considerable speculation as a possible predictor of individuals' union voting behavior, and there is now a considerable body of empirical literature bearing on this relationship. Indeed, it could be argued that the hypothesis that dissatisfied workers are more likely to vote pro-union has received more empirical attention than any other hypothesis in trying to understand union voting behavior. The results of these studies are consistent: Individuals who are dissatisfied with their jobs are more likely to vote in a pro-union manner if given the choice (see DeCotiis & LeLouarn, 1981; Fiorito et al., 1986; Getman et al., 1976; Keaveny, Rosse, & Fossum, 1988; Heneman & Sandver, 1983; Youngblood et al., 1984; Zalesny, 1985).

Most earlier studies only investigated the effects of overall job satisfaction. However, consistent with the trend in organizational psychology away from conceptualizing variables as unidimensional constructs and investigating bivariate relationships toward the study of multivariate relationships between multidimensional variables (see Locke, 1983; Smith, Kendall, & Hulin, 1969), researchers are now asking whether specific facets of job dissatisfaction differentially predict the prospect of a pro-union vote. At its most basic level, dissatisfaction with one's job can be categorized as being of an extrinsic or intrinsic nature. Intrinsic factors are those concerned with the job itself, such as the degree of autonomy, control, and participation in decision making. In contrast, extrinsic aspects are unrelated to the actual job itself, but are related to the context or environment in which the job occurs, such as supervision, pay, and physical conditions.

Much of the research on extrinsic job dissatisfaction as a predictor of union voting preferences has focused on economic issues, including objective (e.g., pay level) and subjective indices (pay dissatisfaction). Underlying the hypothesis that pay level is associated with pro-union voting intentions are general beliefs that unions are effective in raising wages (Fiorito et al., 1986; and see Chapter 8), and the available data consistently show that lower paid employes are more likely to mainfest pro-union attitudes and to vote in favor of union representation (Allen & Keaveny, 1981; Bigoness, 1978; Feuille & Blandin, 1974; Gordon & Long, 1981; Premack & Hunter, 1988; Youngblood et al., 1984; Zalesny, 1985). Premack and Hunter's data (1988) are most informative in this regard. First, they conducted a meta-analysis; hence, their results reflect a better estimate of the relationship between pay and pro-union voting. Second, they showed that, while significant, the relative effect of objective pay level on union voting preferences was meager both compared to other predictors and in terms of its absolute magnitude.

Other hypotheses concerning the effects of pay have been investigated. For example, it has been suggested that *changes* in pay level predict pro-union voting, because employees perceive unions to be responsible for gaining any positive changes (Fiorito et al., 1986). The limited research focusing on this hypothesis has produced mixed results. Some studies show no significant association (e.g., Cooke, 1983), others show a significant positive relationship (Lawler, 1984). In any event, the meaning of these results is tempered because (1) objective pay level and changes in pay over time are highly correlated (Fiorito et al., 1986) and (2) their criterion was on the outcome of the election at a global level rather than on individual voting preferences.

The findings with respect to dissatisfaction with pay are consistent across studies. Dissatisfaction with one's pay predicts attitudes toward collective bargaining (Bigoness, 1978; Hills, 1985), and pro-union voting (Getman et al., 1976; Gordon & Long, 1981; Hamner & Berman, 1981). Perhaps more important, there is increasing awareness that dissatisfaction with pay level and objective pay level itself are not the only aspects of remuneration with which individuals concern themselves. At least as important, if not more so, is perceived pay equity, that is, the question of whether individuals perceive their level of pay to be just and fair in terms of their output, and that obtained by co-workers performing similar types of work. There are increasing suggestions that several aspects related to pay equity are also associated with pro-union voting. Allen and Keaveny (1981) addressed the issue of whether a pay increase was viewed as equitable. The greater the sense of inequity concerning the increase, the more the subjects in their study perceived a need for a union to represent their interests. Barling, Laliberte, Fullagar, and Kelloway's (1990) findings revealed a significant zero-order correlation between pay inequity and pro-union voting sentiment. However, their path analyses, in which the relative contribution of several predictor variables can be tested, revealed that the effects of perceived pay equity influenced union voting behavior indirectly through union attitudes, and this phenomenon was consistent across American and Canadian samples. This indirect effect will be considered in greater detail later.

In summary, findings from these studies are consistent: Objective pay level, pay dissatisfaction, and perceived pay inequity consistently predict pro-union voting attitudes and/or preferences. Despite the fact that unions have traditionally presented their potential attractiveness to employees on the basis of the economic benefits associated with union membership, and drawn up their bargaining agenda accordingly, a comprehensive understanding of the reasons motivating individuals to seek union representation require that we go beyond economic factors. As Bakke (1945) noted in his classic article, "To classify unionism, therefore, merely as a mechanism for collective bargaining for economic advantages is to underrate its importance" (p. 9). Accordingly, we now turn our attention to other aspects of job dissatisfaction.

There is some research on the effects of employee satisfaction regarding specific job conditions on the propensity to unionize. One issue of considerable concern to employees is occupational health and safety. Workers who are exposed to physical hazards in the workplace, and who see themselves in some danger as a result, are more likely to vote in favor of a union (Hills, 1985; Kochan, 1979). Two other issues that have been investigated are satisfaction with promotional possibilities and satisfaction with one's coworkers. Bigoness (1978) showed that satisfaction with promotion was negatively associated with attitudes toward collective bargaining. In contrast, satisfaction with one's coworkers was unrelated to attitudes toward collective bargaining (Bass & Mitchell, 1976; Bigoness, 1978; Hamner & Smith, 1978). These two findings are consistent with the oft-stated goal and perceived strengths of unions: While most unions concentrate heavily on economic issues, and issues of perceived fairness, unions are not typically involved with interpersonal relationships between rank-and-file members. Seen from this perspective, it is understandable that dissatisfaction with one's coworkers would not be associated with attitudes toward collective bargaining.

The studies mentioned thus far have all focused on specific aspects of job satisfaction. Some studies have focused more globally on extrinsic job satisfaction. For example, general dissatisfaction with working conditions, which includes pay, job security, and other extrinsic aspects, predicts a pro-union vote (e.g., Brett, 1980; Gordon & Long, 1981; Keaveny, Rosse, & Fossum, 1988; DeCotiis & LeLouarn, 1981). It seems clear, therefore, that the findings are consistent: Global extrinsic job dissatisfaction and facet-specifc job dissatisfaction invariably predict a pro-union vote. Nonetheless, just as we would be limiting our knowledge of why individuals choose to join unions if we concentrated only on economic factors, there are also some studies that have gone beyond a focus on extrinsic job factors. These studies assess the relationship between intrinsic job factors and voting in union elections. Two points about these studies should be noted here, as they will restrict the discussion. First, there are far fewer studies focusing on intrinsic than extrinsic job satisfaction. Second, some studies deal with intrinsic job characteristics rather than focusing specifically on dissatisfaction. From all these studies, it is possible to contrast the effects of extrinsic and intrinsic job satisfaction on voting decisions.

The findings concerning the role of intrinsic job satisfaction are mixed. In his study, Bigoness (1978) found a significant correlation between satisfaction with work itself and attitudes toward collective bargaining. Allen and Keaveny (1981) also showed that overall intrinsic satisfaction predicted the perceived need for a union. However, some studies have shown no relationship between overall intrinsic job satisfaction and pro-union voting (Keaveny et al., 1988). Allen and Keaveny (1981) also focused on specific aspects of intrinsic job satisfaction. They showed that satisfaction with the skill utilization inherent in the job, the amount of creativity required by the job, and feelings of achievement all correlated negatively with the perceived need for a union. However, no significant relationship emerged between satisfaction with responsibility inherent in the job and attitudes toward collectve bargaining (Allen & Keaveny, 1981). The meaning of the findings relating intrinsic job satisfaction and union voting behavior can be further understood by contrasting them with findings on employees' perceptions of intrinsic job characteristics.

One intrinsic job characteristic that has attracted some attention is the extent to which employees perceive they can exert some control and/or power over their work and working conditions. The rationale underlying this hypothesis is not new. Bakke (1945) had already identified the attainment of control and independence as a major contribution that unions could achieve for their members. Since then, a number of studies have focused on this issue, and the findings support the hypothesis that employees who believe they lack control over working condtions will be more favorably disposed toward the presence of unions (Allen & Keaveny, 1981; Lawler & Walker, 1984). Closely paralleling the need to control one's workplace is the perceived influence one exerts over work-related outcomes. While Decotiis and LeLouarn (1981) showed a significant zero-order correlation between perceived influence and union voting, the meaning of this relationship is called into question, as it was no longer significant after the effects of extrinsic job dissatisfaction and psychological stress were controlled. Another variable that reflects perceived control is the feeling of powerlessness. Whether that feeling derived from the perceived inability to influence managerial decision making (Zalesny, 1985), aspects related to compensation (Hammer & Berman, 1981), or generalized powerlessness at work (Keaveny et al., 1988), the findings remain the same: Feelings of powerlessness predict a pro-union vote.

Bakke (1945) identified another job attribute that might be related to pro-union attitudes and voting which he labeled "justice." The notion underlying this relationship is that employees who believe that company policy is just and is administered fairly are less likely to turn to unions. Studies that have investigated this issue consistently show support for this hypothesis (Bass & Mitchell, 1976; DeCotiis & LeLouarn, 1981; Keaveny et al., 1988). Similarly, findings from various studies show that a lack of trust in management predicts union voting preferences (Hammer & Berman, 1981; Zalesny, 1985).

Aside from variables such as justice, trust, powerlessness, and control, the question has also been asked as to whether factors specifically related to one's job predict union voting behavior. Goal clarity, the extent to which job expectations are made clear by the organization, is negatively associated with the felt need for collective bargaining (Bass & Mitchell, 1976). Similarly, both role conflict and role ambiguity, and psychological stress, are negatively associated with union voting behavior (DeCotiis & LeLouarn, 1981). Satisfaction with the extent to which one's skills are used positively predicts attitudes to collective bargaining (Allen & Keaveny, 1981). Likewise, lack of autonomy on the job predicts positive attitudes to unions (Hills, 1985). Clarity, skill utilization, and autonomy all contribute (together with other job characteristics such as task variety and feedback) to what Hackman and Oldham (1975) would refer to as the "motivating potential" of the job, and research shows that holding a job that is low in motivating potential predicts union voting intentions (Youngblood et al., 1984). Similarly, psychological involvement in, and identification with one's job negatively predicted attitudes to collective bargaining (Bigoness, 1978). To many theorists and practitioners, perhaps the most important attribute of a job is the incumbent's ability to participate fully in decision making. At least three studies have shown that where such participation is not available to university faculty, it may be the strongest predictor of a pro-union vote (Bornheimer, 1985; Feuille & Blandin, 1974; Hammer & Berman, 1981).

All these findings concerning the extent to which intrinsic job factors predict pro-union voting must be seen in a broader context. A number of studies allow us to do so, because they have simultaneously investigated intrinsic and extrinsic job dissatisfaction. The results from these studies initially appear to be somewhat mixed. Some studies suggest that extrinsic job dissatisfaction is a more important predictor of union attitudes or union voting intentions than intrinsic job dissatisfaction (e.g., Allen & Keaveny, 1981; Brett, 1980; Schriesheim, 1978). Others, however, show that intrinsic job dissatisfaction is a more important antecedent of union preferences than extrinsic job dissatisfaction (e.g., Bornheimer, 1985; DeCotiis & Lelouarn, 1981; Hammer & Berman, 1981; Zalesny, 1985).

Several factors might account for these differences. First, whether intrinsic or extrinsic job dissatisfaction serves as the predominant motivator of the vote for union representation depends primarily on the nature of the sample (Kochan, 1979). Keaveny et al. (1988) and Youngblood, Mobley, and DeNisi's (1981) studies are most instructive in this regard. They simultaneously investigated both extrinsic and intrinsic job satisfaction within professional and nonprofessional samples, and showed that intrinsic satisfaction was more important in the professional sample and vice versa. Second, Hammer and Berman (1981) offer a somewhat different explanation. In contrast to need hierarchy theories, they suggest economic concerns only become primary motivators when employees enjoy some participation in decision making. Where employees enjoy little power and distrust management, these factors are the most important predictors, and economic factors would not be important. To Hammer and Berman, therefore, the fundamental question is whether employees enjoy sufficient power and trust in management. If they do, economic factors would achieve greater importance. This implies that different predictors emerge in different organizations: Such differences are contextual, originating in the peculiarities of specific employer-employee relationships.

Union Attitudes and Experiences

Despite the importance accorded to job dissatisfaction as a causal factor in union voting intentions, job dissatisfaction is probably a necessary but insufficient factor in deciding whether to vote for or against a union. Numerous authors have posited that attitudes to unions fulfill an important role in the unionization decision, and different authors accord varying roles to union attitudes in this process. In an attempt to understand just how union attitudes influence union voting preferences, we will make extensive use of Deshpande and Fiorito's (1989) differentiation between general and specific union attitudes. The difference between the two has been illustrated by Kochan, Katz, and McKersie (1986), who note that while three-quarters of American non-union employees certainly believe that unions generally improve wages, working conditions, and so forth (i.e., general union attitudes), most do not believe that the presence of a union would improve *their own* wages and working conditions (specific union attitudes).

There are suggestions that political, social, and economic events of the 1980s influenced public attitudes toward unions (Lowe & Krahn, 1989). Because unions may be seen as institutions serving the interests of workers during times of economic decline, perceptions of their general role may have improved. Alternatively, in a period characterized by government-imposed restrictions, aggressive anti-union management strategies, two-tiered wage agreements, and concessionary bargaining, perceptions of union power and instrumentality in bettering individual working conditions may have deteriorated (Lipset, 1986; Riddell, 1986). Likewise, in Canada the public generally approve of the overall functions of unions and believe that workers would be worse off in the absence of labor organizations. At the same time, however, they also disapprove of the behavior of unions (Lowe & Krahn, 1989). Similar results have been found in British opinion polls, where the majority of respondents surveyed viewed unions as necessary for the protection of worker interests, but too powerful (Rosier & Little, 1986). Such surveys counter the simplistic impression that public attitudes toward unions have deteriorated over the last twenty years. Regardless of whether these attitudes have grown more or less favorable, several academic studies have demonstrated that union attitudes have a significant impact on individuals' propensity to join unions and voting behavior in representation elections.

Without any doubt, strong attitudes have always been expressed, whether pro-union or anti-union. For example, Whyte (1944, p. 222) quotes a non-union employee who stated that "I don't want to have anything to do with an organization that's run by communists and racketeers. When I have to pay an organization in order to hold my job, I'll just quit." Similar attitudes still prevail today. Cook (1983) notes that the Teamsters continue to attract very negative attitudes, largely because they are viewed to be controlled by individuals with ties to organized crime. These attitudes are then held to be important predictors of unionization: As will be noted in the chapter on de-unionization, the Teamsters suffer more decertification elections, and lose a disproportionate share of these elections, again presumably because of the negative attitudes they attract (e.g., Cooke, 1983).

A number of studies have been conducted to assess the effects of individual attitudes to unions on union voting intentions and voting behavior. Perhaps the first and most important study was that conducted by Getman et al. (1976). Although their study was initially designed as a test of the effects of company campaigns during certification elections, and their findings and policy recommendations on this specific issue have been frequently questioned, their findings on union attitudes and job dissatisfaction have been consistently replicated. As Getman et al. (1976, pp. 58–59) stated with respect to the predictive role of union attitudes:

> The correlation between union attitudes and vote was 0.62. ... Union attitude indices ranged from a low score of 8 to a high score of 32 ... employees who had a union attitude index of 22 or higher favored union representation by approximately three to one (381–138); those with an index below 22 were opposed more than four to one (414–71). Knowing whether an employee's union attitude score was greater or less than 22 enables one to predict his vote with 79 percent accuracy.

Recent studies consistently support their findings (Barling, Kelloway, & Bremermann, 1991; Barling, Laliberte, Fullagar, & Kelloway, 1990; Deshpande & Fiorito, 1989; Montgomery, 1989; Schriesheim, 1978). Perhaps more important, critical re-analyses of Getman et al.'s (1976) data (e.g., Dickens, 1983) replicate the relationship between union attitudes and union voting behavior. Nonetheless, one important limit to the generalizability of these findings must be borne in mind. Union elections take different forms. In one situation, only one union seeks recognition as the formal bargaining unit. In another, two or more unions compete against each other for the right to represent the employees. As Martin (1984) notes, general union attitudes would only predict the outcome of the former election. In contrast, as will now be suggested, *specific* union beliefs may be more important in predicting the outcome of elections where different unions are competing against each other for formal recognition: In that case, individuals would presumably choose one union on the basis of the relative power and perceived instrumentality of the two unions.

The importance of separating general attitudes toward unions from attitudes to a specific union had already been acknowledged by Bakke (1945, p. 3) in his oft-cited essay, when he noted that "It is well to remember that the worker does not join unions in general, but rather joins a specific union. Unions vary considerably in their nature and practices." Even before Bakke's (1945) article had been published, the possible effects of beliefs about the effectiveness of specific unions had been investigated. Chamberlain (1935), for example, found that 90% of the union members in his sample believed that textile unions were effective. Most union members in his sample suggested that workers join unions "because that is the only way the working man can get results" (p. 121).

Before presenting the findings, a brief note about the nature of specific union beliefs is in order. These specific beliefs are frequently referred to as "perceived union instrumentality," which accurately reflects its meaning. The issue under consideration is how instrumental the specific union is perceived to be in resolving particular dissatisfactions. Because the individuals concerned would obviously not currently be members of the specific union, any judgments on how instrumental the specific union could be would not likely be based on direct and/or current personal experience. Rather, their judgment would be formed on the basis of vicarious observations, personal contact with members of the specific union, hearsay, and, in very few cases, prior experiences with the specific union. In contrast, as will be seen in subsequent chapters, when currently unionized members consider the instrumentality of the specific union, they base their opinions on direct and current personal experience. On a practical level, union members and nonmembers differ in their judgments about the instrumentality of the same union. For example, Chamberlain (1935) asked 200 men employed in textile plants whether they believed that textile unions were effective. Of the 100 union members, 90 responded affirmatively. Of the 100 non-union members, only 38 thought that textile unions were effective.

The question of whether employees' specific perceptions about the instrumentality of a particular union affect their voting preferences concerning that union has been subjected to much empirical analysis. The results of these studies show consistently that perceiving that a union would be effective in resolving workplace dissatisfactions is invariably linked with a vote in favor of the union (e.g., Barling, Laliberte, Fullagar, & Kelloway, 1990; Beutell & Biggs, 1984; DeCotiis & LeLouarn, 1981; Deshpande & Fiorito, 1989; Fullagar & Howland, 1989; Kochan, 1979; Montgomery, 1989; Premack & Hunter, 1988; Schriesheim, 1978). Moreover, an analysis of these findings shows that the relationship between union instrumentality perceptions and union voting preferences is usually high.

Despite the consistency and magnitude of these findings, two questions remain. First, most of these findings focus on the extent to which unions are perceived as being able to redress extrinsic workplace issues, such as wages, security, and supervision. Intrinsic issues, such as the meaningfulness of work, have been investigated much less frequently. This might represent an important omission, because employees have different perceptions about how instrumental the union might be in satisfying different issues, and different unions may choose to focus on intrinsic issues to varying degrees. For example, consistent with the notion that unions have focused most of their bargaining efforts on extrinsic issues, and have achieved most of their gains in this area (Quinn & Staines, 1977), it is to be expected that workers perceive them to be more successful in this regard. As unions start to turn their focus to intrinsic issues, which includes issues about the quality of worklife, it would be appropriate to investigate multiple dimensions of instrumentality. Certainly, Fiorito (1987) has shown that perceptions of the union's instrumentality concerning political issues predicts pro-union voting.

Second, even though perceived union instrumentality is grounded in expectancy theory (see Pinder, 1984), most of the above studies have not faithfully reflected expectancy theory. Specifically, while the studies discussed all included an in-depth focus on the notion of instrumentality, only a few have also focused explicitly on either or both of the expectancy and/or valence components (Barling & Fullagar, 1990; Beutell & Biggs, 1984; Zalesny, 1985). It remains to be seen whether more accurate predictions of union voting intentions and behavior can be obtained if the theory is assessed more faithfully. For example, including the valence component would enable researchers to understand not only whether unions are perceived as instrumental in satisfying certain issues, but also to weigh each of those issues in terms of their perceived importance to the employee.

In summarizing the effects of union experiences, it is apparent that both general and specific union attitudes predict union voting preferences. One question that has been asked concerns their relative influence on union voting. Certainly if zero-order correlations are used as the basis for answering this question, it would appear as though general and specific attitudes are equally important (e.g., Deshpande & Fiorito, 1989; Schriesheim, 1978). However, studies using multivariate approaches that permit an examination of the simultaneous effect of general and specific beliefs support the conclusion that specific beliefs about the effects of a union in an individual's own workplace are more important than general beliefs in predicting union voting intentions and behavior (Deshpande & Fiorito, 1989; Kochan, 1979). Indeed, based on the findings that specific beliefs supersede general beliefs, Keaveny et al. (1988) suggest that even when employees believe the particular union to be undemocratic and corrupt, employees will still vote for the specific union if they believe its presence will result in better wages and job security. There appears to be a consensus in the literature that most workers join unions for instrumental rather than ideological reasons. Thus, despite the considerable difficulties encountered in judging the anticipated costs and benefits of union membership, it is appropriate to conclude this section by quoting Brett (1980, p. 49): "In the end, a decision to organize a union is instrumental. Do the employees involved believe they will be better off with a union or not?"

Nonwork Effects

Despite the consistent and profound effects of job/work and union experiences on union attitudes and union voting behavior, some causes of general attitudes toward unions and specific decisions whether to vote in favour or against union representation are independent of work and union factors. Community and family characteristics, socialization experiences, and one's current reference group have been hypothesized to be important socializing influences in this regard.

Several sociological studies have attempted to ascertain the impact of communities on union attitudes and unionization (Krahn & Lowe, 1984). For example, when the local community revolves around specific occupational characteristics there is a close relationship between work and community life. Such an "occupational community" influences the industrial attitudes and behaviors of workers (Blauner, 1964; Lipset, Trow, & Coleman, 1956; Strauss,

1977a). The size of a community has also been shown to have an effect on unionization: Workers from smaller communities are more directly exposed to unions (Bowen & Shaw, 1972; Mills, 1956), and the closer social relations of small communities provide greater support for unionizing employees (Krahn & Lowe, 1984), both of which facilitate unionization. Research on American auto workers has indicated that the more integrated the worker is in both the industrial and wider communities, the greater the individual involvement in unions (Form & Dansereau, 1957). Finally, in a Canadian study, Krahn and Lowe (1984) have suggested that such community characteristics as industrial structure, general economic climate, social relations, and union tradition may have an impact on union attitudes (specifically general attitudes toward union power and specific beliefs concerning unions' instrumentality in providing material benefits).

The hypothesis that salient factors in one's family of origin exert an important effect on later union attitudes and intentions is not new. Both Bakke (1945) and Whyte (1944) recognized that family influences during one's early years would exert such an effect later on. Interest in the effects of family socialization on union attitudes and voting preferences continues (e.g., Brief & Rude, 1981; Fiorito et al., 1986) and the available data support the hypothesis that early family socialization influences subsequent union attitudes.

One series of studies has asked whether parents' union status (members or not) exerts any influence on union attitudes or voting intentions. The results from such studies are mixed. Deshpande and Fiorito (1989) and Youngblood et al. (1984) supported the existence of such a link; Laliberte (1986) did not. However, it has since been argued (e.g., Barling, Kelloway, & Bremermann, 1991; Gallagher & Jeong, 1989) that merely focusing on parents' union membership status represents an inadequate test of this hypothesis. The hypothesis positing a link between family socialization and current union attitudes is grounded in the notion that children's attitudes are influenced by the psychological environment in which they develop. Yet parental membership status is an inadequate proxy of parental union attitudes. Union members can be unfavorably disposed toward unions; similarly, employees who have never been presented with the option of joining a union can be favorably disposed. Accordingly, a better test of the family socialization hypothesis would require a focus on parents' union attitudes, or children's perceptions of their parents' attitudes. Studies taking this approach show consistently that parents' self-reported union attitudes, or children's perceptions of their parents' union attitudes, predict the union attitudes of non-unionized employees (Gallagher & Jeong, 1989; Montgomery, 1989; Smith & Hokpins, 1979). Barling, Kelloway, and Bremermann's (1991) study extends these general findings. They showed that (1) children's perceptions of parents' union attitudes influence union voting intentions indirectly, through their direct effects on children's union attitudes, and (2) family socialization exerts a greater effect on children's union attitudes and voting intentions than either work ethic or Marxist work beliefs.

A second hypothesized nonwork influence on union attitude is one's current reference group (e.g., Brief & Rude, 1981; Montgomery, 1989). Again, this hypothesis is by no means recent: Bakke (1945, p. 5) illustrated the role of group factors and family socialization in the decision to join a union:

> Family pressure has led more than one man to reject union membership; so has pressure from his buddies in the shop or from the members of his church . . . The roll of any union contains the names of some men who have joined for little reason other than that, "If the other boys want a union, why then I'm for it too."

Chamberlain (1935) showed that approximately half of his non-union sample stated that a main reason for joining a union was that one's fellow workers did. More recent studies support these earlier findings (Fullagar & Howland, 1989; Montgomery, 1989; Zalesny, 1985). As well as replicating findings that peers' general union attitudes influence one's own attitudes and voting decisions, Montgomery (1989) also showed this effect was greater when subjects believed that their peers wanted them to conform with their own attitudes.

In any attempt to understand employees' union voting decisions more comprehensively, the need for further research on prior exposure to unions, whether direct or vicarious, whether through family or friends, has been noted (Heneman & Sandver, 1983). Following from Montgomery's (1989) findings, one worthwhile direction would be to consider not only the union attitudes of salient others, but also the extent to which they wish the employee in question to manifest similar attitudes. In any such research, however, one intriguing problem identified by Montgomery (1989) in this context, and raised in other contexts as well (Barling, 1990), is worth noting. Namely, any effects of family socialization or reference groups on current union voting decisions may be underestimated. Specifically, when asked about the extent to which parents or coworkers affect our behavior, only a small proportion of respondents will acknowledge such an effect at all, either because they are unaware of the influence or unwilling to acknowledge it.

One remaining question concerns the relative effects of work, union, and nonwork experiences on union voting intentions and preferences. Even if family socialization and reference group effects may be underestimated, the results from Fullagar and Howland's (1989) recent study suggesting that perceived union instrumentality is more predictive of union voting behavior than either normative influences or job dissatisfaction seem justified. However, to answer this question more thoroughly, we should turn to research that has simultaneously examined these work, union, and nonwork predictors of unionization decisions.

Modeling Union Voting Intentions and Decisions

Much of the research that has been presented so far has suffered from one or both of two problems. In the first instance, many studies have investigated whether single variables predict union voting preferences. Yet as Youngblood et al. (1984) suggest, the notion that any single variable predicts an outcome as complex as union attitudes, voting intentions, or voting behavior is simplistic. Second, even though studies have focused on the simultaneous and relative effects of several predictors, these studies are typically more empirically than conceptually driven. It is important to note, therefore, that there have been several attempts to construct rich conceptual models of union voting behavior. Because these models enable us to understand the relative contribution of individuals' work, union, and nonwork experiences to union voting behavior, we now turn our attention to an examination of these models. Another way of viewing the contribution of such studies is that they help isolate the direct and indirect effects of the various predictors.

Arguably, the first psychological model of union voting behavior was developed by Brett (1980) on the basis of the data collected by Getman et al. (1976). According to Brett, initial interest in the possibility of unionization is triggered by job dissatisfaction. This dissatisfaction would most likely be extrinsic, with facets such as wages, security, and supervision being of most importance. If it is accompanied by the perception that the employee alone can do very little to reduce the dissatisfaction, the question arises as to what can be done to improve the situation. Brett (1980) argues that this job dissatisfaction only serves as the initial trigger in the unionization process, and is likely to lead to pro-union voting under certain circumstances.

Brett (1980) includes in her model several additional components discussed earlier in this chapter. First, individuals must believe that the specific union in question is able to redress the particular dissatisfaction. Stated somewhat differently, given high job dissatisfaction, pro-union voting would become more likely when perceived union instrumentality (i.e., specific union attitudes) is high. Second, the attitudes of fellow employees and other salient individuals would be critical. When dissatisfied workers' attitudes are shared with the specific individual, the likelihood of pro-union voting would again be enhanced. In this sense, the role of subjective norms is included. Third, personality factors are also considered important. Brett (1980) argues that some individuals reject the notion of collective action, believing instead that workplace problems should be dealt with individually. Thus, employees may be dissatisfied, and believe that unions could resolve the specific dissatisfaction, but prefer to take individual action. This specific component is somewhat analogous to the Protestant work ethic that was considered earlier in this chapter, and will be considered again (see Chapter 4).

Finally, a prominent role is assigned to general attitudes to unions. According to Brett (1980), even if the first four conditions in the model are fulfilled, a pro-union vote is highly unlikely where employees manifest negative attitudes to unions in general. In addition, some employees in her study who were satisfied with their working conditions nevertheless voted for a union if their general attitudes to unions were favorable. In this respect, general attitudes to unions serve as a final "gatekeeper" in the process leading to the decision to vote for or against union representation.

Interestingly, Brett's (1980) model provides some indication as to why the magnitude of the correlation betwen job dissatisfaction and union attitudes and voting behavior, while consistently statistically significant, is modest. First, job dissatisfaction is a distal cause of union voting; and other more proximal causal factors such as specific and general union attitudes should be expected to exhibit stronger correlations with union voting preferences. Second, job dissatisfaction is an insufficient cause of union voting preferences. Employees who are dissatisfied with their jobs would not vote for a union if they held negative attitudes to unions, especially if they believed the union was not likely to resolve their dissatisfaction. In contrast, individuals who are satisfied with their jobs may still vote for a union if they manifest favorable union attitudes.

One question is the extent to which Brett's (1980) model has received empirical support. As an integrated set of hypotheses, her model has not been subject to empirical scrutiny. Also, important aspects of the model, such as the proposed interaction of job dissatisfaction and general union attitudes (Schriesheim, 1978), have not been tested. When specific aspects of the model have been assessed, questions are raised. For example, it is possible that general union attitudes predict specific attitudes (i.e., perceived union instrumentality), and that specific attitudes are more predictive of union voting behavior (Barling, Kelloway, & Bremermann, 1991; Barling, Laliberte, Fullagar, & Kelloway, 1990; Deshpande & Fiorito, 1989). As such, the contribution of Brett's (1980) model does not rest on its empirical status. Instead, it provided much-needed theory at a time when theoretical formulations were most required (Heneman & Sandver, 1983).

In sharp contrast to Brett (1980), Premack and Hunter (1988) have provided a model of the unionization process that is more empirically than conceptually grounded. Essentially, Premack and Hunter (1988) conducted a meta-analysis of fourteen existing studies investigating employee unionization decisions. The model they arrived at differs from that of Brett (1980) in several substantive ways. First, the trigger in their model is not dissatisfaction with working conditions, but instead objective wage level. Second, they separated satisfaction into two components, namely, satisfaction with extrinsic aspects and satisfaction with administration. Third, general attitude to unions is absent from their model. Fourth, the process leading to the unionization decision roughly paralleled that of Brett, namely, wage level predicted extrinsic satisfaction, extrinsic satisfaction predicted satisfaction with administration, extrinsic satisfaction predicted perceived union instrumentality which resulted in the decision whether to vote for or against the union. However, unlike Brett (1980) who only posited indirect effects on union voting, Premack and Hunter (1988) showed that any of these four predictors themselves could result in the decision to vote for or against a union, presumably because employees differ as to when a union would be seen as desirable (see Figure 3.1). For example, for some workers, low wages could be a sufficient cause for a pro-union vote. For others, low wages alone would be insufficient.

Both models just discussed focus only on union and work-related predictors of union voting decisions. As already noted in this chapter, nonwork factors also influence the decision to vote for a union, either directly or indirectly. As a result, Barling and his colleagues investigated how characteristics associated with the

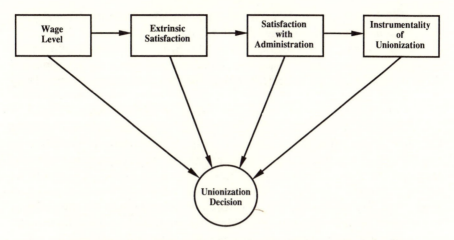

FIGURE 3.1   Premack and Hunter's model of union voting behavior

individual employee interact with work and union-related characteristics. In the first of these studies, Barling, Laliberte, Fullagar, and Kelloway (1990) refined previous models of the intent to vote for a union in several ways. For example, they focused on dissatisfaction with extrinsic aspects of work, and the perceived instrumentality of the union in resolving such extrinsic aspects. Both extrinsic job dissatisfaction and extrinsic union instrumentality predicted the willingness to vote for a union. Extrinsic job dissatisfaction and general union attitudes also influenced the willingness to vote for a union indirectly through their effects on extrinsic union instrumentality. Also, Marxist work beliefs and psychological conservatism (i.e., the fear of change) exerted direct effects on general union attitudes. In addition, they investigated the role of perceived pay equity instead of focusing on objective wage level and found that it exerted a substantial negative effect on extrinsic job satisfaction (see Figure 3.2). Finally, it is worth noting that this model was replicated independently in two separate samples in

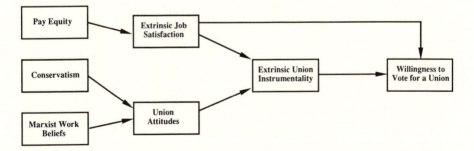

FIGURE 3.2   Barling, Laliberte, Fullagar, and Kelloway's model of work and nonwork predictors of union voting intentions

the United States and Canada, despite the differing labor relations structures and legislation in these two countries (Kumar, Coates & Arrowsmith, 1987).

Noting the importance of union attitudes in understanding union voting preferences, and suggestions that some of the causes of union attitudes lie outside of work and union experiences, Barling, Kelloway, and Bremermann (1991) explored the development of union attitudes and union voting intentions in a sample of pre-employed late adolescents. Because personal work experiences would presumably exert a minimal effect within such a sample, they contrasted the relative effects of beliefs about work (Marxist and humanistic work beliefs) and family socialization (perceptions of parents' union participation and union attitudes) in their sample of pre-employed individuals. Several interesting findings emerged (see Fig. 3.3). First, the effects of family socialization on subjects' union attitudes was at least twice as large as the combined effect of both work beliefs. Second, both family socialization and work beliefs exerted indirect effects on union voting intentions through their direct effects on general union attitudes.

Finally, several studies have attempted to apply social psychological models to the decision to unionize with some success (Montgomery, 1989; Youngblood et al., 1984; Zalesny, 1985). The most recent and rigorous of these is Montgomery's (1989) application of Fishbein and Ajzen's (1975) model of behavior and the formation of behavioral intentions to the decision to vote in a union certification election. This model proposes that there are two main predictors of intention to vote for a union. First, are workers' beliefs that joining a union leads to certain outcomes (e.g., pay increases, facilitation of grievances processes, equalization of salary differentials, improvement of benefits), and the person's evaluations of these outcomes. Second, are various normative pressures that impinge on the worker. These consist of the individual's beliefs that specific individuals or groups (e.g., family, co-workers, supervisors, and management staff) think the individual should or should not vote for a union, and the person's motivation to comply with the specific referents. According to Fishbein and Ajzen (1975), behavioral intention (in this instance, intention to vote for a union)

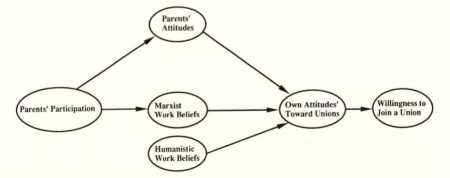

FIGURE 3.3 Barling, Kelloway, and Bremermann's model of pre-employment predictors of union voting intentions

is the single best predictor of behavior (voting for a union). This approach extends the previous models we have discussed in two ways: (1) it incorporates perceptions of union instrumentality but acknowledges that individuals value differently the outcomes that unions are seen as instrumental in achieving; (2) it broadens the focus of normative pressure to include not only one's family, but coworkers and management, and incorporates a measure of compliance. Montgomery's (1989) results also supported the importance of general and specific union attitudes. In addition, normative pressures were found to significantly influence voting intention.

In conclusion, the limited data available suggests that both work and nonwork factors certainly do play a role in the development of union attitudes and union voting preferences. Also, models have been derived with the potential for contributing to our understanding of the unionization process. Given the probable stability of union attitudes, further research is encouraged to understand more comprehensively the development of union attitudes and union voting behavior.

Conceptual, Empirical, and Ethical Issues in Predicting Union Voting Behavior

The preceding discussion concerning the prediction of union voting preferences and behavior raises several important issues, from theoretical, empirical, and ethical perspectives. These will now be discussed in turn, as they both affect interpretations of the results already obtained, as well as the design and conduct of any future research in this area.

One issue that has consistently emerged concerns the way in which the outcome variable is operationalized. In general, the outcome has been operationalized as (1) a dichotomous variable indicating whether the union was successful or not, (2) a proportion indicating the percentage of union non-union votes cast in the election, (3) general attitudes to unions, which include attitudes to collective bargaining and the perceived need for collective bargaining (Allen & Keaveny, 1981; Bass & Mitchell, 1976), (4) intentions to vote for the union (Beutell & Biggs, 1984), or (5) a self-report of actual voting behavior (Premack & Hunter, 1988). The first question that emerges is whether the information obtained using these various criteria is at all comparable. The first two techniques are compatible with a macro-level approach that focuses on the outcome of certification elections; the latter three measures are consistent with a micro-level approach to predicting individual union voting behavior. As argued earlier, the second approach might provide more fruitful information given that the typical certification election is decided by very few voters. Although it is beyond the scope of this review to provide a definitive answer to this question, it is worth noting that Heneman and Sandver (1983) suggest that studies have been more successful in predicting individual voting behavior than the outcomes of elections.

Of considerable concern are the numerous studies in which the outcome of interest was a categorization of the pro- vs. anti-union vote. But what about employees who deliberately choose not to vote in the election? We argue that ignoring such individuals in research (not one study could be found in which a group of abstainers was included!) has critical conceptual and practical implications. From a pragmatic perspective, because certification elections are typically decided by only a few votes, identifying the abstainers is of critical importance. As Whyte noted over four decades ago, "In any closely contested election, it is the votes of the 'on the fence' workers which are decisive'" (1944, p. 229). From a conceptual position, because union attitudes are relatively stable (Barling, Kelloway, & Bremermann, 1991), these undecided abstainers may be most likely to be influenced by a company or union campaign. Yet current research ignores this critical group, possibly because it is believed that undecided voters would vote to support the status quo—that is, vote against union representation (Brett, 1980). Also, researchers may be blinded by the assumption that there are truly only two alternatives, "vote yes or vote no" (Herman, 1973, p. 221). In any event, union organizers and academic researchers would be advised to pay far more attention to this group.

A more in-depth focus on the way in which the outcome has been operationalized in micro-level studies is also appropriate. First, the results of recent research would indicate that general union attitudes predict union voting intentions or behavior, rather than serving as a proxy for them. Second, there is no certainty that intentions to vote for or against union representation function as a suitable proxy for the actual vote itself. On the one hand, some researchers argue so strongly against this notion that any study focusing on voting intentions was deliberately excluded from their empirical review of the outcome of certification elections (Heneman & Sandver, 1983). On the other hand, Premack and Hunter (1988) argue on the basis of their meta-analysis that the population correlation between voting intentions and actual voting behavior is .79; and that the two variables serve as a proxy of voting behavior. Since their study was published, this controversy has continued: Deshpande and Fiorito (1989) noted that while union voting intentions are interesting in their own right, their results suggested that voting intentions do not proxy voting behavior. On the contrary, Montgomery (1989) showed that voting behavior can be correctly classified with 91% accuracy based only on voting intentions. The debate as to whether union voting intentions are synonymous with union voting behavior is important and will undoubtedly continue.

All the research on individual unionization decision making is predicated on the assumption that individuals are free to choose whether to vote for or against the union; in other words, that no situational factors constrain their choice (Herman, 1973). One factor that could limit individuals' freedom in this context is management and/or union intimidation, and it is apparent that individual voting behavior is influenced by management tactics, despite earlier claims to the contrary (Getman et al., 1976). This may have important implications for the interpretation of any findings on the predictors of employee voting behavior. Herman (1973) argued that such external constraints would decrease any correlation between the predictors of interest and union voting. It is possible, therefore, that the extent to which micro-level variables predict pro- or anti-union voting behavior has been underestimated in the past.

From a conceptual perspective, numerous studies have identified job dissatisfaction, general attitudes to unions, and perceived union instrumentality as important predictors of union voting. Clearly, an in-depth understanding of individuals' voting preferences requires a greater comprehension of how these factors develop. There is a voluminous body of research on the predictors of job dissatisfaction (see Locke, 1983). In sharp contrast, there is very little information about the development of general or specific attitudes to unions (Brett, 1980). As Youngblood et al. (1984) perhaps understate, "how one acquires either a positive or a negative impression of labor unions is not completely understood" (p. 579). Recent research has shown the role of nonwork factors in the development of general union attitudes (Smith & Hopkins, 1979), including the influence of family socialization and beliefs about work, which are independent of work themselves (Barling, Kelloway, & Bremermann, 1991). Given the possibility that general union attitudes are stable once they have developed, understanding their formation becomes an even more important task for future research.

One final methodological issue that pervades many of the studies discussed above is the tendency to focus on zero-order correlations between predictor variables and the outcome of interest. This approach is undoubtedly simplistic (Youngblood et al., 1984), and ignores the logical fact that no single variable is sufficiently powerful to cause any individual to vote for or against union representation. The models just discussed (e.g., Barling, Kelloway, & Bremermann, 1991; Barling, Laliberte, Fullagar, & Kelloway, 1990; Brett, 1980; Premack & Hunter, 1988) explicitly assume that antecedent variables interact in predicting union voting. This has important conceptual and practical implications. Conceptually, it becomes possible to isolate the relative effects of different predictor variables. It also provides information to both unions and management that could be of some practical use.

Because much of the research that has been considered has focused on data collected within the United States, whether the findings obtained generalize to other national groups represents a legitimate question. One study has investigated this issue. As noted above, Barling, Laliberte, Fullagar, and Kelloway (1990) empirically cross-validated their model in Canada and the United States. This finding is noteworthy because, as will be noted in Chapter 4, the labor relations climate differs in several important respects between these two countries, with public policy and labor legislation being more receptive to organized labor in Canada.

It might be argued, however, that one substantial similarity between Canada and the United States is their emphasis on "business unionism," where workplace issues dominate the bargaining agenda. A different model of unionism exists when the goal of organized labor is to fundamentally alter societal (i.e., nonwork) conditions, such as that found in Poland in the 1980s, or that which still exists in South Africa today. For example, a primary goal of the National

Union of Mineworkers in South Africa is the attainment of racial equality (Middleton, 1990). The question remains whether such variables as job dissatisfaction, perceived union instrumentality, and general attitudes to unions constitute the primary predictors of employee preferences to vote for or against union representation. Although no studies are available to answer this specific question, we suggest that workplace issues (e.g., job dissatisfaction, organizational commitment) become somewhat less important, and that the extent to which unions are believed to be able to resolve the principal concerns would increase in importance. This suggests that the relative importance of these various predictors must be expected to vary between studies, depending on the nature of the particular workplace (see Hammer & Berman, 1981) and also the goals of the specific union. The critical role of specific union attitudes (or perceived union instrumentality) within this process is also illustrated.

Lastly, one ethical issue emerges that is critical for researchers. When dealing with any socially contentious issue, such as whether workplaces should be unionized, it is almost inevitable that researchers' personal biases affect the research, through its design, conduct, or the way in which any results are presented or interpreted. If we examine the way in which results are interpreted, just how biases could become manifest can be understood. For example, Schriesheim (1978) ends his article: "Thus it seems important to stress that to avoid unionization organizations must seek to satisfy needs *before* they even begin to consider seeking union representation, particularly those dealing with economic job satisfaction factors" (p. 551). In a similar vein, Feuille and Blandin (1974, p. 692) conclude: "it may be worthwhile for administrators to act to increase the faculty's perceptions of equitable involvement in the personnel decision processes," even though the relationships yielded between job satisfaction and union voting preferences could be used as plausibly to suggest implications for labor practitioners. Neither of these two studies included parallel implications for labor practitioners. From an ethical viewpoint, it would certainly be more appropriate for lessons for both management and labor to be identified. For example, when dealing with issues central to public policy (such as labor organizations), the ethical principles of the *American Psychological Association*, which govern the conduct of psychologists, state that "As scientists, psychologists accept the ultimate responsibility for selecting appropriate areas ... most relevant for study. ... They provide *thorough* discussion of the limitations of their data and alternative hypotheses, especially where their work touches on social policy" (p. 1; italics added). Moreover, employees should retain the right not to participate in any research that they might believe compromises their best interests. Presumably, pro-union subjects would be unwilling to participate in research that might have a pro-management bias. "Ethical practice requires the investigator to inform the participant of all features of the research that might reasonably be expected to influence willingness to participate" (*Ethical Standards of Psychologists*, 1977, p. 7). Likewise, given the existence and use of campaign tactics outlined in this chapter, the *Ethical Guidelines* speak to the extent to which these tactics potentially impinge on personal rights. "In providing psychological services, psychologists avoid any action that will violate or diminish the legal and civil rights of clients, or of others who may be affected by their actions" (p. 3).

Some Implications for Unions and Management

The research findings obtained so far offer information from which practical implications for both unions and management can be derived.

Perhaps the most important implication for unions derives from the fundamental role that perceived union instrumentality plays in the decision of whether to vote for a union. As already noted, non-union employees hold expectations about what specific unions can do for them. The greater these expectations, the more likely a pro-union vote. However, a paradox emerges. While it is critical that perceived union instrumentality be high for a pro-union vote to follow, unrealistic expectations can be counterproductive in the long term (Chafetz & Fraser, 1979). As will be seen in Chapter 7, when initial expectations about the benefits of unionization are not realized, the likelihood of decertification is enhanced. It is critical for unions, therefore, to ensure that their members are intentionally given reasonable expectations of what they might expect if they choose to be employed in a specific company. This could be achieved by emphasizing the gains obtained by similar unions in similar workplaces (Brett, 1980; Deshpande & Fiorito, 1989), by promoting formal contacts with shop stewards, and/or informal contacts with other union members, or through union meetings. In effect, a socialization process within the union is required. This becomes particularly important, because management might simultaneously engage in a campaign to champion the benefits of remaining non-union and illustrate the costs of becoming unionized.

One specific issue that unions would encounter in planning meetings that generalizes to other situations in which union meetings are called is the trend for attendance at union meetings to be extremely low (Brett, 1980; Gordon et al., 1980). As Brett (1980) notes, it is far easier to ensure attendance at company-sponsored meetings during work time than union meetings during nonwork times. Clearly, this is an issue for unions to confront and overcome.

There are also sufficient data to emphasize the importance of group cohesion during organizing campaigns. As already noted, the relationship between the size of the bargaining unit and the likelihood of a pro-union vote suggests the importance of cohesiveness between the members of the bargaining unit. Union organizers might be well advised to accentuate group cohesion, especially during closely contested campaigns (Cooke, 1983).

The results of the studies reviewed in this chapter also provide some indication that unions might exercise greater caution in targeting specific units for organizing purposes. On the one hand, it is clear that union organizing efforts are least successful in larger units. As such, it might be worthwhile for unions to focus more of their organizing efforts on smaller units (Heneman & Sandver, 1983). At the same time, some comment is in order following the failure to isolate any demographic characteristics that consistently predict the propensity to vote in favor or against unionization. As Gordon and Long (1981) point out, it follows that union organizers need not limit their efforts on the basis of the demographic constitution of the unit in question. Likewise, it would not be necessary for union organizers to design different messages for the various segments of the unit. A unitary communication emphasizing the instrumentality of the union would seem to be justified on this basis.

If practical lessons can be learned from this literature that might benefit unions, what lessons might there be for management? Perhaps first and foremost, job dissatisfaction triggers the union decision-making process. As Brett (1980) reports, "Union organizers are fond of saying that the best union organizer is the boss" (p. 57). Thus, any attempts to strengthen job satisfaction could have long-term benefits in avoiding and/or defeating attempts to organize unions (Brett, 1980; Heneman & Sandver, 1983). The practical difficulties involved in this should not be underestimated, especially given recent findings suggesting that some of the determinants of job satisfaction lie outside of the control of the organization (Arvey et al., 1989). At the same time, management would undoubtedly benefit by diminishing employees' expectations about potential benefits of unionization, or enhance employees' perceptions of the value of retaining a union-free workplace (Heneman & Sandver, 1983).

The issue of the effectiveness of company campaigns against union represen-tation has already been dealt with in this chapter. To summarize, some of the strategies used are certainly effective. Where such techniques conform with labor relations legislation, management is obviously within its rights to use them. However, two caveats should be borne in mind. First, one issue that management should consider *before* they decide to engage in a campaign against union representation is the post-election climate. Irrespective of who is successful in the ensuing election, the union-management climate would be dramatically altered following a closely fought election, especially if unfair practices are perceived to have been used. Second, an ethical issue can be raised that is especially relevant to public-sector unionism. When management decide to fight against union representation, considerable financial resources are committed to such efforts. In the case of the public sector, the money and time committed to fight against unionization must be taken directly or indirectly from the public coffers. It is important, therefore, to ensure that management campaigns against union representation within the public sector are consistent with public policy. As Hindman (1988, p. 22) asks, "By what authority do they expend public funds for the exclusive purpose of opposing unions?" Even if public institutions face increased operating costs should organizing campaigns be successful, cultural values about unionism and the benefits that accrue to employees (see Freeman & Medoff, 1984; and Chapter 8) must be considered before committing public funds in the fight against unions.

Conclusion

This chapter has considered demographic, personality characteristics and work beliefs, and macro-, and micro-level predictors of unionization. Neither demographic nor personality factors proved to be powerful or meaningful predictors. Micro-level predictors have been shown to be better predictors of unionization activity than macro-level predictors (Heneman & Sandver, 1983). Among the micro-level predictors of union voting behavior, three variables consistently predict pro-union voting intentions and voting behavior, namely, job dissatisfaction, general union attitudes, and perceived union instrumentality. Among these three variables, we argue that perceived union instrumentality remains the most critical, or as DeCotiis and LeLouarn (1981, p. 108) suggest, "perceived union instrumentality ... may be the fulcrum of the unionization process." This premise will become even more apparent when the remaining processes in the unionization process (e.g., union commitment, union participation, leadership influences, and decertification) are considered in subsequent chapters.

4

Union Commitment

Just why individuals would choose to be loyal to a labor union is a question that has captured the attention of unionists, management, social theorists, and academics, often for very different reasons. Union stewards and officials express an interest in members' commitment to the union because their ability to bargain collectively with management from a position of strength depends heavily on the loyalty of their membership. Thus, a knowledge of union commitment is of some practical benefit. As Gordon et al. (1980) note:

> Since the ability of union locals to attain their goals is generally based on the members' loyalty, belief in the objectives of organized labor, and willingness to perform service voluntarily, commitment is part of the very fabric of unions (p. 480).

Management is intrigued by, and frequently wary of, employees' loyalty to unions, partly because they see in this loyalty a possible diminution in their power to direct the organization in a way they think is most appropriate. Social theorists view union commitment as one mechanism for achieving democracy in the workplace. Lastly, academics are now expressing increasing interest in unions because research on union commitment represents an attempt to clarify the relationship between psychological, behavioral, and attitudinal variables and union participation. As such, a more comprehensive understanding of unions as organizations, the process of unionization (with its origins in union attitudes, union voting behavior, and even early family socialization as discussed in the previous chapter) and the nature of commitment might ensue. Gordon and Nurick (1981) go so far as to suggest that union commitment is a "major" variable in any applied psychological approach aimed at understanding unions. A focus on union commitment, therefore, is crucial.

In this chapter, we will first consider the definition and nature of union commitment. Antecedents (causes) and consequences of union commitment will then be discussed. Thereafter, we will review the notion of dual commitment (or allegiance to both company and union), which first attracted attention in the 1950s. Lastly, situational influences on union commitment (such as union vs. closed shop agreements) and national differences will be addressed.

A Definition of Union Commitment

Despite the relevance of commitment to an understnding of union psychology, it was only in 1980 that a concerted attempt was made to formlize a definition of union commitment. A primary basis for this was the data already available on organizational commitment. This is not to suggest that the issue of union commitment had not been investigated previously. Research in the 1950s did examine allegiance and loyalty to the union (Dean, 1954; Purcell, 1954; Stagner, 1954, 1956). However, union commitment was typically investigated in the context of dual allegiance to both the union and the employing company. The definitions of this concept of allegiance were anecdotal and subjective. Purcell (1954) defined allegiance as "an attitude of favorability towards the *union* or general approval of (its) over-all policies" (p. 49). Stagner (1954) described union allegiance more generally as the acceptance of membership within a group and the expression of favorable feelings toward the group. Stagner (1954) differentiates between allegiance and commitment, in that allegiance "has less connotation of depth and intensity" compared to commitment, but "is more intense than passive membership" (p. 42). Rosen and Rosen (1955) suggested that allegiance is a static phenomenon with little relationship to situational variables. Union commitment was also viewed as the outcome of a calculative involvement with the union and a desire for (1) better economic and working conditions, (2) control over benefits, and (3) self-expression and communication with higher management (Sayles & Strauss, 1953). None of these early references to union allegiance, however, constituted a systematic exploration and operationalization of the concept of union commitment.

The issue of dual commitment or allegiance will be considered further at the end of this chapter. At this stage it is sufficient to note that Gordon, Beauvais, and Ladd (1984) summarized the dissatisfaction with dual allegiance and indicated the need to move beyond a focus on dual allegiance. They argue that dual allegiance is "a concept whose tenuous operational and empirical foundation belies its reputation as the most thoroughly demonstrated proposition in human relations in industry" (p. 361).

The Nature of Union Commitment

Gordon and his colleagues (Gordon, Philpot, Burt, Thompson, & Spiller, 1980) were the first to move conceptually beyond the focus on dual allegiance. Drawing on more general research on organizational commitment, they defined the construct of union commitment, and provided a measure of it. What followed was the first systematic research program specifically analyzing union commitment. The assumption underlying Gordon et al.'s (1980) conceptual approach was that commitment was the binding of the individual to the organization, be it labor or company. Their measure of union commitment reflected many of the components identified in previous definitions of organizational commitment (e.g., Buchanan, 1974; Porter & Smith, 1970). It also highlighted the importance of the exchange relationship (Steers, 1977) in the development of commitment. In other words, the member becomes committed to the union in exchange for the union's provision of improved wages, working conditions, and benefits. Gordon et al.'s (1980) definition of union commitment conceptualizes attitudes of commitment as leading to committed behaviors rather than vice versa.

The role of Gordon et al.'s (1980) research should not be underestimated: They legitimized the study of unions within organizational psychology at a time of indifference between organized labor and management, and at a time when the relationship between organized labor and organizational psychologists could be described as one of "neglect" (Fullagar, 1984; Gordon & Nurick, 1981). They also provided the first acceptable measure of union commitment, and precipitated numerous studies attempting to establish the concurrent and construct validity of their criterion of union commitment (e.g., Fullagar, 1986; Gordon, Beauvais, & Ladd 1984; Klandermans, 1989; Ladd, Gordon, Beauvais, & Morgan, 1982; Tetrick, Thacker, & Fields, 1989; Thacker, Fields, & Tetrick, 1989). The results of these studies usually suggest that union commitment consists of four major constructs that have been distilled from factor analytic studies. These four dimensions are (1) an attitude of loyalty to the union, (2) a sense of responsibility to the union, (3) a willingness to exert extra effort on behalf of the union, and (4) a belief in the goals of unionism. Each of these factors will now be discussed in turn.

Union loyalty has three components. First, union loyalty denotes a feeling of pride in the union. Second, it reflects the exchange relationship highlighted by previous research on organizational commitment (e.g., Steers, 1977). In exchange for the gratification of various needs and the provision of benefits, the member develops attitudes of loyalty to the union. Not surprisingly, union loyalty correlates highly with general satisfaction with the union (Gordon et al., 1980). Thus, to some extent, loyalty reflects a "calculative involvement" (Etzioni, 1961; Kidron, 1978) in labor organizations (Gordon et al., 1980; Ladd et al., 1982) based on individuals' perceptions of union instrumentality. In other words, loyalty to the union is likely when individuals perceive that the union will meet their needs. Third, loyalty to the union implies a desire to retain union membership (Klandermans, 1989). This is consistent with definitions of organizational commitment that emphasize "continuance commitment" (Allen & Meyer, 1990), that is, the aim of remaining a member of the organization (Porter & Smith, 1970).

In contrast to union loyalty, responsibility to the union and the willingness to work for the union capture the behavioral essence of union commitment. Responsibility to the union and willingness to exert extra effort for the union reflect Porter and Smith's (1970) notion of organizational commitment, whereby the individual member is prepared to exert high levels of behavioral effort on behalf of the organization and to provide a service to the organization, in this case, the union. Responsibility to the union can be differentiated from the willingness to work for the union. While responsibility refers to those day-to-day behaviors that are *required* for normal role fulfillment, the willingness to work for the union reflects the *voluntary* nature of behavioral acts that go beyond those required for normal role fulfillment. In this sense, Schneider (1985) suggests that the willingness to exert effort beyond that normally required for membership of an organization is the hallmark of commitment. Using Katz's (1964) typology, this effort not only includes the fulfillment of dependable role behaviors, but also encompasses behaviors that go beyond prescribed roles—roles that are necessary just to retain membership. Thus, the willingness to work for the union supersedes the feeling of responsibility to it.

Conceptually, responsibility to the union and willingness to exert effort for the union should predict behavioral indices of participation in union activities. Data support this prediction. Specifically, Gordon et al. (1980) have shown that the greater the behavioral commitment, the more likely the individual is to fulfill those routine responsibilities of membership necessary for the union's effectiveness. These responsibilities include ensuring that the agreement/contract the union has with the company is upheld; ensuring that shop-stewards perform their jobs correctly; and utilizing the grievance procedure. In addition, these behavioral constructs of union commitment are associated with behavioral participation over and above required activities. This includes helping new members learn about aspects of the agreement that affect them; talking about the union with friends; promoting the union's values and objectives; and teaching recruits how to use the grievance procedure.

Finally, belief in the values and goals of unions parallels Kanter's (1968) concept of ideological conformity and support. Thus, this is not a union-specific belief. Instead, this final dimension of union commitment reflects a belief in the goals of unionism. As such, this dimension is consistent with Porter and Smith's (1970) definition of commitment as a belief in the values and objectives of the organization, and is analogous to Etzioni's (1961) concept of "moral involvement."

Since Gordon et al.'s (1980) original study, numerous studies have been conducted to investigate the structure of union commitment and the dimensionality of the measuring instrument they provided. In the first reported test, Ladd et al. (1982) demonstrated the validity of the dimensions of union commitment in samples of engineers, technicians, and nonprofessional workers who were members of white-collar unions. However, because Ladd et al. used a subset of Gordon et al.'s (1980) data, their results cannot be considered an independent replication. Fullagar (1986) conducted a test of the union commitment measure in South Africa, and five factors emerged (essentially Gordon et al.'s four factors plus a factor Fullagar [1986] labeled "Loyalty to the Employing Organization and Work"). Fullagar (1986) argued that the four factor structure was not replicated entirely due to the nature of the sample he used (i.e., blue-collar workers of differing occupational status in South Africa).

The first direct challenge to the four factor structure followed from Friedman and Harvey's (1986) analysis. Although based on Gordon et al.'s (1980) data, they used a different data analytic strategy (namely, an oblique confirmatory factor analytic model), and found support for two dimensions, namely, Union Attitudes and Opinions (which incorporated the loyalty and belief in unionism factors) and Prounion Behavioral Intentions (comprising the responsibility and willingness dimensions). Friedman and Harvey (1986) noted that their findings are consistent with Fishbein and Ajzen's (1975) theory of behavioral intentions.

Given the seeming confusion, two recent studies have been conducted contrasting the two- and four-factor solutions. First, Klandermans' (1989) data collected on a Dutch sample suggested that combining the two attitudinal dimensions was appropriate; but that the two behavioral dimensions of responsibility and willingness should be kept separate. Second, in a direct contrast of the two- and four-dimensional models using confirmatory factor analytic techniques, Thacker et al. (1989) suggested that Gordon's et al.'s four dimensions provide a more accurate perspective of the dimensionality of union commitment than do Friedman and Harvey's (1986) two-factor structure, but that the four union commitment dimensions are substantially interrelated.

Within a separate sample, these same authors (Tetrick et al., 1989) showed that the four factors were stable over an eight-month period. Also, Tetrick (1989) showed that there is some causal ordering among these four dimensions. Specifically, belief in unionism influences union loyalty and feelings of responsibility to the union. In turn, the willingness to work for the union is predicted by loyalty and responsibility. Tetrick (1989) further showed that belief in unionism was the most stable of the four dimensions, and union loyalty the least stable.

Thus, most of the available research suggests that four dimensions of union commitment are stable, valid, generalizable, and operational. In the first developmental stage of any research, the nature of the construct and criterion measure is of some importance. Arguably, research on union commitment has progressed beyond this developmental stage. At this stage, focusing only on the number of dimensions does a disservice to the initial aim of the focus on union commitment, which was to enhance organizational or workplace democracy by strengthening labor unions. The more important question now is whether the four dimensions have different antecedents and outcomes. An understanding of the predictors and outcomes of the four dimensions of union commitment is of conceptual value and pragmatic benefit to unionists (Gallagher & Clark, 1989). Consequently, it is necessary to identify and understand the antecedents and outcomes of union commitment.

A Model of Union Commitment

There is a considerable amount of psychological and industrial relations research that can provide a theoretical basis for a psychological model of union commitment. Not only has this research demonstrated the relevance and applicability of behavioral science concepts to the area of industrial relations, it also represents another step in redressing the historical neglect by psychologists of labor issues. Steps toward the formal development of a model of union commitment were stimulated by Gordon et al. (1980), and culminated in Fullagar and Barling's (1987) conceptual model and more recent empirical research (Barling, Fullagar, McElvie, & Kelloway, 1992; Fullagar & Barling, 1989; Fullagar, McCoy, & Shull, 1992; Thacker et al., 1990). This updated

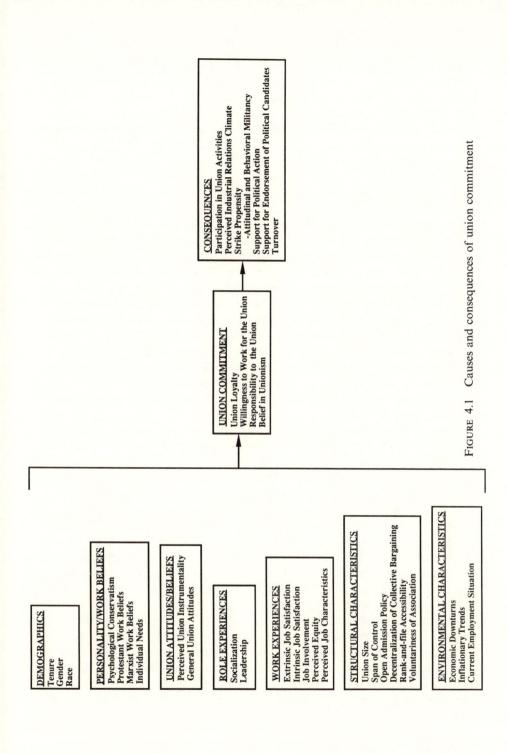

FIGURE 4.1 Causes and consequences of union commitment

model of union commitment is presented in Figure 4.1. In the model, the predictors of union commitment are classified according to whether they are demographic characteristics, personality factors, union characteristics and perceptions, work experiences, role-related characteristics, structural character-istics, or environmental characteristics. The primary consequences of union commitment that have been considered reflect behavioral participation in the union. These antecedents and consequences will now be discussed in turn.

Antecedents of Union Commitment

Demographic/Personal Characteristics. The issue of whether certain demog-raphic characteristics are associated with union commitment has received some attention for at least two reasons. First, parallel findings show that certain personal characteristics predict company commitment (Mowday et al., 1982). For example, there are data showing that organizational commitment is positively related to age and tenure (Angle & Perry, 1981; Hrebiniak, 1975; Morris & Sherman, 1981), and inversely related to education (Angle & Perry, 1981; Morris & Sherman, 1981; Morris & Steers, 1980; Steers, 1977). Moreover, males exhibit higher levels of organizational commitment than females (Angle & Perry, 1981; Hrebiniak & Alutto, 1972). Second, following some research on the predictors of union voting behavior, the question of whether it is possible to paint a profile of the "typical" union member has stimulated some research (Kochan, 1980).

Gordon et al. (1980) found that female members' expression of union loyalty was more positive than male workers. However, despite data showing that union loyalty predicts subsequent participation (Fullagar & Barling, 1989), males participate more in union activities. This apparent discrepancy can be resolved if one realizes that it is not due to gender *per se*, but rather to differences between men and women with respect to diverse variables such as the greater experience of work/family conflict among working women (Chusmir, 1982; Cornfield, Filho, & Chun, 1990; Roby & Uttal, 1988). Family commitments hinder full participation in union activities for women, who may experience interrole conflict differently than males (Hall, 1972). Specifically, while males are afforded the luxury of fulfilling their various roles sequentially (i.e., spouse, parent, worker), social pressure on females is such that they are still required to fulfill these same roles simultaneously. This indicates that lack of active participation in the union does not preclude strong feelings of attachment to the organization. Instead, situational factors may limit the extent to which females can actualize their feelings of loyalty to the union. Also, the distinction between attitudinal and behavioral commitment is highlighted, and the possibility that each may have different causes, correlates, and consequences is suggested (Kelloway et al., 1990).

The second demographic characteristic related to unionization and union commitment is race. Black workers are more willing to join unions than unorganized white workers (see Chapter 3). However, before such differences are attributed to race *per se*, an alternative and more plausible explanation must be considered: Black workers have stronger perceptions of oppression and discrimination, less opportunity to obtain alternative employment, and diminished opportunities for the expression of higher order needs (Buchholz, 1978). The greater proclivity of blacks to join unions, therefore, should not be attributed to race, but racist practices and attitudes that still prevail in American industry. Thus, race can be construed as a "marker" variable denoting the existence of important underlying processes and psychological experience. This explanation is explored in more detail in Chapters 3, 5, and 7.

In Fullagar and Barling's (1989) study on a South African, blue-collar labor sample, race influenced the relationship between union loyalty and union participation. Specifically, the relationship between union loyalty and union participation was significantly stronger for black than white workers. Within the South African context, race denotes differences in privilege, job security, wages, union protection, and access to political, organizational, and social institutions for the satisfaction of both lower and higher order needs.

In trying to understand the relationship between gender and race on the one hand, and union commitment on the other, neither gender nor race is important in itself. Instead, members of different racial and gender groups are subject to different occupational and social experiences, which differentially influence the likelihood that they will look to union representation and/or union commitment as a means of resolving job dissatisfactions. In evaluating the influence of demographic characteristics on union commitment, most evidence suggests that there is little support for the idea of a "union type" (Fullagar & Barling, 1989; Gordon et al., 1980). Thus, attempts at creating a profile of the "typical" union member or union activist would be inaccurate at best, and attempts to use such profiles to intimidate or fire union activists would be misguided at best, and ethically questionable at worst (cf. Kochan, 1980).

Personality Characteristics. In formulating a model of union commitment, it is important to distinguish between personal/demographic variables and personality characteristics as antecedents to union commitment for at least two reasons. Even where demographic variables (e.g., gender, race) predict commitment, these demographic variables merely denote the existence of important underlying processes. In contrast, personality variables represent underlying psychological processes. Second, separating personal/demographic from personality antecedents of union commitment allows for reciprocal relationships between personality antecedents and union commitment to be considered. For example, it is possible that psychological conservatism or adherence to Marxist work beliefs influence and are in turn influenced by union commitment. On the other hand, while age might influence commitment, it is impossible for commitment to affect age .

It has been suggested that the individual's beliefs must be compatible with the goals of organized labor and the process of unionization for the individual to become involved in the union. One pertinent factor is the Protestant work ethic, which emphasizes the values of hard work and individuality. Fullagar and Barling (1989) showed that for privileged workers (i.e., workers with access to decision making), the work ethic predicted union loyalty. However, the work ethic is only one of many belief systems (Buchholz, 1978). Others such as the Marxist belief system and the humanistic belief system may be related to union commitment, particularly because they both predict union attitudes (Barling, Kelloway, & Bremermann, 1991). Likewise, psychological conservatism, which reflects the fear of change, might be particularly salient in the context of industrial relations: First, psychological conservatism predicts union attitudes (Barling, Laliberte, Fullagar, & Kelloway, 1990), and, second, change is a central element of the industrial relations process (Bluen & Barling, 1988).

New members entering labor organizations bring with them different goals and needs that they may seek to satisfy through trade union membership. As with organizational commitment, initial levels of member commitment to the union may be associated with workers' perceptions of the congruence between their own goals and those of the union, and the extent to which they perceive the union as instrumental in attaining those goals. It is also possible that power and affiliation needs influence commitment to the union. Glick, Mirvis, and Harder (1977) have suggested that the relationship between union satisfaction and participation is moderated by personality characteristics. Satisfaction is positively correlated with participation among members who express high needs for participation in decision making, achievement, and personal growth. For union members whose needs for accomplishment and growth are relatively weak, participation may follow dissatisfaction with the union.

It is interesting to note that not only does race (as a proxy for discrimination) moderate the relationship between union loyalty and union participation, it also moderated the relationship between work values and union commitment (Fullagar & Barling, 1989). Among white, "affluent" workers, work ethic beliefs are more important determinants of union commitment. By contrast, among black, disenfranchised workers, Marxist-related work beliefs are stronger predictors of union commitment. The indication here is that greater personal feelings of alienation and exploitation, and a strong development of class consciousness, cause greater loyalty to the union among less privileged sectors of the blue-collar labor force.

Union Characteristics and Perceptions. Several studies have shown that individuals who become members of organizations, and who have realistic expectations of the benefits offered by that organization, are less likely to leave voluntarily than if they hold unrealistic beliefs (Wanous, 1980). There is also research evidence suggesting that the extent to which the expectations of new organizational members are met has a direct, albeit limited, influence on commitment (Grusky, 1966; Steers, 1977). This parallels research on unions that has indicated a significant and strong relationship between instrumentality perceptions concerning the union's effectiveness in improving work conditions and (as noted in the previous chapter) the worker's decision to vote for or against unionization (e.g., Beutell & Biggs, 1984; Bigoness & Tosi, 1984; Brett, 1980; DeCotiis & LeLouarn, 1981; Kochan, 1979; Youngblood et al., 1984).

Recent research, using longitudinal data and adopting a path analytic approach to strengthen causal inferences, has found beliefs about the union's instrumentality to be a strong predictor of both attitudes of commitment to the union, and behavioral participation in union activities in samples of unionized, blue-collar workers (Fullagar & Barling, 1989) and white-collar workers (Kelloway et al., 1990).

Taking research findings on the reasons people vote for or join a union, why they choose to decertify an existing union (Bigoness & Tosi, 1984), together with available data on the predictors of union commitment and participation (Gordon et al., 1980; Fullagar & Barling, 1989; Kelloway et al., 1990), it becomes clear that perceptions of instrumentality fulfill a fundamental role within the total unionization process (see Chapters 3, 5, and 7). This should not be surprising, as perceptions of instrumentality are also important predictors of several organizational behaviors, for example, work motivation (Pinder, 1984).

Given the dramatic decline in union membership in some American unions (see Chapters 1 and 3), one recent study focused on the influence of membership decline due to layoffs on union commitment. Mellor (1990) hypothesized that the crisis of membership decline is similar to other crises the union encounters, such as a strike. Accordingly, following Stagner and Eflal's (1982) study in which a strike enhanced within-group solidarity, Mellor hypothesized that union membership declines would enhance union commitment. Mellor studied 20 unions who had experienced differing levels of membership decline, and used Friedman and Harvey's (1986) two dimensions of union commitment (union attitudes and opinion and pro-union behavioral intentions) as outcomes. He found linear relationships between the percentage decline in union membership due to layoffs and both commitment criteria. Mellor (1990) suggests that these findings are consistent with his crisis scenario hypothesis. It might also be worth considering two additional interpretations of Mellor's (1990) findings. One possibility is that such findings are a statistical artifact. Decisions as to which individual workers are to be laid off in unionized enviornments are invariably based on seniority. Because there are data showing that seniority is also associated with union loyalty (Barling, Wade, & Fullagar, 1990; Gordon et al., 1980), it is possible that the union members remaining in the twenty locals exhibited higher levels of commitment even before the layoffs occurred. A more conceptual explanation worth considering is that union members who retained their jobs would perceive the union as being instrumental; it was, after all, the union that negotiated the seniority clause that saved their jobs. As such, their perceptions of their unions' instrumentality might be enhanced and, as discussed, research shows consistently that instrumentality perceptions predict union commitment.

One observation worth noting is that there are relatively few studies concerning the influence of union characteristics and perceptions on union commitment. The consistency with which aspects of the union (such as instrumentality perceptions) predict union commitment and pro-union voting together with research suggesting that union commitment is more a result of union than organizational characteristics and processes (e.g., Barling, Wade, &

Fullagar, 1990; Bigoness & Tosi, 1984; Kelloway et al., 1990) point to the need for future research to direct more attention to union characteristics and perceptions.

Work Experiences. Perhaps the most prevalent explanation of the process of unionization in the behavioral literature is that workers join unions because of perceived deprivations and various dissatisfactions with the conditions of their employment (Allen & Keaveny, 1983; Brett, 1980; Bigoness, 1978; Dubin, 1973; Duncan & Stafford, 1980; Farber & Saks, 1980; Getman et al., 1976; Kochan, 1978; Premack & Hunter, 1988; Schriesheim, 1978; Walker & Lawler, 1979; Zalesny, 1985). In this section, we will first focus on studies that have specifically considered the consequences of job dissatisfaction on union commitment. Thereafter, we will review studies of the influence of general work processes on that commitment.

The positive relationship between union loyalty and extrinsic and intrinsic job satisfaction in Gordon et al.'s (1980) study gives rise to two suggestions. First, given the instrumental nature of union loyalty and the *positive* correlation between this factor and satisfaction of both higher and lower order needs, Gordon et al. suggest that white-collar workers "regard union membership and the actions of their bargaining units as important influences on all ... facets of their employment." Nevertheless, dissatisfaction with extrinsic factors was more strongly associated with "Willingness to Work for the Union" and "Belief in Unionism." Second, some of the subjects in Gordon et al.'s study were involved in a cooperative effort with management aimed at investigating noneconomic issues. This may have inflated expectations concerning the satisfaction of intrinsic needs and made the results somewhat atypical.

Among unionized individuals, Gordon et al. (1980) found either negative or nonsignificant associations between satisfaction of lower and higher order needs and feelings of responsibility to the union, expressed willingness to work for the union, and general belief in unionism. White-collar workers who were dissatisfied with extrinsic aspects of their job were more willing to be actively involved in the union. Similarly, belief in the philosophy of organized labor was stronger among those workers who felt that their extrinsic needs were not being satisfied. Satisfaction of intrinsic needs was not associated with either beliefs in organized labor or willingness to work for the union. In addition, the relationship between facets of union commitment and extrinsic/intrinsic job satisfaction does not seem to be moderated only by a simple blue-collar vs. white-collar distinction. Several factors, such as the nature of the membership and the type of union under investigation, appear to influence the relationship. For example, Gordon et al. (1984) found that although union loyalty was significantly associated with extrinsic and intrinsic satisfaction in a sample of technicians, a similar association was not found among engineers. Similarly, while job dissatisfaction and union commitment are significantly associated in the United States and South Africa, this is not necessarily the case in Canada (Barling, Wade, & Fullagar, 1990). Later in this chapter, we will consider further how the nature of the union-management contract influences union commitment, as well as the influence of a different situational factor, namely, the national context in which the study is conducted.

Recent research permitting causal inferences has confirmed that dissatisfaction with extrinsic job characteristics predicts union commitment among both black and white union members, and especially among more affluent workers (Fullagar & Barling, 1989). However, among black union members who were more alienated from their jobs, intrinsic dissatisfaction was a more significant cause of loyalty to the union. These findings corroborate the industrial relations perspective that attachment to unions is a consequence of both dissatisfaction *and* perceived deprivation (Begin, 1979; Kemerer & Baldridge, 1975; Walker & Lawler, 1979).

Nonetheless, it should be noted that some studies show no relationship between job dissatisfaction and union commitment. Barling, Wade, and Fullagar (1990) found that while overall work satisfaction predicted company commitment, it did not predict union loyalty, and suggested that situational factors might account for this. The community college teachers they studied had recently been on strike and were legislated back to work. Yet the measure of global job dissatisfaction used in that study probably did not include the specific dissatisfactions the union members had been experiencing, namely, their weekly teaching load. In addition, the source of the dissatisfaction was probably viewed as being the Board of Regents, rather than work per se or direct supervision. In the study by Kelloway et al. (1990), intrinsic and extrinsic dissatisfaction exerted somewhat different effects on the four dimensions of union commitment. Intrinsic job dissatisfaction exerted a direct influence on union loyalty, willingness to work for the union, and belief in unionism. Extrinsic job dissatisfaction exerted no direct effects, but did influence these same three commitment dimensions indirectly through its effects on the perceived instrumentality of the union in resolving union members' dissatisfaction.

As a result, these studies emphasize factors that must be taken into account in understanding the relationship between job dissatisfaction and union commitment. Barling, Wade, and Fullagar's (1990) study suggests that situational factors must be considered in understanding the relationship between job dissatisfaction and union commitment. Kelloway et al.'s (1990) and Barling, Wade, and Fullagar's (1990) findings suggest that the *nature* of the dissatisfaction must be considered. In addition, the likelihood that dissatisfaction exerts indirect effects on union commitment is also raised (Kelloway, Barling, & Fullagar, 1990).

Job factors other than dissatisfaction have been investigated and are important to examine because unlike job dissatisfaction, which reflects the *outcome* of organizational experiences (Locke, 1983), these other factors concern the *processes* involved. As noted in the previous chapter, perceptions of equity correlate negatively with propensity to unionize, especially among white-collar workers (Kochan, 1979). Measures of wage inequity such as perceived underpayment or wage differentials between unionized and nonunionized employees are consistently associated with pro-union attitudes and union membership (Duncan & Stafford, 1980; Farber & Saks, 1980; Maxey & Mohrman, 1980).

Although pay inequity is unrelated to union commitment (Fukami & Larson, 1984), differential relationships may exist between perceived pay equity and union commitment across varying levels of occupational status and differing types of jobs. For example, perceived inequity in wages is positively and significantly related to the willingness to unionize among white-collar, but less so among blue-collar workers (Kochan, 1979). This occurs despite the fact that dissatisfaction with wages is significantly related to support of the union (Kochan, 1979). It would appear, therefore, that (1) the relationship between perceived equity and union commitment may differ among different types of workers, and (2) the effects of objective wage levels and subjective perceptions of pay are very different (see Barling, 1990).

Fullagar and Barling (1987) suggest that workers might be more predisposed to become committed to labor organizations if they were in alienating work situations which: (1) provide the worker with no power or control because the pace of work is controlled and mechanized (powerlessness), (2) break down and simplify the work process (meaninglessness), (3) do not provide sufficient information for the worker to plan and predict his or her work enviornment (normlessness), (4) do not have the potential to satisfy their social needs (isolation), and (5) do not offer the worker the opportunity to self-actualize (alienation). The effects of both job dissatisfaction and alienation, however, are probably moderated by perceptions of the union's instrumentality in improving conditions of work where the organization has been unresponsive (Brett, 1980; DeCotiis & LeLouarn, 1981; Kochan, 1980). The link between intrinsic job satisfaction and union commitment among black workers in Fullagar and Barling's (1989) sample may be related to a strong desire to influence the content (i.e., the noneconomic factors) of one's job, particularly as black employees are unable to influence the noneconomic aspects of their working environment through other more informal, individualistic, or employer-initiated programs.

A few sociological approaches have associated alienation with the process of unionism. Tannenbaum (1952), for example, sees trade unionism as a response to the worker's sense of alienation from both job and society. The union provides workers with a collectivity in which they can relate to employers, fellow workers, and their own job. Unions increase the worker's power and control and reduce feelings of normlessness, isolation, and self-estrangement. The union therefore is not merely an economic organization but also a social and ethical system that attempts to re-establish the values through which the individual has found dignity. Blauner (1964) also sees the union as a reform movement that could counteract powerlessness.

Several studies have empirically investigated the relationship between job involvement/alienation and unionization. Pestonjee, Singh, and Singh (1981) found a significant negative correlation between job involvement and attitudes toward unions ($r = -0.58$) in a sample of 200 blue-collar textile workers in Northern India. In a sample of blue-collar workers in South Africa, Fullagar and Barling (1989) found that the relationship between job involvement and union loyalty was moderated by race (reflecting differing levels of occupational privilege). Affluent, white union members who were loyal to the union manifested higher levels of job involvement than black workers, for whom job alienation predicted loyalty to the union. Thus, as will become apparent later, the direction of the relationship between job involvement and union loyalty is similar to that of the relationship between company and union loyalty in that both are dependent on other organizational experiences. This pattern is also consistent with Purcell's findings that workers who express positive attitudes toward their job will tend to have positive attitudes toward their union (Purcell, 1960).

Two studies, however, have shown no relationship between job involvement and union commitment (Barling, Wade, & Fullagar, 1990; Kelloway et al., 1990). In the study already mentioned in which striking teachers had been legislated back to work, job involvement did not predict union loyalty (Barling, Wade, & Fullagar, 1990), and this can again be attributed to situational factors. First, where the relationship between management and labor is poor, job involvement would attain less importance than current behavioral concerns as a predictor of union loyalty. Second, job involvement would be less important as a predictor of union loyalty among workers of lower occupational status who are more alienated from decision-making processes. A further situational explanation of the findings from these four studies resides in the national context in which these studies were conducted. Studies showing a relationship between job involvement and union attitudes or commitment have been conducted in India (Pestonjee et al., 1981) and South Africa (Fullagar & Barling, 1989). In contrast, no relationship emerges between job involvement and union commitment among Canadian samples (Barling, Wade, & Fullagar, 1990; Kelloway et al., 1990). The possibility that industrial relations factors are specific to the national context will be considered later in this chapter.

To summarize, studies examining intrinsic issues, such as work content and desire for more influence have found that they are as important predictors of unionism as extrinsic factors (e.g., Bigoness, 1978; Duncan & Stafford, 1980; Garbarino, 1975, 1980; Hammer & Berman, 1981; Herman, 1973; Ladd & Lipset, 1973; Walker & Lawler, 1979). The general conclusion from the above studies (and those mentioned in the previous chapter) is that the process of unionization is related to dissatisfaction with both intrinsic and extrinsic factors (Block & Premack, 1983). Thus, jobs that have a low motivating potential and engender greater dissatisfaction with the work environment should also evoke greater union commitment among workers. It also appears that the possible role of situational factors cannot be ignored.

Role-related Characteristics. A focus on role-related experiences (e.g., role ambiguity, conflict, overload) as opposed to work-related experiences (e.g., job dissatisfaction) is appropriate for several reasons. First, considerable attention has been devoted to role experiences since Kahn et al.'s (1964) seminal book. Second, as Kahn et al. (1964) note, substantial numbers of people suffer from role stress. Third, deleterious personal and organizational outcomes are associated with role stressors (Fisher & Gitelson, 1983).

One relevant factor is the socialization into one's union role. Interaction with established union and organizational members is the primary avenue whereby recruits internalize the implicit mores of the organizational or union climate and refine their initial expectations concerning the organization and their roles (Van Maanen & Schein, 1979). Although anticipatory socialization experiences (i.e., socialization that occurs before the individual has become a member of the organization) have been found to influence attitudes (Feldman, 1976; Porter, Lawler, & Hackman, 1975; Van Maanen, 1977), the more important influence may derive from early socialization experiences at the outset of organizational membership (Stagner, 1956). To date, the vast majority of research has focused on the effects of socialization on commitment to business organizations. However, some studies do address the socialization process within labor organizations.

Early socialization experiences are consistently and positively correlated with all aspects of commitment to the union. Positive socialization experiences in the first year (e.g., the extent to which the new member was supported, encouraged, or ignored; whether the goals of the union were clearly set out) were positively correlated with all four dimensions of union commitment (Gordon et al., 1980). Fullagar and Barling (1989) subsequently showed that early union socialization predicted union loyalty. One problem with these studies is that they all rely on data that asks union members to recall their initial experiences in the union. For many members, this would require recall over a considerable period of time, and entails all the problems associated with retrospective recollection. By addressing the problem of retrospective recall, Fullagar, McCoy, and Shull's (1992) data attain some importance. They assessed the influence of union socialization on union loyalty among a sample of apprentices. Both union socialization (the extent to which the journeyman clarified the union's goals, communicated positive attitudes and appropriate information about the union) as well as specific characteristics of the socializing agent influenced union loyalty directly and indirectly.

Two other studies provide some indirect support for the link between union socialization and union commitment. Fukami and Larson (1984) found that a variable they called "social involvement" predicted union loyalty. All four items that made up this social involvement scale focused on the extent to which respondents interacted with fellow workers and hence union members. Through such interactions, some socialization may have occurred (Van Maanen & Schein, 1979). Tetrick (1989) showed that belief in unionism predicted the other three dimensions of union commitment. Because the belief in unionism dimension was relatively stable and may develop prior to formal work experiences (Barling, Kelloway, & Bremermann, 1991; Tetrick, 1989), the belief in unionism may indicate a form of anticipatory socialization that occurs independent of the work environment. Thus, social involvement and the extent and nature of initial socialization experiences are important correlates of attachment to unions.

Structural Characteristics. Stagner (1962) suggested that structural variables may be more important than personal characteristics in influencing labor issues such as the degree to which union members participate in decision making. Certainly, a number of structural characteristics are associated with commitment to organizations. These include size, span of control, the extent of formalization, functional dependence, and decentralization of the organization (Steers, 1977; Stevens, Beyer, & Trice, 1978). Also, the degree of worker ownership and participation in decision making are positively related to organizational commitment (Rhodes & Steers, 1981). This parallels Tannenbaum and Kahn's (1958) findings of a positive correlation between the participation of the rank and file in union activity and control over the union.

Certain structural characteristics of the union affect the extent of union democracy and participation. These include not only such factors as size and span of control, but also degree of open admission policy, extent of decentralization of collective bargaining, and rank-and-file accessibility to political participation. It is probable that the structure of the labor organization facilitates participation and commitment to the extent that it possesses the structures that encourage democracy (see Chapter 2).

So far we have viewed commitment as a consequence of various deprivations and dissatisfactions experienced by the worker. An alternative approach would be to perceive union attachment as a response to the unequal distribution of power and control in organizations. Using Walker and Lawler's (1979) "aggressive/protective" typology, it can be hypothesized that the two types of unions differ in terms of their emphasis on resolving the power imbalance. "Aggressive" unions represent workers who feel alienated from the political processes of the organization and seek to rectify the imbalance in authority structure between management and employees. "Protective" unions, consisting of relatively privileged, skilled workers who have greater access to decision-making structures within the organization, are less concerned with the distribution of power and more concerned with maintaining the status quo. It is quite feasible that these different types of union, which reflect differing needs and interests within the labor force, will have members who exhibit varying levels and processes of commitment. Indeed, Fullagar, Barling, and Christie (1991) showed that members of aggressive unions had higher levels of union loyalty but lower levels of company commitment than their counterparts in protective unions.

Turner (1962) has suggested that different types of unions are associated with different styles of government. These differing styles in turn result in varying levels of member participation. For example, high participation levels are found in "closed" occupational unions with rigid membership controls. Within general, "open" unions which cover a wide range of occupations, a lower level of membership participation prevails. Again, no data exist on the relationship between union type and commitment. Consequently, the predictive effects outlined above remain speculative.

Another structural characteristic of the organization that might influence commitment is the degree of freedom of association. There may be a different *structure* and *level* of commitment in companies where two or more competing labor organizations exist, compared to those governed by a union shop agreement. Research on job choice in organizations has shown that chosen jobs are rated as more attractive and valued more highly than jobs when no choice is offered (Lawler, Kuleck, Rhode, & Sorensen, 1975; Vroom & Deci, 1971). Similarly, using dissonance theory (Festinger, 1957), one would predict that selecting one out of a number of unions would influence new members' attitudes toward the union. Also, as mentioned previously, one of the important behavior characteristics encouraging commitment is their ability to be freely enacted. Salancik (1977) suggests that, given several alternatives, the individual will be more behaviorally committed to his or her final decision in an effort to justify joining a particular labor organization. The presence of a number of unions in any one plant or industry increases the individual worker's freedom of choice. Despite the conceptual importance accorded to volitionality in this context, membership of the union can be a compulsory condition of employment ("closed" shop condition).

Drawing on the work of Salancik (1977), Gallagher and Wetzel (1990) suggested that the perceived voluntariness of association could affect union commitment. Because the four unions they studied all had a union shop agreement, they could not address their hypothesis directly, so they focused on the *perceived* voluntariness of association, asking individual members whether they would have joined of their own volition. Workers who reported being in the union involuntarily reported less union loyalty, willingness to work for the union, or responsibility to the union. Even though Gallagher and Wetzel could not contrast the commitment of members operating in open vs. closed or union shops directly, and problems of retrospective recall might have clouded employees' recollections, the conceptual and practical significance of this issue suggests that it certainly is an area warranting further investigation. Whether the individual joined the union voluntarily or as a condition of employment moderates the importance placed on procedural and distributive justice (Gordon & Fryxell, 1989). Further comparisons between North American unions and many European unions would be instructive in this respect.

Environmental Characteristics. Market context and socio-political variables could also affect commitment to labor organizations. Economic downturns, inflationary trends, the current unemployment situation, and changes in employment and wage rates way well influence commitment levels. Economic recessions are said to produce labor unrest because of retrenchments and a climate that facilitates exploitation of labor market conditions (see Chapter 2). Consequently, a swing in favor of unionization may occur (Adams & Krislov, 1974; Ashenfelter & Pencavel, 1969; Moore & Pearce, 1976). Unions thrive during periods of low unemployment or rapid employment growth (Ashenfelter & Pencavel, 1969; Bain & Elsheikh, 1976; Roomkin & Juris, 1978). Although these trends have not been supported unequivocally (Anderson, O'Reilly, & Busman, 1980; Fiorito, 1982; Mancke, 1971; Moore & Pearce, 1976; Sheflin, Troy, & Koeller, 1981) they do suggest the probable role of labor market influences on union commitment. Researchers investigating union commitment have yet to turn their attention to these macro-economic determinants.

The Consequences of Union Commitment

Perhaps the major factor motivating Gordon et al.'s (1980) initial proposal that union commitment become a major focus of study for individuals interested in understanding the psychology of unions was the desire not only to understand unions, but also to enhance workplace democracy through membership participation in the union. As early as 1956, Stagner had suggested a link between union commitment and union participation. Yet two and a half decades later, very little research had investigated the behavioral outcomes of union commitment. Instead, most research has tended to focus on (1) the psychometric properties of Gordon et al.'s (1980) criterion of union commitment, and (2) possible causes of union commitment. Only more recently has research begun to analyze the consequences of union commitment. We now consider this research and suggest directions for further work on this subject.

In their study, Gordon et al. (1980) found that all the factors of their union commitment scale correlated significantly and substantially with participation in such union activities as serving in an elected office, voting, attending general membership meetings, knowledge of the union contract, and grievance-filing behavior. Also, all four union commitment factors correlated positively with recent participation in activities supportive of the union. Nevertheless, their study used a cross-sectional design that can only provide indications of the static relationship between union commitment attitudes and behavioral participation in union affairs, and precludes causal or directional inferences.

Several studies focus specifically on the hypothesized outcomes of different aspects of union commitment (Fullagar & Barling, 1989; Kelloway et al., 1990; Klandermans, 1989; Thacker et al., 1990), two of which are based on longitudinal data. The first longitudinal study investigated the causal nature of the relationship between union loyalty and behavioral participation in such formal union activities as attendance at union meetings, voting behavior, knowledge of the agreement, and grievance filing behavior (Fullagar & Barling, 1989). To enhance causal inferences about the causal or temporal effects of union loyalty (a primary dimension of union commitment) on behavioral participation in the union, cross-lagged regression analyses were computed. These analyses consistently demonstrated the causal priority of attitudes of loyalty to the union on subsequent participation in union affairs. This conforms with the prediction that affective commitment contributes to the development of behavioral participation in the union, and supports the theoretical causal presumptions behind attitudinal commitment (Buchanan, 1974; Ferris & Aranya, 1983; Mowday et al., 1982). More specifically, the results indicate the causal direction of the relationship between commitment to the union and union participation (Gordon et al., 1980). However, although union loyalty is the major dimension of union commitment, the direction and nature of the relationship between other dimensions of commitment and behavioral participation may be different. Kelloway et al. (1990) investigated this in a separate study, also based on longitudinal data. They found that after controlling for the influence of willingness to work for the union, union loyalty predicted industrial relations climate, but did not predict union participation. By contrast, after controlling for union loyalty, willingness to work for the union predicted union participation, but not industrial relations climate.

Given the strong relationship between union loyalty and participation in union activities (e.g., grievance filing), one direction for further research would be to ascertain the influence that union loyalty exerts on other aspects of union participation. Grievance filing and other more militant forms of union participation are important criteria for two reasons. First, they require members to go beyond the role behaviors normally required of union members. Second, the strength of the union depends on the power of its leadership to impose sanctions. Some research has attempted to understand militancy (i.e., attitudinal support for and active participation in organized conflict with management) in terms of the individual's organizational position, social background, and sources of job dissatisfaction (Schutt, 1982). In one study, Barling, Fullagar, Kelloway, and McElvie (1992) showed that union loyalty significantly and substantially predicted the propensity or willingness to strike after controlling for the influence of union tenure.

A separate way in which unions achieve their goals is by engaging in political activities to influence the course of legislation that affects workplace conditions (e.g., occupational health and safety, restraints on the right to bargain collectively) and social conditions. More specifically, unions often lobby for the election of political candidates sympathetic to their position. Again, union loyalty has been shown to predict political action by the union (Fields, Masters, & Thacker, 1987) as well as membership support for the endorsement of specific political candidates in elections (Thacker et al., 1990).

One final factor of importance to the strength of the union is its size (see Chapter 2). Consequently, the extent to which unions retain their membership in union (or open) shop climates is of some significance. Indeed, Katz and Kahn (1978) define one characteristic of a successful organization as the ability to attract and retain members. This is as relevant for labor organizations as it is for commercial ones. If union commitment is predictive of members' participation in essential activities, and is influential in determining voluntary performance of actions that ensure the union's attainment of its goals, commitment is a crucial determinant of union success. However, although a consistent relationship exists between organizational commitment and voluntary turnover, only two studies have addressed the relationship between union commitment and retention of members.

In Gordon et al.'s. (1980) seminal study, none of the four dimensions of union commitment predicted whether members would leave the union. However, so few members actually chose to leave (only 6.9% of their sample quit the union) that it is possible that statistical factors such as range restriction account for their findings. In a study on a Dutch sample, Klandermans (1989) focused on the *intent* to withdraw from the union, thereby avoiding problems involved in measuring actual quitting. In his study, fully one-third of the sample had contemplated leaving their union, and the intent to withdraw from the union was predicted significantly by all four dimensions of union commitment.

All the outcome criteria discussed thus far reflect behavioral participation in the union. One potential attitudinal outcome is perceived industrial relations climate, a derivative of organizational climate (Dastmalchian, Blyton, & Abdollahyan, 1982; Nicholson, 1979). Kelloway et al. (1990) have shown that after controlling for behavioral commitment to the union, union loyalty also predicts industrial relations climate. In developing future models of union commitment, therefore, other attitudinal outcomes (e.g., perceptions of the union-management relationship) must be considered.

Before concluding this discussion of the model of the causes and consequences of commitment to the union, several cautionary notes are necessary. First, notwithstanding some previous research (Fullagar & Barling, 1989; Kelloway et al., 1990), the processes of commitment described here are based primarily on correlational data derived from cross-sectional research. Therefore, one of the major shortcomings of most of this research on antecedents and outcomes of organizational commitment is that causal inferences are not necessarily justified. Second, with few exceptions (e.g., Kelloway et al., 1990; Klandermans, 1989), this research has focused on the causes, correlations, and consequences of either overall union commitment or union loyalty, and ignored the other three components of union commitment. This is of some consequence given indications that the four dimensions have different outcomes (e.g., Kelloway et al., 1990; Klandermans, 1989). Nevertheless, the available research is still a valuable empirical base for developing a model of union commitment. Finally, research has shown that union commitment predicts behavioral participation in the union. It is now critical that researchers go one step beyond such correlational research, and investigate whether union participation can be increased by changing union commitment. One avenue for investigation emerges from Tetrick's (1989) findings that belief in unionism was the most stable of the four dimensions, with union loyalty the least stable. She concludes from this that any attempts to increase participation in union activities should focus on modifying union loyalty rather than the ideological belief in unionism.

Dual Loyalty to Company and Union

As noted earlier in this chapter, the study of union commitment is by no means a recent phenomenon. There was a considerable body of research on dual commitment in the 1950s. However, the extent to which that early literature can guide our knowledge and understanding of union commitment per se is questionable. Research was invariably descriptive rather than inferential, empirically driven and atheoretical, and frequently concerned allegiance to organizations other than unions. For example, Stagner (1954) noted that interest in the topic was generated at least partially by the need to understand simultaneous loyalty to different political systems: "I need mention only the problem of the American communist, with his dilemma based on his loyalty to the Soviet Union and his asserted loyalty to the United States" (p. 41). Nonetheless, the issue of dual loyalty to company and union has continued to attract the attention of social theorists, management, and organizational scholars. Gordon and Ladd (1990) suggest that "Perhaps because of the compelling notion of industrial harmony implicit in the concept, dual allegiance to the company and the union has been a subject of recurring interest to behavioral scientists over the past 40 years" (p. 37). Gordon and Ladd posit two major reasons for what they see as the current resurgence of interest in dual loyalty to company and union. First, they suggest that the notion of dual allegiance is fashionable whenever external constraints increase the pressures on management and labor for greater cooperation. Second, the development of a reliable and valid criterion to assess union commitment has rendered the issue more amenable to empirical research. In this section, we will briefly outline the research findings on dual loyalty to the union and the company that have been generated over the past four decades.

Different trends can be discerned in the literature on dual loyalty to company and union. In the first instance, numerous studies have attempted to classify dual loyalty in terms of the direction and magnitude of the relationship between company and union loyalty. This approach is consistent with early questions as to whether dual loyalty was indeed possible following concerns that cognitive dissonance would exclude any dual allegiance, and with the attractive idea of industrial harmony that it conveys. In their Table 1, Gordon and Ladd (1990, pp. 39–41) summarize the results of much of the research that has assessed dual loyalty in terms of the magnitude and direction of the relationship between the two loyalties. What is immediately apparent is that there is no consistency whatsoever. In some cases, substantial positive correlations emerge (i.e., $r = 0.74$), such as in Gottlieb and Kerr's (1950) study, or the correlation of 0.66 in Gallagher et al.'s (1988) study. Other studies have found no significant correlations between company and union loyalty (e.g., Sherer & Morishima, 1989). In still other studies, significant negative correlations have been yielded between loyalty to the union and the company (e.g., Barling, Wade, & Fullagar, 1990; England, 1960).

Not surprisingly, researchers have devoted some attention to understanding why discrepancies in such correlations have emerged. As Gordon and Ladd (1990) note, consistent with the taxonomic approach, researchers have focused on the characteristics of the union members concerned and on the nature of the situation. As one example of the focus on union members' characteristics, Magenau, Martin, and Peterson (1988) contrasted the dual loyalty of stewards and rank-and-file members. They showed that dual loyalty (i.e., a significant positive correlation between loyalty to the union and the company) emerged only for union stewards. In a separate line of research, Conlon and Gallagher (1987) investigated the strength of the relationship between union and company loyalty in three subgroups: Current employees who were members of a union, employees who had never been members of a union, and those who had resigned their union membership. They found significant differences between the patterns of dual loyalty for these three groups. There was no correlation for the "never-member" group and positive correlations for the other two. However, the amount of information that can be gained from these studies is questionable. First, the utility of focusing on dual loyalty between company and union loyalty among individuals who had never been members is debatable. Second, even if consistent patterns are yielded, their conceptual implications are limited. Third, there is always the potential for deliberate abuse of such data, for example, compiling profiles of individuals unilaterally committed to or active in the union and using this information to exclude or punish these individuals (Kochan, 1980; Lawler, 1990).

The research focusing on attributes of the situation as an explanation for dual loyalty has produced somewhat more consistent results. When union-management relations are favorable, positive correlations occur between commitment to the company and the union. By contrast, when union-management relations are strained, negative correlations emerge. Several studies can be cited to support this. For example, Gallagher et al.'s (1988) substantial correlation of 0.61 between company and union loyalty was obtained on a Japanese sample, in which positive union-management relations are the norm. Fukami and Larson (1984) studied dual loyalty in a situation where the union had agreed to cooperate with management in exchange for a guarantee of no layoffs; the correlation between company and union commitment in their study was 0.27. Yet when Fukami and Larson partialled out the effects of union-management relations, the correlation between company and union loyalty was no longer significant.

In situations where the union-management relationship is strained, the correlation between union and company commitment is negative. For example, Barling, Wade, and Fullagar (1990) studied a group of community college teachers two months after they had been legislated back to work without a settlement following a legal three-week strike. The correlation between union and company loyalty was -0.25. In England's (1960) earlier study, the correlation between union and company commitment was either nonsignificant or negative during and following union-management negotiations. Thus, it would appear that the strength and direction of the dual loyalty relationship between union and management are conditioned by the quality of union-management relationship.

In trying to understand and predict the emergence of dual loyalty, Walker and Lawler (1979) suggested a differentiation between protective and aggressive unions. The membership of aggressive unions is primarily composed of alienated workers who are somewhat removed from decision making and seek to gain greater control in the workplace. In contrast, members of protective unions are relatively empowered, and seek to use their union membership to retain their control. There is some support for their notion. Walker and Lawler (1979) found that members of protective unions displayed higher levels of commitment to their employing organization. Martin (1981) also posited that dual allegiance is moderated by the "protective" or "aggressive" nature of the union. The information gathered from these studies is limited by small sample sizes (Martin, 1981), and a focus on members (and nonmembers!) of a protective union that had initially been aggressive (Conlon & Gallagher, 1987).

Fullagar, Barling, & Christie (1991) contrasted the correlation between company and union loyalty of union members in the same organization in South Africa who were affiliated with different unions. Their results clearly support Walker and Lawler's (1979) typology. There was a significant and positive correlation ($r = 0.43$) between company and union loyalty in the protective union. In the aggressive union, this correlation was significant but negative (-0.26), and these two correlations differed significantly from one another. Like Fukami and Larson (1984), Fullagar, Barling, & Christie (1991) controlled statistically for all factors contributing to the union-management climate, and again the correlation between union and company loyalty was no longer significant. Also, as already noted, average union loyalty scores were higher in the aggressive union. In contrast, the levels of company commitment were greater in the protective union.

Thus, it can be concluded from this research that the existence of dual allegiance is strongly dependent on the nature of the union and union-management relations (Angle & Perry, 1986). This is consistent with Tannenbaum and Kahn's (1958) suggestion that dual allegiance is more likely among union workers who perceive the primary function of their union to be that of protecting their interests on the job, and less likely at the lower, more alienated levels of the organizational hierarchy because there is less opportunity for organizational involvement and the satisfaction of higher order needs. However, this should perhaps come as no surprise: As early as 1954, Lois Dean had advised us that dual allegiance would be moderated by the nature of union-management relations.

Finally, the conceptual, practical, and legal significance of the dual loyalty concept remains a major concern. Conceptually, the research on dual loyalty has pointed to two important conclusions. First, specific situations can be identified under which dual loyalty is more likely to occur. Second, dual loyalty should be viewed as an *outcome* rather than a *cause* of more fundamental organizational processes. It is doubtful whether more conceptual advances are likely from this program of research. On a practical level, it is questionable whether such information can be used either by labor leaders or management, especially if dual loyalty is merely an epiphenomenon of more fundamental organizational processes. Lastly, in terms of its legal significance, Gordon and Ladd (1990) warn of potential problems. Use of the taxonomic approach would result in individuals manifesting high levels of unilateral union commitment being more easily identified by management. For example, Fullagar and Barling (1990) and Thacker and Rosen (1986) all identify specific organizational and union factors that characterize employees unilaterally allegiant to the union. Yet simple identification of such organizational and personal factors is not necessarily the ultimate goal of classification; specific interventions targeting individuals who manifest such attributes is. As Gordon and Ladd (1990) caution us: "Unfortunately, questions have yet to be raised, no less answered, concerning the unstated interventions that might be visited on workers who possess the personal characteristics that typify the members of certain taxons identified in DA (dual allegiance) research" (p. 57). The potential utility of future research on dual loyalty, therefore, must be questioned.

Situational Influences on Union Commitment

One truism about most behavioral research is that findings generated within one culture or country are not necessarily generalizable to other cultures. However, even though generalizability is an empirical issue (Cook & Campbell, 1979), it is assumed all too often that North American findings are generalizable to other countries. National differences may be particularly important because of the way in which different countries choose to structure their labor relations system. For example, in some jurisdictions, union or closed shop agreements are the norm (e.g., Ontario, Canada); in others, such as the right-to-work states in the United States, they are illegal. This may be of considerable importance if Salancik's (1977) notion of volitionality is considered: He proposed that commitment is higher in situations where people voluntarily join an organization.

The level of union commitment varies across different countries. Thacker, Tetrick, Fields, and Rempel (1991) tested whether the mean levels of the four dimensions differ across Canada and the United States. They noted that significant differences between these two countries could influence industrial relations, such as differential rates of unionism, and their economic base. The mean score for the willingness to work for the union in both countries was the lowest of the four dimensions in both countries, and no differences accounted for this dimension. Nonetheless, the meaning of these differences remains unclear. Although they showed that there were statistically significant differences on the remaining three union commitment dimensions (union loyalty, responsibility, and belief in unionism), they propose that the meaning of these differences be de-emphasized because there were as many significant differences *within* the two countries as *across* them. Several other factors suggest that caution is appropriate before it is concluded that union commitment levels are meaningfully influenced by national origin. First, the magnitude of the between-country differences was relatively modest. Second, we do not know whether the results obtained are confounded by the nature of the contract between management and labor (i.e., closed vs. open shop unions in North America and Canada, respectively), which would compromise any results obtained. Third, Thacker et al. (1991) also showed that the multidimensional structure of union commitment was consistent across the two countries.

Data are also available from different countries examining the predictors of union commitment. Indeed, much research on union commitment has been conducted in countries other than America (e.g., in South Africa, Canada, and Holland) where Gordon et al. (1980) did their original research. This is important because the predictors of union commitment could still differ across countries or contexts, even if there are no differences in mean levels. For example, even though union loyalty is predicted by job involvement for white-collar workers and by job alienation for blue-collar workers in South Africa (Fullagar & Barling, 1989), no such relationships emerged in Canada (Barling, Wade, & Fullagar, 1990). Likewise, extrinsic job dissatisfaction had a direct effect on union loyalty among white-collar workers in South Africa, but not in Canada. Also, while the four union commitment dimensions did not predict union turnover in America (Gordon et al. 1980), they did in Klandermans' (1989) Dutch sample.

However, because numerous factors other than national origin differed between these studies, any conclusion that the predictors or levels of union commitment do not generalize across countries is premature. As Thacker,

Tetrick, Fields, and Rempel (1991) note, "This leads us to conclude that union commitment is influenced more by the proximal, micro-level work situation than the larger economic, political and cultural systems" (p. 69). Nonetheless, because of its conceptual and practical significance, future research might profitably focus further on this issue.

Conclusions

This chapter has attempted to illustrate the importance of the concept of union commitment and to develop a model of its antecedents and outcomes. It is important to understand commitment, not only for the purpose of psychological research on unions, but also for labor leaders to improve deteriorating levels of participation and increase the democratic involvement of rank-and-file members (Gallagher & Clark, 1990), and for management better to understand why employees would turn to unions in the first instance. Levels of commitment could be utilized as a measure for judging the effectiveness of labor organizations, assessing training programs for shop stewards, and ascertaining the success of negotiations and the strength of the union (Gordon et al., 1980). However, additional research of both a theoretical and an empirical nature will be required to develop a full understanding of the conditions that foster member commitment and the processes through which union commitment grows. Undoubtedly, our knowledge of union commitment would be enhanced if such research were to make greater use of longitudinal data and focus specifically and simultaneously on the four dimensions of union commitment.

5

Union Participation

Are you an active member, the kind that would be missed?
Or are you just contented, that your name is on the list?
Do you attend the meetings, and mingle with the flock?
Or do you stay at home to criticize and knock?
Do you ever go to visit with a member who is sick?
Or leave the work to just a few and talk about the clique?
Think this over, member—you know right from wrong?
Are you an active member, or do you just belong?

(Attributed by Perline & Lorenz to an anonymous union member)

Throughout this book we have concentrated on the psychological process of individual attachment to labor unions. This process formally starts with the individual's decision to join a union. Influences on this decision have been traced back to family socialization. The process continues with the development of affective attitudes of attachment to the union (union commitment), and results in the behavioral participation of members in various union activities. If union commitment is a crucial attitudinal component for unions to function effectively, union participation is an equally important contributor to "the very fabric of unions" (Gordon et al., 1980, p. 480). Union participation is also central to union democracy (Pateman, 1970), and to transforming social institutions and restraining union bureaucracy (Nicholson, Ursell, & Blyton, 1981b).

Taking an organizational perspective, union locals can be viewed as organizations that require the continued involvement of their members in a variety of expected behaviours and roles. The survival and efficiency of any organization rely on how well its members fulfill these roles (Katz & Kahn, 1978). Participation in such union activities as grievance filing, meetings, officer elections, strikes, and committees is essential for both union efficiency and democracy: Participation encourages majority rule at union meetings, acts as a check on any oligarchic tendencies within the union leadership, and provides the means for informing union leaders about membership needs (Anderson, 1978). In many ways, participation in union activities is as important to the union as individual productivity is to the organization. Yet, despite its importance, union participation has not received the attention it deserves; and it is still variously defined and inadequately operationalized.

The Nature of Union Participation

Early research on participation in union activities was characterized by inconsistent conceptualization of the construct, and either poor quality or a lack of empirical evidence, and simplistic and bivariate analyses. Earlier definitions of participation treated the construct as a static and dichotomous phenomenon (individuals were classified as either active or inactive). More realistically, union participation varies over time and in degree: Most of the time, little participation is required of the union member. Periods of high activity (e.g., during elections, contract ratifications, strikes) are followed by stretches of dormancy and stability, depending upon events within the union and between the union and management. One contribution of recent research has been to extend the definition of participation toward a more continuous concept which includes a wider variety of union activities (e.g., Fosh, 1981; Huszczo, 1983; McShane, 1986a; Strauss, 1977a).

There is a some debate in the literature as to whether union participation is a unidimensional or a multidimensional construct. Several authors (Nicholson et al., 1981a; Portwood, Pierson, & Schmidt, 1981; Strauss, 1977a) have suggested that different kinds of union activity have different determinants. For example, members with a high need for affiliation tend to engage in such social union activities as attending meetings, but affiliative needs do not predict nonsocial union activities, such as grievance filing behavior. McShane (1986a) has attempted to demonstrate empirically the multidimensionality of union participation by showing that different kinds of union activity are distinct and have different predictors.

McShane has identified at least three forms of union participation: (1) participation in the administration of the union, such as running for an elected office, holding a union position, and serving on a committee; (2) involvement in union voting, be it a strike vote, a certification or decertification vote, a contract ratification vote, or a union election; and (3) attendence and involvement in union meetings. Using factor analysis, McShane (1986a) found that these three sets of union activities formed three distinct factors, each with high internal consistency. Furthermore, the three forms of union participation were differentially associated with predictors such as education, seniority, employment status, salary, union attitudes, extrinsic job satisfaction, and job involvement. For instance, salary was related to union meeting attendance but not to administrative participation, and attitudes to unions were associated with active participation in union administration but not with voting participation. These results suggest that union participation is a multifaceted construct, and that different types of union activity are independent of each other.

McShane's (1986a) empirical findings must be interpreted with caution both for conceptual and statistical reasons. On a conceptual level, the orthogonal solution McShane imposes on his data (i.e., that the three factors are unrelated to each other) is unrealistic. Although orthogonal solutions such as those imposed by McShane ease the interpretation of results, they strain reality. For example, it is not realistic to expect administrative participation to be unrelated to attendance and involvement in union meetings. On the contrary, being a union officer is probably an excellent predictor of meeting attendance. Furthermore, a far greater proportion of the research on union participation has reported highly reliable unidimensional scales (e.g., Fullagar & Barling, 1989; Huszczo, 1984; Kelloway et al., 1990). Statistically, if we inspect McShane's participation dimensions, two of the three factors identified had only two items loading on them. Such factors are usually unreliable and must be interpreted with caution or ignored, because one never knows whether they are "real" or "artifactual" (Harman, 1967). Second, the dichotomous nature of McShane's data inhibits the interpretation of factor analysis except for a purely heuristic set of criteria. It is difficult if not impossible to express dichotomous variables within the factor analytic model (Kim & Mueller, 1978). Last, subsequent research (e.g., Kuruvilla, Gallagher, Fiorito, & Wakabayashi, 1990) has failed to replicate McShane's analysis. In addition, most research has conceptualized union participation as unidimensional and measured the construct using a checklist of participatory acts. Consequently, we will assume that union participation is a unidimensional construct, while acknowledging that additional research is needed to establish the construct validity of union participation.

There are ways of conceptualizing union participation other than whether it is unidimensional or multidimensional. One distinction is between participation in "formal" and "informal" union activities (e.g., Fullagar & Barling, 1989). Formal participation consists of those behaviors that are necessary for the union to operate effectively and democratically. This includes participation in such traditional union activities as involvement in elections, meeting attendance, familiarity with the terms of the contract, filing a grievance, and serving as an officer or on a committee. Informal participation denotes those activities that reflect support for the union but are not necessary for its survival. They consist of such behaviors as helping other members file a grievance, talking about the union with friends, and reading the union's literature and newsletters. Although informal participation does not imply the same intensity of involvement as formal activities, it is probably more characteristic of a larger proportion of the union membership and highly supportive of the formal function of the union.

Another distinction made is between behavioral and psychological involvement in union activities (Nicholson et al., 1981a). The behavioral vs. psychological distinction was precipitated by Child et al.'s (1973) two-dimensional typology of membership attachment. The behavioral dimension consists of the degree of active involvement in union affairs, and the psychological dimension is defined as the congruence between union policies and member expectations. Using these dimensions in a 2 × 2 matrix, Child et al. (1973) categorized union members into one of four types: the "Stalwart," the "Card-holder," the "Trouble-maker," and the "Alienated" member. These four types could be distinguished in terms of the extent of their active and subjective involvement in the union. Behavioral involvement can be defined as the individual's active participation in union activities, and psychological involvement as the member's belief in unionism and attitudinal attachment to his or her local. Sayles and Strauss (1952) explicitly excluded beliefs or values from their definition of participation, arguing strongly that participation is a purely behavioral construct. We believe that psychological or subjective involvement is similar, if not identical, to union commitment (see Chapter 4) and consequently have treated it independently and as an antecedent predictor of behavioral participation.

One of the issues with conceptualizations of union participation that emphasize behaviors such as attendance meetings, voting in elections, holding union office, and serving on a committee, is that they ignore the *degree* of involvement in such activities, and the *extent* of their influence on union decision making. When adopting a participatory view of union democracy, it is important to remember that participation does not imply influence. Participation is a necessary but insufficient condition of democracy (McShane, 1986b). Traditionally, participation has been defined solely in behavioral terms, with little or no emphasis on the influence over union decision making. Only one study (Anderson, 1979) has defined and operationalized union participation more broadly by assessing both member's involvement in, and influence over, union decision making. Anderson (1979) investigated three areas of participation: (1) active participation in several union activities over a twelve-month period (e.g., meeting attendance, involvement in union committees, voting in the last election, filing a grievance, and reading the union newsletter); (2) participation in union decision making (e.g., developing contract proposals, accepting contracts, electing local and provincial union leadership, proposing constitutional changes, filing and processing grievances, formulating union policy, managing union funds, hiring union staff, and disciplining members); and (3) the individual's desire for participation in the above areas. The results of this research suggest that these different facets of participation not only have different correlates but may be linked together. Behavioral participation in union activities may lead to involvement in a greater number of decisions, which in turn increases the member's influence over union decision making. Union participation, therefore, is necessary because it leads to, but cannot guarantee, union democracy. Influence is an outcome of union participation. Accordingly, we emphasize again that union participation must be seen as distinct from the concept of influence.

The extent of union participation is also variable, ranging between minimal to full union participation. Consultative participation exists when members are consulted and are capable of making suggestions and offering opinions that affect decision making. Veto participation is when members can affect union activities due to a system whereby decisions by union officers have to be ratified or approved by members before taking effect. Finally, full participation is where members fully participate in suggesting, developing, approving, and implementing policy. Full participation in all areas of union activity would obviously be neither practical nor desirable as it would detract from the union's functional efficiency. Perhaps most important from the perspective of union democracy is that members have veto power and the opportunity to express views.

Whatever the optimal level of participation for effective and democratic labor organizations, the *extent* of participation as well as the *types* of participation have to be considered simultaneously for a full understanding of participation. For example, during contract negotiations, members may participate fully in the formulation of demands, have no participation in the actual negotiations, but have the right to veto the conditions of the final contract. Also certain areas or facets of participation, such as holding a union office, serving on a committee, and regularly attending union meetings, imply more intense participation than voting in union elections, reading the union literature, and even using the grievance process. Nevertheless, even though the degree or extent of participation is critical, there is no research focusing on this aspect of union participation.

Previous research that has attempted to define and operationalize union participation has highlighted several aspects worthy of further investigation. First, the stability of union participation is interesting. To what extent does union participation fluctuate over time? Second, future research needs to broaden the assessment of the number and nature of activities in which the union member is involved to obtain a more comprehensive understanding of the multifaceted nature of participation. This should not only include formal activities but also informal behaviors. Furthermore, the construct and discriminant validity of these participative behaviors need to be established to resolve the dimensionality of union participation. Third, most research has assumed that participation implies active involvement in, and influence over, union decision making. Studies have tended to measure participation by using checklists of activities. Future research must measure *levels* of activity, and *degrees* of participation. In contrast, the question of the *extent* of influence is more appropriately viewed as an outcome of the success of the union. Fourth, most operationalizations of union participation have relied on self-report measures, and objective measures of union participation would be useful in research (e.g., union records of meeting attendance). Dean (1958) suggests that members over-report their involvement in union activities and meeting attendance, thus exaggerating actual levels of participation. McShane (1986a), on the other hand, reports a correlation of 0.79 between self-reports of meeting attendance and official union lists of attendees, suggesting that self-report measures in this instance are relatively valid. It must be noted, however, that union records of participation are frequently unreliable or non-existent. Thus, we define union participation as "the extent of the individual's active involvement in, and influence over, both formal and informal union activities."

Before considering the causes and consequences of union participation, it is worth noting that previous operationalizations of union participation have invariably excluded strikes as an examplar of union participation. We argue that an understanding of union participation would be enhanced by also studying strike involvement. Therefore we explicitly consider the causes and outcomes of participation in strikes. Apart from being the most extreme, visible, and dramatic example of membership participation, there are other reasons why we have chosen to include strikes in this chapter on participation in union activities. First, involvement in strike activity shares many correlates with the other forms of union participation, as well as having several unique predictors and conse-quences. Second, strikes are socially important participatory acts that provide valuable insights into the dynamics of industrial relations and the processes of power and conflict in industry (Kelly & Nicholson, 1980a). Third, most of the strike literature has been written from economic and sociological perspectives, and several important psychological questions concerning strikes remain unanswered. For example: Why do individuals participate in strikes, given the financial, occupational, and social risks involved? What factors predict whether individuals will actively engage in a strike (e.g., walking the picket line), thereby increasing its chance of success? What are the personal consequences of involvement in a strike? For these reasons, we will explicitly include a focus on strikes in considering union participation.

For our purposes, we define strike activity as involving a variety of behaviors including the initial vote to go out on strike, picketing, sit-ins, sleep-ins, consumer boycotts, work to rule, and corporate campaigns. However, because of the infrequency of strikes and the conflict-laden atmosphere in which they occur, access to the union membership for behavioral researchers during a strike is invariably difficult. Consequently, researchers have had to rely on proxy variables such as the propensity to strike (Barling, Fullagar, McKelvie, & Kelloway, 1987; Martin, 1986). Similar measures of behavioral intention have been used successfully in studies on union voting behavior (see Chapter 3), and those on employee turnover (Mobley, 1982).

Causes of Union Participation

The causes and correlates of union participation have elicited interest for some time, and a considerable amount of research has focused on establishing the correlates of trade union participation. Much of the earlier research in the 1950s was aimed at establishing whether an active "unionist type" existed, and investigating which individuals were more likely to participate in union activities and why they would do so. The rationale for this research was to discover and describe the social characteristics and motivations of union activists. Fosh (1981) suggests that much of this early American research was fostered by a climate of MacCarthyism and the Cold War, and attempted to ascertain whether individuals active in unions were social agitators, Communist Party sympathizers, or more acceptable "solid citizens."

To further understand union participation, we have classified its predictors and outcomes into broad categories: namely, demographic predictors, personal or personality predictors, work-related factors, union-related factors, and nonwork factors. This is consistent with the categorization used in discussing certification, commitment, and decertification (Chapters 3, 4, and 7 respectively).

Demographic Predictors of Union Participation

In the same way that there is some interest as to whether a specific "type" of individual is more likely to vote for a union, become committed to the union, or decertify the union, the issue of whether specific types of individuals are more likely to become active in the union has long been of concern.

Several demographic characteristics have been associated with participation in labor organizations. When compared to less active members, members who are active in the union are more likely to be married and older (Perline & Lorenz, 1970), male (Fiorito & Greer, 1982), with the union longer (Glick et al. 1977; Hoyman & Stallworth, 1987; McShane, 1986a; Perline & Lorenz, 1970; Strauss, 1977a), night shift workers (Strauss, 1977a), and raised in urban areas (Sayles & Strauss, 1953; Tagliacozzo & Seidman, 1956). In contrast to many stereotypes, union activists have also been found to be better educated (McShane, 1986a), to enjoy higher salaries (Kolchin & Hyclak, 1984; Spinrad, 1960; Strauss, 1977a) and greater occupational status (Nicholson, Ursell, & Lubbock, 1981; Spinrad, 1960; Strauss, 1977a), and to have been socialized in families whose members were unionized and actively involved in union activities (Purcell, 1953; Seidman et al., 1958). Research focusing on union militancy and strike behavior paints something of a different picture. Although the findings are not entirely consistent, strike behavior, the willingness to go out on strike, and union militancy are more likely among young males (Alutto & Belasco, 1974; Catano & Rodger, 1986; Dubey, Uppal, & Verma, 1983), and members of a minority group, with blue-collar family backgrounds (see Klandermans, 1986; Schutt, 1982).

However, like the research on demographic predictors of voting in certification and decertification elections (see Chapters 3 and 7), much of the research that has attempted to outline a demographic profile of the active union member is limited by several factors. These include its failure to investigate the *relative* predictive value of these demographic characteristics, and the extent to which demographic variables are proxies for other processes, and a lack of clarity concerning the definition of union participation. With regard to the relative role of demographic predictors, Hoyman & Stallworth (1987) have shown that when such variables as socio-economic status, sense of efficacy, trust in political systems, attitudes toward civil rights legislation, and confidence in ability to achieve union office are controlled, no differences exist between black and white members in terms of their overall participation in union activities. Other studies (Anderson, 1979; Chacko, 1985; Huszczo, 1983) that have adopted multivariate approaches to understanding participation and its correlates have found that demographic variables are of no significance. Instead, attitudinal, social, and role-related variables are more important predictors of union participation.

With regard to the way in which participation is operationalized, black subjects in Hoyman and Stallworth's (1987) study were less likely than their white counterparts to have held a union office or served on a union committee and to have participated less frequently in state-level elections, strike votes, and contract votes. Yet there were no significant race differences in terms of voting in local elections and attending meetings. Furthermore, there were no race differences in such occasional, more sporadic, and informal union activities as picketing, participating in union-sponsored recreational activities, political activity, and involvement in training and educational programs. In fact, Hoyman and Stallworth (1987) found that black union members participated more than whites in strikes, community activity, and health and welfare programs. Likewise, McShane (1986a) found that temporarily employed union members engaged significantly less in union voting behavior (union by-laws restrict it), but that there was no significant difference in the frequency of attendance at union meetings.

The importance of understanding the meaning of the particular proxy variable (race in Hoyman and Stallworth's [1987] and part-time status in McShane's [1986a] studies) can be illustrated. In a study of officers in local Canadian unions, Chaison and Andiappan (1989) identified several barriers associated with gender differences in participation in local union activities. The most important barriers were those related to the traditional roles into which women are socialized. Women have to control the greater inter-role conflict and responsibilities with holding two jobs (one at home, the other at work). Child care duties, which traditionally have been the role of women, also prevent them from participating in unions outside working hours. Also, Fiorito and Greer (1986, p. 162) have shown that gender differences in union membership are due to factors other than gender per se. They conclude that:

> "women's issues" are women's issues only in the sense that women share low levels of satisfaction with pay or similar phenomena. Overall, the factors that influence unionism measures appear to be the same for both men and women.

Similarly, the effects of race on union participation are attributable to minority groups' low levels of income, education, political participation, sense of efficacy (the belief that the individual can make a difference), and pesonal, economic, and social discrimination. Any differences in union participation between white and black members are not attributable to race per se but to expectations that individuals can exert an influence on union decision making. Research tends to indicate that demographic-related variation in union participation is attributable to factors such as industrial and occupational distributions, exposure to or experiences with unions, different levels of satisfaction with particular job facets, differences in union attitudes, instrumentality and efficacy beliefs, and other factors that may vary with demographic characteristics.

In addition to the above problems, Gordon and Miller (1984) have raised an ethical concern associated with research that attempts to determine the demographic characteristics of workers who participate in union activities. Because much of this research is atheoretical, and empirically driven, it is more vulnerable to managerial abuse. In particular, less scrupulous managements may discriminate against workers who possess the demographic characteristics or profile of an active member. Indeed, Gordon and Nurick (1981) have identified one source of the mistrust between labor organizations and applied psychologists as the latter's moral myopia when it comes to considering the social implications of their research. For this and other reasons outlined in this book, we hesitate to identify a "union type," and offer little justification if any, to continue to search for a "union type."

Job-related Attitudes and Characteristics

The influence of job-related attitudes and experiences as predictors of unionization cannot be ignored. As we've seen from prior chapters, certain work factors exert consistent effects on both union voting behavior and union commitment. In summarizing the pre-1970 literature on the correlates of trade union participation, Spinrad (1960) concluded that union participation was greater among workers whose jobs have relatively high occupational status and pay. Participation levels are higher in craft locals compared to industrial locals (Lipset, Trow, & Coleman, 1956; Seidman, London, Karsh, & Tagliacozzo, 1958). Part-time and temporary employees are less active in unions; indeed, such employees are often prevented by union by-laws from holding union office (Geare et al., 1979).

A more fruitful avenue in the search for predictors of union participation may lie in work experiences rather than work status or work characteristics just discussed for several reasons. First, changeable work experiences (such as job satisfaction) are more psychologically meaningful from a psychological perspective than are static job-related characteristics (like full-time vs. part-time employment status). Second, a focus on work experiences as predictors of participation allows for a comparison with the literatures on union voting and union commitment. Third, as will become apparent, objective job-related characteristics (e.g., job status) serve as proxies for critical organizational experiences such as job satisfaction.

Undoubtedly, the work experience that has been implicated most as a cause of union participation is job dissatisfaction. However, the nature of this relationship remains equivocal. On the one hand, several reviews of the earlier literature concluded that job satisfaction is positively correlated with union participation (e.g., Perline & Lorenz, 1970; Spinrad, 1960; Strauss, 1977a). Compared to their non-active counterparts, active union members appear to be more satisfied with their jobs, have a greater interest in work (Tannenbaum & Kahn, 1958), perceive themselves as having more influence over decision-making processes (Anderson, 1979), and are more satisfied with their job content as opposed to their job context (Strauss, 1977a). Spinrad (1960) explains these relationships by arguing that union participation enriches the individual's overall job situation and provides a means for greater interpersonal influence, status, and meaning. This explanation is partially supported by evidence indicating a positive association between job status and extent of union activity (Blyton, Nicholson, & Ursell, 1981; Clegg, Killick, & Adams, 1961; Form, 1976; Meissner, 1971; Sayles & Strauss, 1953; Van de Vall, 1970). Higher status jobs provide greater potential for job satisfaction, they also facilitate greater opportunities for social interaction with other workers and the development of social skills, many of which are necessary for participation in labor organizations (Form, 1976; Meissner, 1971). Pateman (1970) has argued that participation in democratic institutions is stimulated by jobs that develop participative competence and reinforce perceptions of efficacy to engage in union activity. Individuals in higher status jobs may possess a greater desire to exercise influence and consequently extend their work-related power into the union setting (Blyton et al., 1981). These findings are consistent with the view that job satisfaction is an outcome of union participation.

On the other hand, empirical evidence has also demonstrated that job satisfaction is *negatively* correlated with participation in union activities. Not only does job dissatisfaction predict the willingness to participate in local union activities (Chacko, 1985; Hamner & Smith, 1978; Kolchin & Hyclak, 1984), but specific dissatisfactions with pay, promotional decisions, and supervision have been related to attendance at union meetings and union voting behavior (McShane, 1986a). Studies typically report that dissatisfaction with economic factors is more influential in predicting union participation than dissatisfaction with job content, especially among blue-collar workers (Brett, 1980; Kochan, 1979; Schriesheim, 1978). Several studies on union participation have distinguished between intrinsic and extrinsic job dissatisfaction (Blyton et al., 1981; Huszczo, 1983; Kuruvilla, Gallagher, Fiorito, & Wakabayashi, 1990; Nicholson et al., 1981b). Two of these studies found a positive correlation between intrinsic satisfaction and participation (Huszczo, 1983; Nicholson et al., 1981b). Blyton et al., (1981) suggest that the relationship between union activity and extrinsic job dissatisfaction (i.e., dissatisfaction with pay, job security, and opportunities for promotion) is mediated by the individual's job status in that high status provides greater access to resources and people. However, more recent reviews of the reasons workers join unions have concluded that dissatisfaction with job content and status are also important influences, especially among white-collar workers (see Chapter 3).

Most of the evidence concerning the relationship between job dissatisfaction and union participation has been extrapolated from the literature on certification elections. Joining a union or voting for union representation can be regarded as a set of behaviors that constitute one area of participatory activity, perhaps one of the first steps in the continuous development of involvement in union activities. As outlined in Chapter 3, dissatisfaction with working conditions is a major trigger of whether individuals will choose to vote for a union.

One theoretical foundation used to explain the association between job dissatisfaction and strikes as a form of union participation is not new. Ross Stagner (1956) utilized Dollard's (1939) frustration-aggression hypothesis thirty-five years ago to understand the psychology of labor organizations. Briefly, this approach suggests that when a person's attempts to achieve a goal are blocked, feelings of frustration will occur, which will be channelled into aggressive behavior. Following from this view, workers strike to vent feelings of frustration over working conditions beyond their control. Although the frustration-aggression hypothesis gained support in animal studies, its application to human studies has been discredited and its explanatory potential in strike causation (and union participation) is questionable at best (Hartley, 1984). The frustration-aggression hypothesis does not specify the level or kind of frustration that is necessary for aggressive behavior; nor does it address either the target or form the aggression will take. Kelly and Nicholson (1980b) argue cogently that no psychological studies have attempted to demonstrate a link between personal aggression and strikes. Given the multiple individual and collective goals in strikes, at best the frustration-aggression hypothesis is only likely to be supported in a few wildcat strikes caused by unexpectedly blocked work goals and dissatisfactions (Kelly & Nicholson, 1980b). A further reason why this hypothesis may not be supported is that the assumption equating strikes with aggression may be incorrect.

Both propensity to strike and actual strike participation have been related to job dissatisfaction (Klandermans, 1986). For example, Dubey et al. (Dubey et al., 1983; Dubey, Chawla, & Verma, 1984) compared job dissatisfaction scores of striking and non-striking administrative employees of two Indian universities. In both studies, strikers reported significantly higher levels of job dissatisfaction than non-strikers. Interpretation of the data is somewhat limited because job dissatisfaction was measured after the strike had begun. In contrast, as part of an employee attitude survey, Thompson and Borglum (1973) obtained data from 1133 hourly paid employees of five geographically separate plants of a meat-packing firm. Several months after the data were collected, the three unionized plants went on an eight-month strike when negotiations at one plant failed to produce a contract. Work attitudes were compared between employees at the three striking plants and those at the two non-striking plants on seven dimensions of what Thompson and Borglum refer to as "job satisfaction," namely, attitudes toward organizational policy, supervision, job pressure, peer relations, compensation, identification with the company, and equipment. The non-striking group recorded significantly more favorable responses on all dimensions. Thompson and Borglum's study also highlights the importance of considering a variety facets of job dissatisfaction when attempting to understand strike causation and, like others (e.g., Schutt, 1982), they concluded that dissatisfaction with job-related factors (e.g., pay, organizational policy) con-tributed to the decision to strike.

While job dissatisfaction may be a necessary condition for strikes to occur, it is not a sufficient condition in itself. The importance of multiple causes of strikes as a manifestation of union participation may help explain why the relation-ship between job dissatisfaction and strikes is neither consistent nor substantial (see Kelly & Nicholson, 1980b). Failure to find consistent significant relationships between job dissatisfaction and strike activity does not imply that striking employees are not dissatisfied. Rather, it suggests that, in most cases, dissatisfied workers do not go on strike (Klandermans, 1986). Dissatisfaction may be resolved before a strike commences. Even if not resolved, dissatisfaction may be suppressed, lie dormant (Kelly & Nicholson, 1980a), or declared illegal (MacBride, Lancee, & Freeman, 1981). Dissatisfaction is most likely to be suppressed by members themselves if the strike is not viewed as being instrumental in resolving the specific job dissatisfaction. Also, the perceived personal costs of striking (e.g., job loss, loss of earnings, compromised promotion opportunities, and victimization) may be too high to risk going out on strike, despite high levels of job dissatisfaction. Like research findings concerning the predictors of union certification, commitment, and decertification, the role of perceived union instrumentality is suggested. Thus, the notion that union participation is the result of a rational decision is emphasized.

One analogy to this emerges from the labor turnover literature, because it is clear that dissatisfied workers do not necessarily leave their jobs. In Mobley's (1982) intermediate linkages model of turnover, several processes occur before dissatisfied employees leave. For example, individuals explore alternative ways of reducing job dissatisfaction, initiate a job search, and evaluate the availability and attractiveness of alternative jobs. In a similar vein, job dissatisfaction represents but one factor in the prediction of strikes (and union participation). To obtain a more comprehensive and accurate understandig of strike causation, additional characteristics must be considered because no single factor is sufficient in predicting all strike behavior. Instead, other job factors (e.g., organizational climate, perceived union instrumentality) need to be examined.

Another work experience that has attracted considerable interest as a possible predictor of union participation within the social science literature is alienation (and its corollary, job involvement). Unlike job dissatisfaction, however, understanding of the relationship between work-related alienation and union participation has not benefited from much empirical scrutiny. The major determinants of alienation are the inability of the employing organization or the specific job task to satisfy the salient needs of the individual, together with inadequacies in organizational structure (Seeman, 1959). Kanungo (1979) believes that alienation and its resultant cognitive states of powerlessness, meaninglessness, normlessness, isolation, and self-estrangement arise from the inability of the organization or work to satisfy the salient needs of the individual. Workers might be more predisposed to participate in union activities if they are in work situations that (1) do not have the potential to satisfy their social needs, (2) do not provide sufficient information for the worker to plan and predict his or her work environment, (3) break down and simplify the work process so that it becomes meaningless, (4) provide the worker with no power or control because the pace of work is controlled and mechanized, and (5) do not offer the worker the opportunity to self-actualize.

Sociological theories of alienation have their source in the writings of Marx, Weber, and Durkheim. Marx conceived alienation as the product of job conditions that separated workers from the products of their labor and the means of production. Alienation is the result of work characterized by a lack of autonomy and control by the individual over his or her own behavior (Marx, 1844/1932). Redefined in motivational terms, the Marxian concept of alienation reflects the frustrated needs for independence, achievement, and power (Kanungo, 1979). Weber also conceived of alienation as arising from a work environment that does not satisfy the individual's needs for autonomy, achievement, and responsibility. Durkheim's (1893) work on alienation focused on the concept of anomie, that is, the perception of a lack of socially approved means and norms to guide behavior for the purpose of achieving culturally prescribed norms (Kanungo, 1979). Kanungo notes three characteristics associated with sociological approaches to alienation. First, they concentrate mainly on the analysis of the state of *alienation* rather than the opposite state of *involvement*. Second, the emphasis in sociological studies has been on group or social alienation instead of on individual feeling states. Third, sociological approaches describe alienation in terms of "epiphenomenal categories" which are difficult to verify empirically due to lack of operationalization.

A few sociological approaches have associated alienation with the process of unionization. Some forty years ago, Tannenbaum (1952) viewed trade unionism as a response to the worker's sense of alienation from both job and society. The union provides the worker with a collectivity in which he or she can relate to employers, fellow workers and his or her job. Unions increase the worker's power and control and reduce feelings of normlessness, isolation, and self-estrangement. The union, therefore, is not merely an economic organization but also a social and ethical system that attempts to re-establish the values in which the individual has found dignity. Blauner (1964) also sees the union as a reform movement that could counteract powerlessness. Neither Tannenbaum's (1952) nor Blauner's (1964) observation, however, have been subject to empirical scrutiny.

Psychological interest in the concept of alienation is relatively recent, and has tended to concentrate on empirical investigations of job involvement (Kanungo, 1979). Psychological descriptions of involvement focus on the extent of psychological identification with work or one's job and the extent to which work affects one's self-esteem (Lodahl & Kejner, 1965). Job involvement is seen as conceptually and empirically distinct from job satisfaction (Brooke, Russell, & Price, 1988). Whereas job satisfaction reflects the extent to which job-related expectations are fulfilled (Locke, 1983), job involvement is associated with the process of work itself.

Despite the considerable amount of speculation about the relationship between job involvement or job alienation and union participation, few studies have investigated the relationship between job involvement and union participation. In a study of white-collar workers in Britain, Nicholson et al. (1981a) showed that union members who were less involved in their jobs were more involved in the union. Corroborating this finding, McShane (1986b) showed that individuals less involved in their work were more willing to participate in union activities than their more job-involved counterparts. More recently, Fullagar and Barling (1989) found that alienation among a sample of blue-collar workers in South Africa was significantly and negatively correlated with participation in essential union activities.

Thus, the results do show that job dissatisfaction predicts union participation. There are even fewer studies focusing on job involvement or alienation. However, the results of these studies suggest that alienation or a lack of job involvement are also associated with union participation.

Union-related Attitudes and Characteristics

Research in the organizational literature indicates that perceptions of the organization's role, together with behavior and attitudes toward the organization, predict active participation in the organization (Mowday et al., 1982). It is not surprising to find that the individual's participation in union activities is more strongly associated with his or her perceptions of the union's instrumentality in achieving valued outcomes, and attitudes toward the local union and unions in general, than it is to either demographic characteristics or job-related attitudes. Several studies have indicated that individual attitudes toward the *local* union, in other words, perceived union instrumentality (Anderson, 1979; Fullagar & Barling, 1989; Kelloway et al., 1990; Kuruvilla et al., 1990; McShane, 1986b), unions in general and union leaders (Glick et al., 1977; Huszczo, 1983; Kelloway et al., 1990), and the perceived value or instrumentality of unions (Anderson, 1979; Fullagar & Barling, 1989; Kelloway et al., 1990; Kolchin & Hyclak, 1984; Kuruvilla et al., 1990; McShane, 1986b) are important predictors of union participation.

Chacko (1985), for example, provides evidence to indicate that perceptions of (1) the union's ability to ensure that intrinsic (participation in, and control over, work) and extrinsic benefits (e.g., pay, fringe benefits) are provided, and (2) the union's responsiveness to its membership are important predictors of participation. Interestingly, the findings of this study indicate that those workers who are dissatisfied with the *union* participate more in union activities. Chacko (1985) interprets this as an indication of the operation of union democracy.

Interest in both the local union and the labor movement has also been shown to affect participation. McShane (1986a) found that those members who had a keen interest in the affairs of the local union tended to be more active in the administrative functions of the union and to more frequently attend union meetings. Similarly, Kolchin and Hyclak (1984) found that individuals who were generally interested in, and committed to, the labor movement were more likely to have served on a union committee or held a union office.

One attitudinal variable that has attained considerable importance for an understanding of unions is union commitment (Gordon et al., 1980). As we discussed previously, union commitment is multidimensional in nature but has been predominantly defined as an affective attachment to the union. In Gordon et al.'s (1980) original cross-sectional research which established the validity of the construct, all four dimensions of union commitment (union loyalty, responsibility to the union, willingness to work for the union, and belief in unionism) were associated with both participation in formal activities (such as serving in an elected office, voting in elections, attending union meetings, willingness to file a grievance) and informal participation (e.g., helping a new member learn about the union, encouraging other members to support the union on an issue, and reading the union newsletter). More recent studies have provided additional evidence that aspects of commitment are associated with participation in union affairs (Fields, Masters, & Thacker, 1987; Fullagar, 1986).

Other empirical evidence also shows that union attitudes correlate with strike-related aspects of militancy (Beutell & Biggs, 1984; Black, 1983). For example, Black (1983) found a significant association between commitment of union membership and strike militancy as reflected in attitudes toward (1) going on strike, (2) the union's being more militant in wage negotiations, (3) the radical nature of the union, and (4) the union's establishing a strike fund. Likewise, Barling, Fullagar, McElvie, and Kelloway (1990) showed that union commitment predicted strike propensity.

When evaluating this line of research, we should remember that the cross-sectional nature of the data prohibits causal inferences concerning the relationship between union commitment and union participation. This is particularly important, because there are theoretical rationales for justifying the hypotheses that attitudes of commitment cause union participation and that participation in union activities shapes individuals' commitment attitudes. One recent study has utilized a longitudinal design to ascertain the nature of the causal relationship between attitudes of union commitment and participation in essential union activities (Fullagar & Barling, 1989). Cross-lagged regression analysis indicated that attitudes of commitment (union loyalty) predicted subsequent participation in such union activities as voting in elections, meeting attendance, familiarity with the union contract, grievance filing, and serving as a union officer or on a union committee. In contrast, union participation did not predict union commitment. However, these findings need to be replicated using more multidimensional facets of union commitment and more comprehensive conceptualizations of participation before the causal direction between commitment attitudes and participatory behaviors is truly established.

The importance of beliefs in the functionality of union activities (Spinrad, 1960) and the perceived influence of unions (Glick et al., 1977) have been emphasized previously as important determinants of union participation. Strauss (1977a) pointed out that "for members to participate they must feel that such action will result in some sort of payoff" (p. 223). In other words, individuals will participate in union activities (e.g., filing a grievance, attending a meeting, serving on a committee, and engaging in voting behaviors) if they believe such behaviors will lead to valued outcomes (e.g., greater pay, more job security, more social esteem). Recent psychological research on unions has found perceived union instrumentality to be an increasingly important variable for understanding other aspects of the unionization process (see Chapters 3, 4, and 7). Perceptions of instrumentality have been shown to be predictive of (1) pro-union voting and intention to vote in certification (DeCotiis & LeLouarn, 1981; Montgomery, 1989; Youngblood, DeNisi, Molleston, & Mobley, 1984; Zalesny, 1985) and decertification (Bigoness & Tosi, 1984) elections, (2) attitudes toward unions (Beutell & Biggs, 1984), and (3) union loyalty (Fullagar & Barling, 1989; Kelloway, Barling, & Fullagar, 1990). Despite the large body of literature on instrumentality theory in organizational psychology (e.g., Campbell & Pritchard, 1983), the focus on perceived union instrumentality represents a relatively recent attempt to understand union behavior and involvement, and assumes that union involvement depends on members' beliefs that their union is instrumental in achieving important work-related outcomes (Anderson, 1979; Strauss, 1977a).

In a longitudinal study investigating the antecedents and consequences of union loyalty, Fullagar and Barling (1989) showed that perceived union instrumentality influences union participation in several ways. First, perceived union instrumentality affects union participation directly. Second, perceived union instrumentality acts as a moderator of the effect of union loyalty on union participation. In other words, individuals who are loyal to the union *and* perceive the union as being instrumental in attaining valued outcomes are more likely to participate in formal union activities (such as attending meetings, voting in elections, holding a union office, and grievance filing) than their counterparts who do not see the union as being instrumental in this respect. Third, perceived union instrumentality influences union participation indirectly by affecting union commitment, which in turn leads to union participation (Kelloway et al., 1990; Kryl, 1990). Thus, more specific attitudes toward the local union have been found to be important predictors of participation (Anderson, 1979; Huszczo, 1983; Kuruvilla et al., 1990; McShane, 1986a).

Other union attitudes associated with active involvement in union affairs include attitudes toward union leadership and organized labor (Glick et al., 1977; Huszczo, 1983), interest in union business (McShane, 1986b), and the perceived value and effectiveness of unions (Anderson, 1979; Kolchin & Hyclak, 1984; Kuruvilla et al., 1990; McShane, 1986b). The *relative* predictive role of union attitudes can be appreciated from studies in the United Kingdom that have shown union attitudes to be stronger predictors of union participation than job characteristics or job-related attitudes (Nicholson et al., 1981). Research on union attitudes and union instrumentality (i.e., general and specific union attitudes respectively) is also important in that it provides an indication to unions as to what they could do to influence member participation. For example, should unions focus on extrinsic, intrinsic, or responsiveness issues? Is the union providing its members with the opportunity to fulfill needs they are not able to fulfill in their jobs?

The emphasis on perceived union instrumentality lends itself to the adoption of a rational choice framework. Traditionally, the literature on individual participation in unions has focused on explaining involvement using demographic variables, work-role characteristics, work attitudes, and union-related attitudes without locating the research in any specific theoretical framework. Although rational choice theories have been utilized in macrocosmic studies of union growth and decline (e.g., Bain & Price, 1980; Cornfield, 1986; Fiorito & Greer, 1982) and in the analysis of strike statistics (e.g., Friedman, 1983; Shalev, 1983), only recently have psychologists begun to apply such theories to individual decision making with regard to union participation (Klandermans, 1984a, 1986). Klandermans has used a basic rational choice theory— expectancy-value theory—to develop a model of union activity. In general, expectancy-value theories consider the individual's action to be related to the person's expectations and subjective value of the consequences that are perceived to follow the actions (Feather, 1982). According to this approach, union participation is a function of the material, social, and goal-related costs and benefits of participation and the perceived value of the outcomes of participation (Klandermans, 1984a, 1986). When the benefits of union activity are perceived as high, and the costs low, then willingness to participate will be high.

Klandermans' findings support research that has used similar rational choice theories to predict union-certification voting behavior (Montgomery, 1989; Zalesny, 1985). Thus, expectancy-value theory, with its emphasis on cognitive factors, has considerable utility in explaining not only why individuals vote for unions, offer loyalty to their bargaining units, and actively participate in them, but, as will be seen in Chapter 7, why they choose to decertify them. Expectancy-value theory also has considerable flexibility in that it accounts for differing perceptions and expectations across different types of membership, union, and situation. Consequently, union participation is regarded as varying over time and situations rather than being a stable phenomenon.

There are several implications for unions of viewing union participation as a function of the perceived costs and benefits of involvement (Klandermans, 1984b). Primarily, unions need to improve the cost-benefit ratio more in their favor by either increasing the benefits associated with participation or by raising the costs of non-participation. Furthermore, member expectations can be changed to perceiving the union as open and accessible, and essentially democratic. The more individuals believe that their participation will achieve certain valued outcomes, the more likely they will participate.

Nonwork Predictors of Union Participation

The question of whether personal characteristics or personality factors influence union participation has long been of interest. For example, the possibility that "union activists" (or agitators as they would be referred to in this context) are driven by ideological considerations independent of work factors is not new. Certainly, some causes of individuals' union-related behaviors lie outside the work context. For example, early family socialization predicts subsequent union attitudes (Chapter 3). Also, under certain conditions, such as when unions take an active role in ameliorating social inequities, life dissatisfaction predicts union loyalty (Fullagar & Barling, 1989). Several variables concerned with union member's early socialization experiences, social behavior, political ideology, work values, and need structure have also been implicated with active participation in union affairs; these will now be considered.

Earlier research found that the active trade unionist tends to be less involved in nonwork and family activities, perhaps because of the amount of time taken in fulfilling union responsibilities (Gouldner, 1947; Kyllonen, 1951; Purcell, 1953; Sayles & Strauss, 1953). More recently, however, in a study of blue-collar workers in the United Kingdom, Fosh (1981) found a moderate correlation between union participation and membership in other formal, social, and political organizations. Active union members were *more* likely to participate in non-union voluntary associations. Generally, active members undertook a greater number of both formal and informal social activities compared to their inactive counterparts. However, no differences existed in terms of the number of outside interests and hobbies and involvement in family activities.

Huszczo (1983) also found that one of the most significant predictors of participation in union activities was the extent of involvement by members in non-union community and political activities. Thus, Huszczo describes the activist personality profile as a "person of high energy level, active in community and political behaviors, and politically liberal" (p. 296). Although Huszczo's study used a large American sample, a wide range of predictors, a broader measure of participation, and a cross-validation design, it was still cross-sectional in nature and causal inferences may be compromised. For example, these results could be used to support the notion that union activity stimulates broader political and community interest, or that involvement in political and community activities results in union participation. Also, participation in general (whether in unions, political, or community groups) could be a function of other factors such as personality characteristics. Nonetheless, the results of recent research do suggest that active members perceive the union's function as going beyond merely an economic and protective one, to being part of a broader, social-political movement, and that union activity is related to a belief in group goals, a concern with the political and social goals of trade unionism, and political attitudes and behaviors. Furthermore, Huszczo's findings refute claims that union activity in the United States is less ideologically bound in comparison to British trade unions (Nicholson et al., 1981b). Research in the United Kingdom (Fosh, 1981; Nicholson et al., 1981a, 1981b) and Europe (Klandermans, 1986) has consistently found political affiliation, and political-economic ideology to be associated with activism in unions.

One of the most enduring beliefs about the causes of union participation concerns the role of ideological beliefs. Several studies have attempted to ascertain whether active union members are more "class conscious" in the sense that they believe in collective as opposed to individual effort, and perceive themselves as members of a working class (Perline & Lorenz, 1970; Purcell, 1953; Sayles & Strauss, 1953; Tagliacozzo & Seidman, 1956). Fosh (1981) found participation in union activities to be strongly associated with what she terms "a commitment to collectivism," where collective action is seen as a means to achieve the goals of trade unionism as a social movement, or, in other words, the group pursuit of group goals. She identified two major sources of commitment to collectivism: (1) socialization experiences that include the extent of social contact with working class and pro-union persons, and (2) the direct or vicarious experience (through one's parents) of such significant events as unemployment, poverty, and collective action (e.g., strikes). Fosh concludes from her research that active union members manifest a strong commitment to collectivism in that they have a firm belief in the political, social, as well as economic goals of trade unions rather than an instrumental belief in trade unionism as a means for acquiring individual ends extrinsic to trade unionism.

In discussing political ideology or class consciousness, we are referring to employees' beliefs about the structure of power and the way in which power is exercised in economic, political, and employment relations. Stated somewhat differently, we are referring to the way in which work is organized. Buchholz's (1978) concept of Marxist work-related beliefs mirrors this: Work is seen as providing self-fulfillment, but the way in which the power balance and employment relations are currently organized thwarts such self-fulfillment at work. To redress this imbalance, collective action is necessary. Fullagar and Barling (1989) found a significant correlation between participation in formal union activities and Marxist-related work beliefs in a sample of alienated, black, South African workers. These subjects manifested class consciousness through (1) a belief in the existence of a class structure, in which classes have conflicting interests, (2) self-identification as a member of the working class, and (3) as a member of that class, an awareness that common material and social disadvantages give rise to collective interests that have to be pursued collectively. Thus, there is evidence for the proposition that individuals are more prone to unionization if (1) they are dissatisfied with the conditions of their employment, and (2) they are "philosophically or demographically predisposed toward the idea of collective action" (Maxey & Mohrman, 1980).

Aside from the issue of whether ideological beliefs predict union participation, the question of whether individuals' psychological needs predict union participation has been raised. There are data to show that growth needs (Hagburg, 1966; Van de Vall, 1970), the need for affiliation (Nicholson et al., 1981a), and a willingness to participate (McShane, 1986) all predict union participation. Klandermans (1986b) suggests that the need for influence, together with the expectation that one can exert influence in the union, are important predictors of union participation. Other basic psychological needs that correlate with active participation in unions are the need for power, recognition, and influence (Seidman et al., 1950), need for involvement (Nicholson et al., 1981a), and the need for social interaction (Purcell, 1953; Seidman et al., 1958; Tannenbaum & Kahn, 1958). With respect to the need for social involvement, active union members are provided with a close social network with other union members outside work (Fukami & Larson, 1984; Lipset, Trow, & Coleman, 1956). This latter finding is consistent with Strauss' (1977a) emphasis on the importance of the occupational community. It may also reflect the influence of group factors and pressures on union participation.

In a more elaborate model of participation based on data from a white-collar sample in the United Kingdom, Nicholson et al. (1981a, 1981b) interpret members' need for involvement as a moderator of the relationship between demographic variables (such as educational status), work-related variables (such as job dissatisfaction), and employment climate (i.e., anxiety concerning job security) on the one hand, and union attitudes and subsequent participation on the other. Other research (Glick et al., 1970; Van de Vall, 1970) has suggested that the job dissatisfaction/participation relationship is moderated by the individual's decision-making needs. Nicholson et al. (1981a) also emphasize that the need for involvement is associated with a more general need to participate in both union and management affairs and decision making. There appears to be a personal component associated with union participation that continually emerges in research under different guises. For example, Form and Dansereau (1957) found union activists to have more social interests as opposed to being economically motivated. Strauss (1977a) also distinguishes between the participation levels of "hard-core" activists whose high level of involvement stems from their interest in internal union business, and "sporadic attenders" whose participation is related to specific grievances or collective bargaining issues. A considerable amount of evidence supports Glick et al.'s (1970) contention that those individuals who have strong needs for participation, influence, accomplishment, and growth, who possess certain political attitudes, and are socially and politically active are more likely to participate in union activities. Indeed, Strauss (1977a) believes that union members are active not because of any antagonism to management, but because their involvement satisfies important personal needs. The sources of these needs and such factors as political affiliation, class consciousness, and political-economic ideology are all strongly rooted in early socialization experiences.

Another major influence on union participation is the individual's social context. In reviewing the literature on union participation thirty years ago, Spinrad (1960) noted that "the likelihood of union participation is enhanced by personal contact with pro-union colleagues, union leaders, family members, and ethnic associations; it is diminished by personal contacts with superiors and non-union or anti-union friends and non-working-class neighbours" (p. 241). Both Spinrad (1960) and Strauss (1977a) emphasize the importance of identification with the occupational community or group as a strong predictor of participation in union activities.

In this context, it is argued that close-knit working communities facilitate greater participation in union affairs and involvement in union decision making (Lipset et al., 1956; Seidman, 1953; Seidman et al., 1958). Spinrad (1960) concludes that "those whose jobs facilitate and encourage frequent contact with fellow workers are more likely to be union activists" (p. 239). The closeness of the occupational community and the working relations between workers have been consistently associated with union activity. Consequently, the homogeneity of the work group regarding pay, background, ethnicity, and skill also facilitates greater levels of participation in union activities (Sayles & Strauss, 1953). Indeed, social interactions with coworkers, friends, and family combine to shape the socialization process and the individual's social identity.

The sense of occupational community is enhanced if the living and working conditions of union members encourage frequent interaction with other members. Thus, it is not surprising that union participation has been found to be high in small plants, among night-shift personnel, in geographically isolated communities and among members who have relatively homogenous work, ethnic, and cultural backgrounds. Members with strong needs for affiliation who are socially well integrated into the occupational community tend to participate more in union activities (Anderson, 1979; Glick et al., 1977; Kolchin & Hyclak, 1984; McShane, 1986a; Strauss, 1977a). The importance of the occupational community corroborates Kerr and Siegel's (1954) work. These researchers examined strike records in eleven countries across different industries and found that strike rates were consistently highest in mining and dock working and lowest in agriculture, trade, and rail transport. They explained their findings in terms of the "isolated mass" hypothesis: Minors and dock workers form isolated communities in which workers are clustered in a homogeneous, undifferentiated mass. Their shared frustrations are not resolved by individual action. The group is isolated from the rest of society and mobility is difficult. Thus, individual means of resolving problems, such as moving to a different job, are replaced by collective action and an increased potential for strike activity

(Kerr & Siegel, 1954). However, more recent research has failed to support Kerr and Siegel's proposition that communities in which low-strike mines are located are less isolated, less occupationally homogeneous, and have a better quality of life than communities in which high-strike mines are found (Brett & Goldberg, 1979; Shorter & Tilly, 1974). Nonetheless, their hypothesis is still historically important, as it helped to legitimize the focus on predictors of strikes other than the demographic characteristics of the strikes themselves.

Still focusing on nonwork factors, the solidaristic approach to unionism proposes that individuals join unions out of a sense of identification with or ideological attachment to the values of trade unionism. These values may develop through socialization or through experience (Guest & Dewe, 1988). The major socialization influences are the member's family background and involvement in unions and coworkers and friends (see Chapter 3). Such collectivist and solidaristic orientations are found more in blue-collar and craft-based unions (Cook et al., 1975; Goldthorpe et al., 1968; Rose, 1974) than in white-collar unions, where there is a stronger instrumental concern for improved wages and working conditions (Goldthorpe et al., 1968; Mercer & Weir, 1972; Nicholson et al., 1981a). The normative and social influence of important others (employers, union representatives, coworkers, family, and friends) has been recognized as exerting a strong role in the union membership decision (Gordon & Long, 1981; Seidman et al., 1958; Warner, Chisholm, & Munzenrider, 1978) and voting decisions in union certification elections (Montgomery, 1989; Youngblood et al., 1984; Zalesny, 1985). This is anecdotally illustrated in the following advice to employers concerning election campaigns:

> A letter addressed to both the employee and his wife is often effective because the average wife has an interest in her husband's job and any matter affecting it, particularly union activity. She will discuss the union with her husband, and her opinion often influences her husband's vote. And a working wife's vote can likewise be influenced by her husband (Hunt, 1979, p. 42).

There is no empirical research directly asking about the effects of normative and social influences on union participation. However, results from studies on union voting behavior, which may reflect a first phase in union participation, suggests the importance of group norms (see Chapter 3). We expect similar normative and social pressures to have an impact on individual participation in union activities.

Klandermans (1986) classifies these approaches to understanding union participation as "interactionist theories," in that they associate participation in union affairs with social networks both inside and outside the employing company. Participation is believed to be a function of group culture and the social pressures exerted by the occupational community. Worker or class consciousness, images of labor organizations, and the perceived instrumentality of unions are all rooted in their social contexts, namely, family socialization, neighbourhood and work experiences, and the union itself. Klandermans (1986) found that member willingness to participate in union activities was significantly influenced by the perceived support of significant others, such as friends, colleagues, and superiors. If groups are important influences on participation, then socialization into the group, whereby the individual learns its purposes, objectives, and norms becomes an important process with ramifications for later involvement in union activities. Thus, it can be seen that nonwork factors also exert a significant effect on union participation.

Structural Predictors of Union Participation

We have already discussed the structural correlates of union democracy (see Chapter 2). Aside from personal, demographic, and work/union experiences that predict union participation, several structural characteristics also predict trade union participation. In particular, most of the strike causation research focuses on strikes from a macro-environmental perspective (i.e., identifying economic, historical, political, sociological, and industrial relations causes of strikes located in the broader society). For example, Shalev (1983) examined the relationship between participation in strikes and unemployment in eighteen countries from 1960 to 1982, using aggregate data. He found that the impact of unemployment on strike activity varies between countries and across time. In general, strike activity is reduced during periods of mass unemployment. Kochan (1980) reports that industrial relations factors that predict strikes include decentralized bargaining structures, high percentage of the workforce being organized, and absence of integration of the union movement into the society. Kochan also discusses certain structural-organizational causes of strikes, namely, inadequate decision-making powers of negotiators, intraorganizational conflict, and negative management of union policies.

There are suggestions that the size of the plant affects union participation. Specifically, plant size might impact on participation through its effect on the work community. The smaller the plant, factory, or organization, the more intimate the work community and the closer the working relations, thus facilitating greater participation in union activities and involvement in union decision making (Lipset et al., 1956; Seidman, 1953; Seidman et al., 1958). The data support this notion. Spinrad (1960) found that the size of the plant in which members worked was negatively associated with participation in union activities.

Not only has the size of the plant been found to affect union participation levels, but so has the size of the union. Within larger unions, a greater tendency exists for enlarging administration and complex union structures to result in ideological differences between the membership and leadership, thus reducing the union's representative function and control (Anderson, 1978; Perline & Lorenz, 1970). As a result, it is suggested that larger unions inhibit participation. The data show that membership involvement and contact between members and union leaders is lower in smaller rather than larger unions (Huszczo, 1983; Strauss, 1977a), and that membership participation in union activities is lower in larger unions (Anderson, 1978; Perline & Lorenz, 1970).

The stability of the workforce has also been found to influence the extent of participation by the union membership (Kolchin & Hyclak, 1984; Spinrad, 1960). Job mobility correlates negatively with union participation (Kolchin & Hyclak, 1984). Union members who perceive scarce opportunities for different jobs, either inside or outside their company, tend to participate more actively in union affairs than those whose job mobility is greater.

In the literature on organizational psychology, considerable attention has been directed toward the effects of leadership on individual and organizational functioning. In contrast, much less research has investigated the effects of the characteristics of union officers and leadership on union participation (see Chapter 6). Research suggests that such characteristics in union officers as ability to communicate, availability for assistance, individual consideration, and accessibility enhance members' participation in the union (Fullagar, McCoy & Shull, 1992; Kahn & Tannenbaum, 1954; Nicholson et al., 1981b). What little research there is indicates that participation is affected by union representatives and officers, and that the characteristics of these people mediate the effect of various antecedents on union participation. Consequently, the behaviors and attitudes of elected representatives themselves and the quality of their relationships with the rank and file needs to be investigated further.

With respect to the effects of union leadership, a frequent accusation leveled against union leaders is that they instigate strikes for selfish or political reasons. The "union agitator" notion was particularly popular between the two world wars (Kelly & Nicholson, 1980b; Nicholson & Kelly, 1980). Certainly, there are data suggesting that positive personal outcomes of strikes do accrue to union leaders. For example, external threats on groups (such as unions) yield positive consequences for group leaders and result in more centralized decision making (Brett, 1980). Consistent with the union agitator hypothesis, Stagner and Eflal (1982) found that attitudes toward union leadership were more favorable during a strike than either before or after. Their data showed that union leaders do attain additional prestige and influence over members during a strike. However, although strikes can enhance union leaders' positions, not too much emphasis should be placed on the role of union leaders in causing strikes. First, any positive effects for union leaders are time limited (Stagner & Eflal, 1982). Second, Brett (1980) cautions that although groups facing external threats tend to close ranks, they may not unite around their leaders and a change in leadership could ensue. Third, the decision to strike could be a result of the current leaders' incompetence at the negotiating table (Brett, 1980).

The view that union leaders choose to initiate a strike solely for personal gain reflects only one possible perspective, and has been criticized for being reactionary (Hyman, 1984). Union leaders may choose to initiate a strike for many reasons other than self-aggrandizement. By overpersonalizing the causes of strikes, there is the risk of de-emphasizing the inherent structural conflict of interests between labor and management (Fox, 1966) and presenting a unitary view of labor-management conflict (i.e., that strikes are caused by agitators, greed, or ignorance). Also, such a perspective is extremely narrow: It is questionable indeed whether union leaders can create job dissatisfaction to serve their own needs (see Brett, 1980). So-called agitators are likely only to be successful in articulating and supporting existing grievances and discontents (Brett, 1980; Kelly & Nicholson, 1980b).

Still, the extent to which various individuals influence the occurrence of strikes (as an extreme and unusual manifestation of union participation) should not be underestimated. Certain influential people (such as union leaders and shop stewards) do influence strikes (Nicholson & Kelly, 1980). This does not imply that they are agitators. Rather, they may be performing their legitimate functions as union leaders in initiating members' strike action. Nicholson and Kelly (1980) state that most "led" strikes (i.e., where the union leadership mobilizes its membership to engage in collective action) are in the pursuit of pay claims. The importance of union leaders' roles in strike initiation was demonstrated by Batstone, Boraston, and Frenkel (1978) who reported that shop stewards influenced the strike process by convincing workers (1) of the existence of problems and (2) that such problems would best be solved by strike action. Although the shop stewards' actions were not initiated for self-gain, they still played a leadership role in the strike.

A focus on union leadership reflects a consideration of the power of specific individuals. For various reasons, different unions have differential access to power, and the power of the union is a pivotal factor in strike causation. For collective bargaining to be effective, a power balance must exist between labor and management (Bluen, 1986). The economic climate influences this power balance and, in turn, strike rates (Stern, 1978): In periods of economic expansion, power resides with labor since there are fewer workers than jobs and strike rates increase. Conversely, in recessionary climates, jobs become scarce and strike rates decrease, and the power balance leans in management's favor. However, power derived from the strength of the economy is but one of the bases of a union's power (Stern, 1978), and we will now examine other behavioral factors that influence the union's power and hence strike rates (Allen & Keaveny, 1983).

Any union's power represents its ability to get management to agree with its viewpoint and accept its demands. If we view strikes as a strategy to achieve union goals (Nicholson & Kelly, 1980), then power is an important predictive factor of strikes. Strikes represent the deliberate use of power to secure greater gains for the union membership. Powerful unions can influence the occurrence and timing of strikes to ensure maximum impact (Klandermans, 1986). Factors influencing the union's strike efforts include the availability of strike funds, internal union agreement to heed a strike call, the union's ability to cater to strikers' financial commitments (e.g., by arranging suspension of mortgage repayments), and other unions' willingness to honor the picket line (Allen & Keaveny, 1983). Ironically, powerful unions also have less need to resort to strikes, and can prevent industrial action (Klandermans, 1986). It is important to remember that union gains are achieved (1) via collective bargaining, where the strike weapon would be an important strategy, and (2) by political lobbying, where strike action would not form part of the strategy. In Shalev's (1983) analysis of strikes in eighteen countries, the results suggest that the greater the unions' political influence to achieve goals, the less the economy affected strike rates. Conversely, where unions relied mainly on collective bargaining, the economy greatly influenced strike rates.

An alternative hypothesis concerning the role of power in strike causation is that strikes are more likely to occur if the union is weak. Seeman (1984) interviewed French and American workers and found that powerlessness correlated with subsequent strike participation. Similarly, Keith (1984) suggests that because physicians are faced with decreasing control over their professional careers, their attitudes toward industrial action have changed. They are becoming more prepared to adopt collective tactics used by other professional groups to resolve issues (Keith, 1984).

These findings concerning the relationship between the union's power and strikes need not be viewed as mutually exclusive. Dubin (1960) proposed a curvilinear relationship between propensity to strike and relative power of the parties that would account for the discrepant hypotheses. However, Dubin suggested that it is not the amount of power held by the union that predicts strikes. Rather, the greater the *disparity* between the power held by the parties, the greater the conflict. However, while plausible, this notion has yet to receive appropriate empirical attention (see Kelly & Nicholson, 1980b).

Another structural variable that has been found to influence union participation is industrial relations climate, i.e., the perceived nature of the relationship between labor and management (Anderson, 1978; Strauss, 1977a). Industrial relations climate is a component of the total organizational climate that focuses on the nature of the union-management relationship. Anderson (1978) suggests that union participation will be greater under conditions of a more hostile relationship between management and labor.

Several studies support this perspective (Bluen & Donald, 1991; Brett & Goldberg, 1979; Kelly & Nicholson, 1980b; Stagner & Eflal, 1982). Recent research has shown that industrial relations climate is not a global construct; instead, it is multidimensional in nature (Dastmalchian, Blyton, & Adamson, 1989). For this reason, future researchers should investigate whether the specific components of industrial relations climate differentially influence strike behavior and union participation.

In summary, it can be seen that participation in union activities is multiply determined. Like other aspects of unionization, demographic characteristics exert a minimal impact on union participation. In contrast, work-related (e.g., job dissatisfaction, alienation), union-related (e.g., perceived union instrumentality, specific and general union attitudes), and nonwork (e.g., personal beliefs about work) factors do predict union participation. It would certainly be interesting at this stage for research to investigate the relative contribution these diverse factors play in union participation, and whether they differentially predict different aspects of union participation.

Consequences of Union Participation

Participation in union activities is seen as having several beneficial consequences: It creates a unified rank-and-file membership, it prevents union oligarchy, and it facilitates the representative function of the union by establishing a framework whereby member needs can be articulated (Ramaswamy, 1977). Perhaps the greatest impact that union participation has is on union democracy in that it increases members' involvement and influence on decision making, selection of leadership, and implementation of policies. With respect to the simplest level of union democracy, participation increases membership control over union activities (Hochner et al., 1980). As Hogan noted more than four decades ago: "In a democracy people get about the kind of government they deserve and this is true of union government as well as of other forms of government" (1948/49, p. 334).

However, no empirical research has investigated the relationship between union participation and democracy. This is partially because little agreement exists about the conceptualization and operationalization of both union democracy and union participation. In Chapter 2, we outlined three criteria of union democracy. These include participation in union activities, the influence of members over union decision making, and the extent of opposition. It is interesting to note that all these criteria are synonymous with the characteristics of participation discussed earlier in this chapter. Consequently, one should expect democracy and participation to be strongly associated, although which precedes which is still a question to be empirically determined.

The consequences of worker participation in union activities also have an impact on organizational performance and various behavioral outputs. Opposing economic theories have been used to explain the effects of involvement in union activities on organizational performance. On the one hand, the traditional economic view is that unions lead to higher labor costs and job regulations that limit managerial flexibility, resulting in a general deterioration in organizational performance. On the other hand, the "Harvard Schools" argue that unions bring about higher productivity: Although unions promote higher wages, such increases lead to a better calibre labor force and the need for fewer workers (Freeman, 1976; and see Chapter 8). Freeman (1976) applies Hirschman's (1970) exit-voice-loyalty model to explain how membership participation in unions improves rather than hampers union-management relations and organizational effectiveness. Unions provide discontented workers with a participatory forum and a collective "voice" at the workplace by means of which they may articulate their feelings rather than "exiting" temporarily (i.e., absenteeism) or permanently (i.e., labor turnover). The choice between exit and union participation (voice) may be determined by the worker's loyalty to the organization and the expectancy that participation can improve the dissatisfying conditions. Thus, it is possible that unionism precipitates confrontation and resolution of issues rather than withdrawl from the organization. In so doing, unions can improve general organizational effectiveness.

Until recently (Bluen & Barling, 1988), the psychological consequences of participation in union activities were largely ignored. Research has ascertained the financial costs of strikes to both individuals (Gennard, 1981, 1982) and organizations (Ackerman, 1979; Becker & Olson, 1986; Chermesh, 1979; Imberman 1979), but financial costs are only a part of the personal consequences of strike involvement. Because much of the literature on the consequences of strikes is economic, personal costs are overlooked, For example, none of the over 300 references included in Pettman's (1971) strike bibliography focused directly on individual psychological consequences of strikes. Even Gordon and Nurick's (1981) agenda for the field of psychological approaches to labor organizations did not include the potentially stressful role of membership involvement in union actions.

Bluen and Barling (1988) argue that strikes (and participation in the industrial relations process) are inherently stressful for the actors involved. For example, union leaders are faced with the dilemma of trying to maintain internal union democracy while at the same time being pressured into adopting a more bureaucratic structure to meet environmental demands (Anderson, 1978). Also, union leaders have to tread a delicate balance between the demands of their membership and the willingness of management to meet those demands. Poor funding means insufficient union officials to do the required work, which leads to the experience of role overload (Warr, 1981). Indeed, 75% of stewards reported medium to high levels of quantitative overload as a result of their excessive workload (Nicholson, 1976). Also, because they possessed neither the experience nor the training to perform their tasks adequately, many stewards experienced qualitative overload. Stewards reported high levels of (1) role ambiguity because they had received no clear-cut guidelines and (2) role conflict because they were continually required to interact with members of both management and workers, who made conflicting demands on them (Nicholson, 1976). Union members are subjected to various other sources of stress, such as management victimization. Allen and Keaveny (1983) cite cases of pro-union employees being discharged, threatened with dismissal and plant closure, denied privileges, and being transferred to lower paying jobs.

Finally, participation in strikes has several stressful behavioral outcomes. For example, Wood and Pedler (1978) report feelings of fear among striking workers, and instances of threats, lies, obscenities, and physical violence. Union officials felt pressured by their members and frustated by the concomitant lack of progress in the union-management negotiations. Non-striking workers were confronted by hostile pickets as they tried to enter premises. MacBride, Lancee, and Freeman (1981) measured the psychological responses of Canadian air traffic controllers during a labor dispute in which the right to strike was withdrawn after a positive strike vote. They found that during the dispute the subjects exhibited high levels of psychological distress (such as feelings of worthlessness, depression, and strain) and a marked deterioration of perceived general functioning, physical health, and psychological well-being.

The preceding examples illustrate that stress is associated with participation in various union activities. However, only a few studies have specifically examined the stress inherent in industrial relations activities. Bluen and Barling (1987) found that industrial relations stress was positively related to measures of role conflict, role ambiguity, propensity to leave, and job dissatisfaction and inversely related to organizational commitment. The design of the study, however, precludes any causal inferences because of the cross-sectional nature of the data. Barling and Milligan (1987) found that psychological distress increased after involvement in strike activity. Stoner and Arora (1987) found that the psychological health of strikers was predicted by five variables reflecting their functioning during the strike: the level of savings, changes in number, scope, and variety of free time activities during the strike, number of people available to offer social support, attitudes supportive of union activities, and expected length of the strike's duration. These studies go beyond previous research on strike behavior in showing that negative personal consequences can accrue to striking employees. For example, Haywood and Taylor (1981) described how spouse and citizen support groups provided invaluable support in offsetting the stressful effects of a protracted strike, and Gennard (1981, 1982) calculated the financial costs incurred by strikers, but did not examine the psychological effects of such costs.

Thus, organizational psychologists can provide information on the personal effects of strikes, a major weapon in the collective bargaining process, and other forms of union participation. Nonetheless, because one of the ethical responsibilities of psychologists is to enhance the psychological functioning of the groups they serve, an ethical issue arises from the fact that negative personal consequences can accrue to strikers: Should psychologists work together with those who would prefer to eliminate strikes? Barling and Milligan (1987, p. 135) commented fairly extensively on this dilemma. They suggest that despite the potential negative consequences of union participation (and strikes), it is still not the function of organiational psychologists

> ... to devise ways of avoiding or breaking strikes. Strike activity in many cases remains a legitimate technique for obtaining organizational change. ... In addition in the same way that unions offer their members an alternative to exit behaviours (e.g., withdrawal), strikes may provide an additional alternative to withdrawl when all other attempts at organizational change have failed. Thus, organizational psychologists must accept the inevitability, legitimacy and even the positive function of strikes. ... This might involve ideological and attitudinal changes for some organizational psychologists, who must redirect their focus to psychological processes that mitigate the harmful effects of being involved in a strike.

Conclusions

In this chapter we have attempted to provide a comprehensive understanding of the concept of union participation, and to outline its causes and some of its consequences. One problem with previous research on participation is that it has relied mainly on cross-sectional data and correlative analyses. As such, it becomes misleading to distinguish between the antecedents and consequences of union participation based on correlational data. As Kryl (1990) points out, significant correlations between a variable X and union participation could have at least four different meanings. First, X could indeed predict union participation. Second, union participation could predict X. Third, X and participation in union activities could have a reciprocal and simultaneous effect on each other. Finally, both variables may be influenced by a third, extraneous factor. Furthermore, the problem of causal inference is frequently exacerbated by operational definitions of union participation that consist of asking members which union-related activities they have been involved in over the preceding twelve months. In these instances, researchers attempt to "predict future participation behavior while presently assessing past participation behavior with potential predictors, all measured simultaneously" (Kryl, 1990, p. 20).

Nevertheless, the literature points to a number of variables as significant work-related, union-related, nonwork, and structural predictors of union participation. These should provide valuable guidelines for future reasearch in ascertaining the nature and direction of the relationship between variables in the participation process. In any future research, investigators could advance our understanding still further by using more direct observations of behavior (e.g., union records of meeting attendance, company records of grievance filing behavior, stewards' assessments of member participation, and so forth). Although many unions do not possess the facilities to collect such data, and others might not be willing to provide such information even if it is available, research of this nature would be useful in assessing the causal nature of the relationship between union participation and its proposed correlates. For example, participation in union activities might cause an awareness of inequlities in the political structures of organizations, which in turn facilitates dissatisfaction and stronger attitudes to the union. Alternatively, greater participation in union affairs might conceivably cause greater conflict among job, family, and union roles.

Furthermore, we have tried to emphasize that union participation is a dynamic and continuous process that develops and fluctuates with union tenure, development, success, and history. Research on union participation therefore, must assess how socialization practices, negotiations, strikes, and their outcomes, the prevailing economic and legal climate, and the union's previous bargaining history (e.g., its success in satisfying members' needs) influence participation in union activities. Consistent with the research on union commitment is a relative wealth of research on the proposed antecedents of union participation, compared to the paucity of information on the potential impact of union participation on union democracy, bargaining effectiveness, and other consequences. Since an understanding of both causes and consequences of union participation is required for a comprehensive model of the concept, further research focusing on the consequences of union participation is overdue. Any such research should assess similarities and differences in the predictors and outcomes of diverse aspects of union participation. In addition, given that many of the factors that predict union participation also predict union voting decisions and union commitment (e.g., general and specific union attitudes, job dissatisfaction), it would be intriguing for further research to explore to what degree the different components of unionization share similar predictors.

To conclude, this chapter has attempted to illustrate the importance and complexity of the concept of union participation, and to outline some of its causes and consequences. An understanding of participation is important for psychological research on unions, for a comprehensive understanding of organizations, and also for labor leaders who wish to address the deteriorating levels of union participation and increase the democratic involvement of rank-and-file members.

6

Union Leadership:
The Role of the Shop Steward

Shop stewards occupy a key role ... acting as decision-makers in their own right, and as facilitators of rank and file involvement in decision-making.
(Nicholson, Ursell, & Blyton, 1980)

In the previous chapter we considered the predictors and consequences of members' participation in union activities. This chapter now extends that discussion by focusing specifically on the topic of union leadership and its influence on the unionization process. There are several reasons why a specific focus on union leadership is warranted. First, union leadership is the highest form of participation in union activities. Acceptance of a leadership role within the union implies a greater involvement in union activities than do other forms of participation such as voting in union elections or attending union meetings (Nicholson, 1976). Moreover, participation in a leadership role in the union necessitates participation in other union activities including decision making (Anderson, 1979). Second, union leaders facilitate the involvement of rank-and-file members in the union. Members' participation in union activities varies with shop stewards' interpersonal skills (Kahn & Tannenbaum, 1954) and accessibility (Nicholson et al., 1980). Attitudes toward the union, such as union commitment, predict members' participation and, in themselves, are influenced by the leadership styles of union officials (Fullagar, McCoy, & Shull, 1992). As the individuals responsible for the orientation of new members and the dissemination of information to members, union leaders are critical for the development of union relevant attitudes and behaviors and union democracy (Kahn & Tannenbaum, 1954). Third, shop stewards play a key role in union-management relations. As the union representative on the shop floor, stewards influence diverse aspects of industrial relations; perhaps most important, stewards fulfill a critical function in the handling of individual grievances (Dalton & Todor, 1979, 1981, 1982a). Fourth, despite calls for increased research on union leadership (e.g., Gordon & Nurick, 1981; Strauss, 1977a), little research has been conducted on union leadership in North America.

This is not to say that union leadership is a neglected research topic. Instead, the bulk of union leadership research has been conducted and published by industrial relations researchers in the United Kingdom and Australia. The report of the Donovan (1968) commission on trade unions and employee associations in the United Kingdom identified the central role of shop stewards in local industrial relations and union government and provided a vast amount of descriptive information on the duties and characteristics of shop stewards. Following this report, researchers in the United Kingdom have addressed a variety of union leadership issues empirically. Even in the United Kingdom, however, conventional wisdom suggests that despite a mountain of data addressing the rule of the shop steward, little is actually known about shop stewards (Partridge, 1977). Finally, union leadership has been identified as the very essence of leadership (Ginzberg, 1948). Unlike leaders in many business organizations who have formal power bestowed on them by the organization, the union leader has limited power resources that are highly dependent on his or her constituency. Anecdotal accounts suggest that union leaders are both sensitive and responsive to the needs of their membership (White, 1988). As such, greater understanding of the union leaders' role may lead to insights regarding both labor unions and leadership.

While some researchers have adopted behavioral definitions of leadership (e.g., Miller, Zeller, & Miller, 1965), the vast majority of union leadership research has focused on the role of the union leader rather than the behaviors required for successful performance of that role. Thus, the emphasis has been on individuals who occupy formal leadership roles in the union rather than on informal leadership. For the most part, the specific focus has been on shop stewards. There are several reasons for this almost exclusive concentration on shop stewards. First, the influential Donovan (1968) commission examined the role of shop stewards in the United Kindgom in considerable detail (e.g., McCarthy, 1967; McCarthy & Parker, 1968), and concluded that shop stewards play a pivotal role in both union government and local industrial relations. As mentioned previously, the Donovan report was influential in shaping subsequent research on union leadership. Second, shop stewards fulfill a significant role in local unions (Kahn & Tannenbaum, 1954) and union-management relations. Peck (1963, p. 15) emphasizes the central role of shop stewards in unions.

> In short, the shop steward is *the* rank-and-file leader in the shop. No other level of action leadership possesses such intimate, direct contact with the membership. Moulded and shaped by the attitudes and opinions of his [sic] fellow departmental workers, the union steward also conditions and affects the ideology of the membership.

Third, while not all shop stewards go on to assume other leadership roles in the union, many full-time union officials began their involvement in union leadership as shop stewards (Clegg, Killick, & Adams, 1961). In this sense, a greater understanding of the shop steward role may generalize to other levels of union leadership. Finally, the shop steward holds a unique role in both the workplace and the union. Being simultaneously a worker and a leader, the shop steward is subject to unique role constraints and pressures (Moore, 1980). As such, the steward role is inherently ambiguous and conflictual.

In this chapter we address four related aspects of the literature dealing with shop stewards. We start by setting the stage for the ensuing discussion by considering in some detail the role of shop stewards in unions. Specifically, we focus on exactly what stewards do in the performance of their daily duties. We then consider how individuals come to assume a leadership role in the union. We have previously discussed factors predictive of participation in the union (see Chapter 5). In this chapter we extend this discussion by focusing on participation in a specific form of union activity; that of voluntarily holding union office. Arguably, this form of participation is critical to the survival and success of the union. Having considered the formal role of a shop steward, we then focus on individual differences in the performance of that role. Specifically, the discussion moves to a consideration of leadership styles and attempts to identify factors that influence the way stewards perform their union duties. Finally, we present some evidence on the effects of shop steward behavior on union-relevant attitudes and behaviors, union-management relations, and the stressors unique to the steward role.

The Shop Steward Role

The term shop steward is by no means universal; different terms are used in different countries and different unions. In the United States, terms may include shop delegate, chairlady, deputy patrolman, chapel chairman, and committeeman (Nash, 1984). In the United Kingdom, terms such as staff representative, father or mother of the chapel, corresponding member, local departmental committee member, and workplace representative are used (Clegg et al., 1961; McCarthy, 1968; Nash, 1984). Whatever the term, the *function* of the shop steward is consistent across countries. For example, in the United States the role of the shop steward as defined by the AFL-CIO is

> His [sic] most important one [job] is the handling of grievances. Among the others are: Organizing and helping to make better union members of the workers in his department, informing the workers of union meetings and urging them to attend, acting as a 'transmission belt' between union officers and the membership, supporting the political education work of his union, supporting labor's community activities and knowing labor legislation (see Nash, 1984, p. 9).

The Trades Union Congress in the United Kingdom describes a similar role for shop stewards.

> He [sic] has responsibility for the state of union organization and his duties often include recruiting new members, collecting union dues and maintaining membership. ... In general ... he [sic] has three main functions—to act for members with a grievance arising at work; to negotiate improvements in terms

of employment; and to participate in joint consultative bodies (see Nash, 1984, pp. 3–4).

Thus the shop steward is primarily described as a representative of the rank-and-file members (McCarthy, 1968; Peck, 1963) charged with the responsibility of representing union members to both management and the union (e.g., Clegg et al., 1961). As such the shop steward is the main communication link between the workers and the company/union and is variously responsible for building the union, informing members on union policies and activities, encouraging participation in all levels of union activity, and, most important, processing individual grievances (Davis, 1980; McCarthy, 1968; Nash, 1984; Peck, 1963).

The range and extent of additional duties assigned to the steward will vary both across and within organizations. For example, the institution of centralized collective bargaining has substantially reduced the stewards' role in the formulation of collective agreements (Kessler, 1986; Peck, 1963). Similarly, in environments where the automatic checkoff of union dues is the norm, stewards may not be directly involved in the financial affairs of the union. Notwithstanding these differences, it is clear that the duties of the shop steward require close contact with the union membership. It is not surprising that the shop stewards' leadership role is seen as being crucial in union-member and union-management relations. Kahn and Tannenbaum (1954, p. 285) indicate the duties and importance of the steward role in unions by commenting

> Through his [sic] role as a grievance processor, decision maker and communicator, the steward appears to be an important instrumentality for the promotion or the weakening of union democracy.

In understanding the role of shop stewards it is important to note that stewards are not typically full-time employees of the union. Rather, stewards perform their union-related duties *in addition to* their responsibilities as employees. Most typically, in North America, stewards perform some part of their duties in the workplace (for which the collective agreement typically mandates compensation from the employer) with additional duties continuing outside working hours. Both diary and survey data converge in suggesting that stewards spend approximately 10 to 15 hours per week on union activities, in contrast to full-time union officials who may spend in excess of 50 hours per week on union activities (Clegg et al., 1961; Robertson & Sams, 1978).

Schuller and Robertson (1983) conducted a diary study of eighty-six shop stewards from both the private and public sector over a period of twelve weeks. Stewards in this study devoted an average of 2 hours and 40 minutes per week to union duties. At least two factors suggest that this is an underestimation. First, stewards in this study were asked to record only time spent in contact with *groups* of union members. Thus the stewards who were subjects of this study did not record time spent in individual interactions or time spent alone doing record keeping or correspondence. Second, other studies have resulted in substantially higher estimates of the time stewards spend on their union duties. For example, McCarthy and Parker (1968) estimate an average of 6 hours per week is devoted to their duties. Clegg et al. (1961) concluded that stewards spend approximately 11 hours per week on union activities with 6 of these hours spent during working time. Similarly, Partridge (1977) conducted a diary study of twenty-four stewards over 10 weeks. He concluded that stewards on average spent 2 hours *per day* on union activities with the majority of this being during working hours. After excluding the convenor (i.e., chief steward) and deputy convenor from the analysis, the estimate fell to 98 minutes per day. Finally, Miller et al. (1965) reported that a majority of union officials (excluding full-time officers) in their study spent between 0 and 9 hours per week on union business.

By far the single most important determinant of the amount of time stewards spend on union activities is the size of their constituencies (Clegg et al., 1961). Estimates generally converge on an average constituency of approximately fifty union members (e.g., Clegg et al., 1961; Donovan, 1968; Lund, 1963; McCarthy & Parker, 1968; Warr, 1981) although other researchers report substantially smaller constituencies (e.g., modal constituency = eleven to twenty members; Schuller & Robertson, 1983). However, there is a wide range in the size of shop stewards' constituencies, from less than ten to over one hundred members (Davis, 1980; McCarthy & Parker, 1968; Schuller & Robertson, 1983).

The relationship between constituency size and the amount of time stewards spend on union activity follows naturally from the stewards' primary role in handling and resolving individual grievances (Nash, 1984). Studies of stewards' and union officials' behavior consistently suggest that the majority of time devoted to union business is spent dealing with individual members and their grievances (Clegg et al., 1961; Miller et al., 1965). Based on his survey of 162 union safety representatives, Beaumont (1981) suggested that approximately half the representatives' time was spent on processing individual complaints; the next most frequent activity was routine monitoring of the workplace for safety hazards. Schuller and Robertson's (1983) diary study of eighty-six shop stewards similarly suggested that the bulk of stewards' time was spent dealing with individual grievances and disseminating information to individual members. Similarly, Partridge (1977) suggests that most of stewards' time is spent liaising with management on individual grievances, monitoring the workplace, and disseminating information to the members.

In addition to constituency size, a variety of other factors may determine how much time stewards spend on their union duties. Geographical dispersion (e.g., representing workers in more than one geographical location) may inhibit interactions between stewards and members (Kessler, 1986). Moreover, the role of the steward may be differentially defined across, and even within, unions. That is, the opinions of the membership have a critical influence on shop steward behavior (Broad, 1983). Therefore, the exact role assumed by the steward will be determined largely by the desires of his or her constituency. Finally, the quality of union-management relations or industrial relations climate in the workplace might reasonably be expected to influence the behavior of the shop steward, with a poor industrial relations climate resulting in a higher rate of grievance activity on the part of the stewards.

Thus, while the general nature of steward duties seems to be similar across unions, one would expect considerable variation in the implementation of these duties both across unions and within unions (e.g., across stewards). Two inter-related factors that predict such differences are the means through which stewards assume their roles and individual differences affecting performance of the duties associated with the steward role. We now turn our attention on these two factors.

Becoming a Union Leader

Given the democratic ethos of labor unions (Fullagar & Barling, 1987), it seems reasonable to accept that union leaders are closer to political leaders than to business leaders (Ginzberg, 1984). That is, the popular perception of union leaders is that they are elected by, and therefore accountable to, the union membership. Unfortunately, this perception ignores an often widespread lack of membership participation in labor unions. While many union leadership positions are formally defined as elected positions, it is clear that the practice falls far short of the ideal.

Consistent evidence suggests that a large number of union officials assume office unopposed. Schuller and Robertson (1983) report that 70% of the stewards in their study came to office unopposed, while McCarthy and Parker (1968) report that 71% were unopposed. In the latter study, approximately 40% of the stewards had to be persuaded to take on the job (McCarthy & Parker, 1968). Similarly, Nicholson et al. (1980) found that not only did 45% of white-collar shop stewards come to office unopposed, but 16% had to be persuaded to take on the job. Nicholson (1976) goes even further in showing that not only were the majority of shop stewards acclaimed to their position, several were appointed as shop stewards over their own personal protests. Moore (1980) reports that 38% of the stewards he studied accepted the position reluctantly and a further 31% were not actively seeking it. This phenomenon is by no means recent. In 1953, Strauss and Sayles reported that, although there was competition for the top union positions, competition for the post of shop steward was much less active.

The lack of democratically elected officials may appear to pose a problem for union democracy. As institutions that value and espouse democratic principles, unions may have considerable difficulty in justifying the lack of duly elected officials. However, several factors mitigate this apparent contradic-tion. First, Won (1964/65) suggests that the definition of union democracy is based on a procedural guarantee; the *potential* for participation rather than participation *per se* is the defining characteristic of union democracy. In this sense a lack of competitive elections for union positions assumes less importance. Rather, the defining characteristic of union democracy is that any individual member has the *opportunity* to run for an elected office. If union members do not avail themselves of this opportunity, this does not, in itself, provide the basis for declaring unions undemocratic (see Chapter 2 for a discussion of the issues involved in defining union democracy). Second, as Schuller and Robertson (1983, p. 332) point out,

> ... a formal election is not the only way in which colleagues can decide who should represent them. Someone may be the obvious choice, or the selection may be made in an informal way during the period preceding the offical election date so that only one nomination goes forward.

This observation is particularly salient in reference to the selection of shop stewards who are "elected" by a relatively small (i.e., $N = 50$) group of constituents, typically found in one workplace.

Finally, Clegg et al. (1961) note that approximately 80% of the stewards in their sample were subject to regular re-election; about half weré opposed at first re-election and a quarter at subsequent elections. Thus while competition for the role of shop steward may not be intense, there are procedural mechanisms through which union members can express their displeasure with the performance of the shop steward thereby rendering stewards accountable to the membership. Moreover, the findings of Clegg et al. (1961) suggest that rank-and-file members do, in fact, avail themselves of these opportunities. In short, the procedural guarantee of democracy (Won, 1964/65) renders stewards accountable to the rank-and-file membership. Taken together, these findings suggest that the preponderance of stewards who assume their position as the result of acclamation has less to say about union democracy than it does about the perceived costs and benefits of being a shop steward.

Recognizing that stewards may assume office through election, acclamation, or appointment, it is instructive to consider what factors are related to becoming a union steward. Nicholson (1976) focused on two broad factors associated with union leadership: external events beyond the control of the individual and internal or individual factors. First, as external factors, Nicholson points to selection of shop stewards by crisis, popularity and appointment. In a crisis, the incumbent steward relinquishes office (e.g., resigns, retires, transfers to a new job) and the least apathetic or most accessible worker gets the job. It is clear that accessability is a factor in selecting shop stewards. One hypothesis offered to account for the predominance of high-status employees among union officials (e.g., Blyton et al., 1981; Kolchin & Hyclak, 1984; McShane, 1986b; Nicholson et al., 1981) was that such employees had more contact with other union members due to their job which allowed them to move about the workforce (Blyton et al., 1981). One may also become a steward by accident—by taking on a related role, the individual finds him or herself saddled with the role of steward as well. As Nicholson (1976) points out, in the face of widespread apathy, the individual displaying the slightest interest beyond the lowest common denominator gets the job. Stewards may also be chosen on the basis of personal popularity or the perception that he or she is the best person for the job. The latter explanation is consistent with findings that education (McShane, 1986a, 1986b, Nicholson et al., 1981), organizational tenure (Dean, 1954; McShane, 1986b; Nicholson et al., 1981; Strauss & Sayles, 1953), and job status (Blyton et al., 1981; Kolchin & Hyclak, 1984; McShane, 1986b; Nicholson et al., 1986) have all been associated with holding union office. Finally, officials of the union (e.g., chief steward, union president) may appoint an individual to act as the shop steward. Such appointments may be made on the basis of experience, organizational tenure, and/or verbal fluency (Nicholson, 1976).

Second, Nicholson (1976) has identified internal factors that motivate becoming a shop steward. The external factors Nicholson described paint a picture of "the reluctant steward." Certainly this is consistent with the numbers of stewards who assume their role unopposed and, at times, despite their own personal protests. It is important to note, however, that Nicholson's description of how shop stewards come to office is predicated on an individual showing *more* interest than the majority of rank-and-file members. While the available literature does not support the view of shop stewards as being "wild-eyed labor radicals," a consistent body of literature suggests that individual work beliefs, union attitudes, and interests are predictive of being a shop steward. Nicholson (1976) refers to such influences as internal factors, which includes both task orientation and ideological beliefs.

The task orientation discussed by Nicholson refers to the recognition by the individual that there is a job to do and that he or she is the person to do it. In this view, taking on the role of shop steward is seen as a moral obligation or personal responsibility. In contrast to the concept of collective instrumentality discussed as a predictor of unionization, union commitment, and decertification, the task orientation identified by Nicholson (1976) reflects a sense of *personal* instrumentality.

Several studies support the notion of task orientation as a predictor of union leadership. Moore (1981) contrasted various hypotheses about why members become union stewards (e.g., innate leadership potential, commitment to opposing the capitalist system, high individual need for power, need to be of service to others, status incongruence, need for self-actualization, authoritarian personality, and personal responsibility). The only hypothesis that received any support was "the responsible person hypothesis." In other words, the single most predictive factor was an individual's inability to stand the distress associated with ineffective or non-existent leadership and a desire to have some control over matters of personal concern. Similarly, Seidman et al. (1950) found that the desire to win improvements for fellow workers was a motivating factor for twenty of the forty union leaders in their study. Organizational involvement (i.e., concern for what happens in the organization), and individual needs for decision making have also been associated with union leadership (Glick et al., 1977). Finally, in an analysis of the leadership styles of union officials, Simpson and Peterson (1972) found that officials scored highly on the initiating structure scale of the Leader Behavior Description Questionnaire (Stogdill & Coons, 1957). This would indicate that shop stewards clearly define their roles and help rank-and-file members know what is expected of them.

Also consistent with the suggestion that stewards experience a sense of personal responsibility is the finding that union officials attribute their participation to the desire to improve the functioning of the union. Won (1964/65) reported that 22% of the 108 United Automobile Workers officials he surveyed were motivated to run for union office either by dissatisfaction with the administration of the union or the perception that they were better qualified than incumbent officials. Similarly, Seidman et al. (1950) found that union officials attribute their activity to dissatisfaction with working conditions (which may reflect a perceived lack of union instrumentality—see Chapter 5) or the lack of other qualified leaders.

Another internal factor identified by Nicholson (1976) is an ideological commitment to unionism. Several lines of evidence support the suggestion that union officials are more likely to be ideologically committed to the goals of the labor movement. In validating scales of work beliefs, Buchholz (1978, 1979) contrasted the belief systems held by individuals in various occupational groups. In contrast to clerical, professional, managerial, and unionized hourly employees (rank-and-file members), union officials manifested higher Marxist and organizational work beliefs and lower work ethic beliefs. In other words, union officials strongly believed that work is fundamental for human fulfillment, but as currently organized represents exploitation of the worker and consequent alienation. Furthermore, work should be undertaken for the good of the "group" or collectivity, rather than for the enhancement of individual self-interests. The cross-sectional nature of these studies does not lend itself to causal interpretation, thus leaving open the question of whether holding union office is predicted by, or predictive of, ideological commitment to unionism. However, union leaders did seem to be more oriented to traditional union beliefs than members of other groups. Somewhat similarly, individuals who have an interest in the labor movement (Kolchin & Hyclak, 1984) and union business (McShane, 1986a), report positive union attitudes (Glick, Mirvis, & Harder, 1977), greater commitment to the union (Kelloway & Catano, 1989), and positive perceptions of union instrumentality (Chacko, 1985), are more likely to hold union office. While not conclusive, these findings suggest that ideology does play a role in determining who will become a shop steward. As an aside, it is worth noting that stronger effects of ideological beliefs may emerge in the United Kingdom where shop stewards are more radical and less controlled than their North American counterparts (Nash, 1984). Consistent with this suggestion is the finding that shop stewards in the United Kingdom were significantly more radical and progressive than the people they represent (Nicholson et al., 1980).

Further evidence for ideological commitment to unionism as a motivating factor in becoming a shop steward emerges from the self-reported motives of elected union officials. Over 49% of the officials surveyed by Won (1964/65) identify factors such as concern for workers' well-being, concern for the working class, and concern with working conditions as motivating factors in the decision to accept the role of shop steward. Interestingly, an overwhelming majority of union officials surveyed by Seidman et al. (1950) claimed union sympathies *prior* to joining the union and cited family background as an important influence. The influence of family background was also identified by 9% of the officials surveyed by Won (1964/65). In conjunction with recent research documenting the influence of family socialization on the development of union attitudes (Barling, Kelloway, & Bremermann, 1991), these findings may be taken as additional support for the role of ideological commitment to unions as a motivating factor in assuming the role of shop steward. Finally, Fosh (1981) found several ideological factors associated with union activity in a British steel mill. Specifically, more active union members (including voluntary branch officers) (1) were more committed to the collective pursuit of group goals, (2) were ideologically identified with the aims of trade unionism, (3) perceived the goals of unions to be social and political, as well as economic, and (4) were more politically aware and interested when compared to their inactive counterparts.

Consistent with the literature on union certification (see Chapter 3) and union commitment (see Chapter 4), research on union leadership offers little support for the notion of a "union type." Thus while union leaders tend to express more positive attitudes toward, and interest in, unions than do rank-and-file union members, (1) they manifest only slightly more interest than rank-and-file members and (2) most of the research has been cross-sectional in nature, thereby precluding causal inferences. Similarly, as with certification (see Chapter 3) and decertification (see Chapter 7), the effect of demographic factors differs across studies and is minimized in multivariate analyses. This raises the question of the relative importance of demographic predictors of union leadership. While demographic factors correlate with union leadership, they may be less important, and indeed proxies for, other variables such as ideological beliefs and the influence of socialization practices.

We may note at least two exceptions to this general conclusion. First, there is the consistent finding that employees in highly skilled jobs and/or high-status jobs are disproportionately represented among union officials (Blyton et al., 1981; Kolchin & Hyclak, 1984; McShane, 1986b; Nicholson et al., 1980). Moreover, after being elected to office, stewards who hold high-status jobs are more likely to be active participants in union activities. Thus, based on behavioral observation of shop steward committee meetings, Blyton (1981) reports that active participation in committee meetings varied directly and positively with job status. A compelling explanation for the association between status and holding union office deals not with job status *per se*, but rather with the increased opportunities for contact with other union members afforded by higher-status jobs (Blyton et al., 1981). Furthermore, higher-status jobs not only provide greater opportunities for social interactions with other workers, they also facilitate the development of the kind of social and organizational skills that are necessary to participate in union activities (Form, 1976; Meissner, 1971). The argument that individuals in higher-status jobs may wish to extend their influence in the workplace by assuming a leadership position in the union has also been advanced (Blyton et al., 1981). As we have implied earlier, union leadership and particularly the role of shop steward involves considerable contact with individual union members. Individuals with jobs that allow them such contact may be more likely to be nominated to, and selected for, union leadership positions. Moreover, individuals in high-status jobs may also have more access to managerial information and opinion (Blyton, 1981). Thus, individuals in high-status jobs may be more accessible to both management and rank-and-file members. It is also possible that the association between job status and union leadership is attributable to third variables such as verbal fluency, education, and tenure, all of which are related to both job status and holding a union office (Nicholson, 1976).

Second, several lines of evidence suggest that women are less likely to hold union office than men (e.g., Benson & Griffin, 1988; Chaison & Andiappan, 1989; Fryer, Fairclough, & Manson, 1978; Heery & Kelly, 1989; Strauss & Sayles, 1953; Wertheimer & Nelson, 1975). As with other forms of participation in union activities (see Chapter 5), the explanation for this finding is based on the role women play in society rather than in their commitment to the union. Chaison and Andiappan (1989) suggest that the most important barriers to becoming union officers for women are that women hold two jobs (at work and at home), and that child-care responsibilities inhibit taking on a union leadership role. These findings echo those of previous research on women's involvement in the union (Wertheimer & Nelson, 1975) reporting that women did not engage in union activities largely because of their family and child-care responsibilities. It is important to recall that at least 50% of the stewards' duties are performed outside work hours (e.g., Clegg et al., 1961) and, therefore, may conflict with family responsibilities.

When women do accept a position, such as that of shop steward, the same factors may inhibit their full participation in the union. Thus Roby and Uttal (1988) report an "inverse" effect on participation whereby married men and single women stewards were more active in the union than either single men or married women. Single female stewards were far more active in the union than female stewards with partners or children. Thus child-care and domestic responsibilities continue to fall disproportionately on women and discourage their active participation in the work of the union (Barling, 1990). These findings suggest both the importance of unions providing means for women to participate in the union (see Chaison & Andiappan, 1989; Roby & Uttal, 1988) and the danger in interpreting participation in union activities as a measure of support for the union. Underscoring the notion that it is not gender *per se* that is operative but rather social and familial constraints on women, Gordon et al. (1980) found that, although women were less likely than men to participate in the union, they expressed *greater* support (commitment) for the union than did their male counterparts. Similarly, Benson and Griffin (1988) report that men and women expressed similar levels of attitudes toward unions but that women were less likely to participate in the union and hold union office.

Although job status is positively related to influence within the union (Blyton, 1981), being female is negatively related to influence in the union. Izraeli (1985) examined the self-reported influence of 148 male and 111 female union officials in Israel. Significant differences emerged between self-reported influence of male and female officials although this effect was moderated by the sex proportion (i.e., ratio of female:male members) in the union. Thus, when women composed less than 30% of the membership, female stewards reported less influence than their male counterparts. When the proportion of females in the union exceeded 70%, there were no gender-based differences in self-reported influence. Moreover, the self-reported influence of male officials did not vary as a function of the proportion of males in the union. The reported influence of female officials did vary positively as a function of the proportion of females in the union. Thus, like job status, gender is related to both becoming a union official and subsequent performance in that role.

Styles of Leadership

In previous sections we have considered the principle responsibilities of the shop steward and the routes through which individuals assume a leadership role in the union. In this section we focus more specifically on factors influencing how stewards perform their role. Both structural (McCarthy, 1967) and individual (Batstone, Boraston, & Frenkel, 1977; Dalton & Todor, 1979, 1981, 1982a,b) factors have been identified as influences on shop stewards' behavior.

McCarthy (1967) identifies six structural factors that may influence shop stewards' behavior: (1) labor market conditions, (2) the socio-technical system of the plant, (3) the level of decision making, (4) the wage structure, (5) the scope of collective agreements, and (6) employer, union, and workgroup attitudes. More specifically, stewards may be more willing to press grievances, and management more likely to make concessions, in times of high labor market demand. The socio-technical system, and more particularly the nature of the work performed by the steward's constituency, may also influence steward behavior by facilitating steward-member communication and workgroup cohesion. As noted earlier, steward behavior may also be influenced by the degree of centralization of both collective bargaining and human resource management. Thus, stewards involved in collective bargaining who deal directly with management decision-makers may exert more influence in the workplace. Stewards also acquire more influence when they are in a position to directly influence the wages of their members. For example, in payment by results (i.e., piece-rate) wage systems, stewards may become directly involved in wage issues by becoming directly involved in the setting of rates. Similarly, the scope of the collective agreement establishes the range of issues stewards can become involved in. The collective agreement largely determines the range of issues that can be negotiated at the shop-floor level (i.e., by stewards). Finally, the attitudes of employers, unions, and rank-and-file members all have the potential to influence steward behavior. As noted throughout this chapter, attitudes of rank-and-file members toward stewards largely constrain their effective range of actions. Similarly, unions vary widely in the support and training they provide for stewards, and managers' attitudes to shop stewards range from real opposition and resentment to acceptance and a marked preference for dealing with shop stewards as opposed to other union officials (e.g., Clegg et al., 1961). Stewards' behavior may reasonably be expected to vary according to the quality of local union-management relations and, in particular, the degree of managerial acceptance and cooperation with stewards.

While the structural factors identified by McCarthy (1967) undoubtedly influence steward behavior, there are at least three reasons for focusing more directly on individual differences in stewards. First, where structural factors are constant, stewards in a single workplace exhibit wide variation in their behavior. Second, although not denying the importance of structural influences, it is instructive to consider the *process* through which such factors influence steward behavior. Specifically, structural factors may be an indirect cause of steward behavior through their influence on stewards' leadership styles and role perceptions. Third, it may be easier to change individual factors (e.g., through training) than it is to change structural characteristics in the workplace. Consquently, a focus on individual factors affecting steward behavior has a greater utility for unions. A good deal of the research on union leadership and, in particular, shop stewards has been given over to the development of "typologies" of union leadership, i.e., the attempt to categorize shop steward behavior along some theoretically or empirically derived set of conceptual dimensions. As a result, they are worthy of attention.

One of the earliest attempts to classify stewards was Gouldner's (1947) distinction based on whether stewards saw their role as improving wages and working conditions (business unionists), or were highly committed to the goals of unionism and saw union leadership as a calling (progressive unionists). As we will discuss further, Gouldner's (1947) distinction has influenced much of the subsequent research, which has incorporated an "orientation to unionism" dimension. Moreover, this emphasis on individual commitment to unionism as an influence on stewards' leadership style is consistent with the empirical evidence suggesting that ideological beliefs influence the assumption of a leadership role in the union (see preceding section).

Perhaps the most influential typology of steward behavior was that proposed by Batstone, Boraston, and Frenkel (1977), who suggested that steward behavior could be classified along two dimensions: first, whether stewards emphasized a delegate rather than a representative leadership role and, second, the degree of steward commitment to trade union principles. In combination, these two dimensions produce four ideal types of stewards, namely, the leader, the cowboy, the nascent leader, and the populist (see Figure 6.1).

The representative-delegate dimension identified by Batstone et al. (1977) deals with the individual steward's approach to leadership. Stewards are classified as representatives if they shape the majority of issues (e.g., grievances) they deal with, initiate grievances on their own, and tend to handle issues by themselves without reference to other union stewards. In contrast, delegates see their role as responding to the wishes of their constituency. Delegates therefore tend to deal only with grievances brought forth by the membership and do not shape or suppress individual grievances. In this sense, the representative-delegate dimension distinguishes between active and passive shop stewards. While the former are pro-active in defining and processing workplace issues, delegates assume a more reactive role and are dependent on rank-and-file members' definitions of problems.

Commitment to trade union principles was the second dimension identified

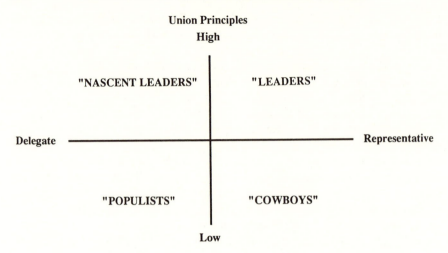

FIGURE 6.1   Batsone, Boraston, and Frenkel's typology of steward behavior

by Batstone et al. (1977). In this context trade union principles refer to the ideals of unity, collectivity, social justice, and the norms of steward leadership (Batstone et al., 1977; Benson, 1989). In the Batstone et al. (1977) typology, stewards are classified as manifesting either high or low commitment to these principles.

The intersection of these two dimensions produces the four types of stewards depicted in Figure 6.1. Leaders were defined as displaying a representative role and manifesting a strong commitment to trade union principles. In contrast, cowboys were able to play a representative role but were more concerned with maximizing the short-term gains of their constituencies, and displayed little commitment to trade union principles. Populist stewards similarly lack a commitment to union principles and assume a delegate role; i.e., being more concerned with carrying out the wishes of the membership than in stirring the membership into action. Finally, nascent leaders display a commitment to union principles but, like populists, act primarily as delegates responsible for carrying out the wishes of the membership.

Batstone et al. (1977) assessed the validity of their typology by examining the behavior of 152 shop stewards representing staff and twenty-six stewards representing manufacturing employees. The results of their analyses offer some support for the typology. Relatively few stewards were classified either as cowboys (none of the staff stewards and seven of the shop floor stewards) or nascent leaders (four staff stewards and ten shop floor stewards). Batstone et al. suggest that the difficulty in assigning individuals to these categories is attributable to the transitory nature of the nascent leader and cowboy styles. That is, stewards tend to move toward either a leader or a populist style. Very clear behavioral differences emerged between stewards classed as leaders and populists. As predicted, leaders were more likely to agree that they had to sometimes stir the membership into action, to espouse the importance of socialism and the defense of workers rights and commitment to trade union principles. In contrast, populists emphasized the need to carry out the wishes of the membership and saw the union as being primarily instrumental. These differences in steward attitudes were also reflected in actual behavior. In handling grievances, stewards classified as leaders were more likely to initiate grievances and amend or suppress grievances raised by other members. In contrast, populists were dependent on their members to raise grievances and were more likely to process the grievance without changing it. In arguing the merits of an individual grievance, leaders tended to use more sophisticated arguments based on trade union principles, negotiated agreements, the role of the steward as a leader, and efficacy. Populists based their arguments on the needs/wants of the membership and the union leadership and were reliant on convenors and other stewards for the resolution of disputes. In union-management relations, leaders were found to have more frequent contact with senior management and a more equal relationship with managers than populists. Leaders relied heavily on the use of informal bargaining and less on strike action and formal dispute procedures compared to populists. Possibly as a result of improved union-management relations, workgroups represented by leaders received substantially higher production bonuses and recorded lower weekly overtime hours than those represented by populist stewards.

Other features of Batstone et al.'s (1977) study are worthy of comment. First, there were distinct differences between stewards from the staff and shop-floor organizations with the former being overwhelming classified as populists ($N = 78$, only 18 of the staff stewards were classified as leaders). Shop-floor stewards were more evenly distributed with thirty-eight classified as leaders and forty-five classed as populists. Second, the distribution of types across the two unions reflected the desires of their respective memberships. Thus while members of the staff union were critical of the union and saw the steward's role as carrying out membership wishes, members of the ship-floor unions saw the need for leadership from the stewards. Batstone et al. (1977) comment appropriatetly that responsibility for leadership rests ultimately with the membership. In a similar vein, Broad (1983) points out that, while the choice of leadership style depends on a variety of factors (e.g., the issue involved, management tactics, individual skills), the most salient factor influencing leadership style is the opinions of the stewards' constituents who substantially constrain the opportunities available to stewards.

The Batstone et al. (1977) typology was cross-validated by Marchington (1983) based on data from 135 white- and blue-collar shop stewards representing eighteen organizations. In general, Marchington's (1983) findings support the validity of the Batstone et al. (1977) typology although the categories were somewhat redefined. As in the original typology, Marchington identified four leadership groups based on steward behavior. The largest category was the leaders ($N = 61$) who were highly committed to unionism and able to lead the members. Leaders believed in being proactive and taking initiative and had a wider conception of the membership than their own constituency. Highly committed to the principles of unionism, leader stewards emphasized collectivity and unity and many espoused social principles as a goal of unions.

Marchington (1983) also identified a group of twenty-five populist leaders who were neither committed to unionism nor acted as leaders. Populist stewards saw their roles as being spokespeople for the members. They dealt primarily with individual, rather than collective, issues and relied on the membership to identify issues. Politically conservative and relatively inactive in the union, the populist stewards often kept their jobs as stewards because no other members were willing to take on those responsibilities.

A third group of thirty-two stewards were classified as workgroup leaders. Similar to the cowboy category (Batstone et al., 1977), the workgroup leaders displayed little involvement in the steward committees but were keen to lead and protect their own members. Marchington (1983) suggests that these stewards were less sectional, militant, and disruptive than would be implied by the cowboy designation. Moreover, little evidence supports Batstone et al.'s suggestion that this was a transient leadership category; while workgroup leaders were not overly keen on union principles, they were active within their own constituency. The number of stewards classified as workgroup leaders was interpreted as evidence that this category did not represent a transitory behavioral style (Marchington, 1983).

Finally, Marchington identified a fourth group of seventeen stewards termed cautious leaders. This group comprised primarily inexperienced stewards who were highly supportive of union principles but felt more bound to follow the wishes of the membership. Thus these stewards (classed as nascent leaders by Batstone et al., 1977) had ties to both their membership and the steward committee but felt bound to follow the wishes of their membership and, consequently, dealt with the steward committee cautiously. Marchington (1983) suggests that this sense of caution is the defining characteristic of this group of stewards.

Thus, the findings of Marchington (1983) largely support the Batstone et al. (1977) typology. In other respects, however, Marchington's findings provided only partial support for Batstone et al.'s findings. First, there was no difference in the distribution of steward types between white- and blue-collar unions. Second, although there was little evidence that workgroups leaders represented a transient type, Marchington (1983) suggests that the model may represent a developmental process. The experience of individual stewards distinguished between both cautious leaders and leaders and populists and leaders (in both cases, more experienced stewards tended to exhibit the characteristics of leaders). The latter finding may also suggest a selection effect where ineffective stewards are not re-elected whereas stewards providing effective representation (i.e., the leaders) are returned to office.

Additional data on the validity of the Batstone et al. (1977) typology comes from a recent study reported by Benson (1989) who developed a literature-based typology substantially similar to that of Batstone et al. (1977). Benson (1989) validated the model using data collected from 202 Australian shop stewards representing approximately twenty different unions. Both blue- and white-collar stewards were included in the sample. Based on their responses to a questionnaire measuring leadership and orientation to unionism, fifty-five stewards were classified as leaders and fifty-five as delegates (substantially similar to Batstone et al.'s populist category). Forty-four stewards were categorized as work group leaders and a further forty-eight stewards were categorized as committed delegates (substantially similar to Batstone et al.'s nascent leader category).

The fact that three separate studies have been able to substantially reproduce Batstone et al.'s (1977) typology argues for the validity of the classification they propose. This support is augmented when one considers that the three studies have used different methodologies (i.e., questionnaire and direct observation), and have been conducted in both Australia and the United Kingdom. However, several problems emerge that question the usefulness of this approach. First, Pedler (1973) has criticized the use of leadership typologies in that they ignore the flexibility stewards demonstrate when dealing with different issues. Specifically, Pedler (1973) suggests that stewards may have a repertoire of leadership styles that will vary with different issues and workgroups. Reliance on leadership typologies does not capture this intra-individual variation. Second, despite claims to the contrary (e.g., Benson, 1989), the Batstone et al. (1977) typology and its derivatives have been poorly operationalized. For example, the questionnaires Benson (1989) used to categorize stewards had unacceptable internal consistency (i.e., alpha < 0.50) which threatens the validity of the measurement instruments. Thus while reliability is not a sufficient condition for validity, it *is* a necessary condition and the failure to reliably operationalize the proposed typology detracts from the validity of the resultant conclusions. Third, and of considerable importance, the Batstone et al. (1977) typology offers little information on the development and effects of union leadership. As noted earlier, the research on steward leadership has been largely descriptive in nature and provides little information as to how stewards develop as leaders. Other than some suggestions that stewards may change their leadership style with experience (e.g., Marchington, 1983), and that stewards are influenced by their constituencies (Batstone et al., 1977), the existing research does not consider the process through which stewards become and develop as leaders. As a result, little is known about the individual, structural, and workgroup characteristics associated with effective steward representation. Finally, despite the initial intent of Batstone et al. (1977), subsequent research has emphasized the refinement of the proposed categories and has not demonstrated a link between steward types and steward behavior. This observation is particularly disappointing considering the variety of behavioral effects that Batstone et al. (1977) attributed to differences in leadership style.

Although not explicitly conducted as tests of individual leadership styles, investigations of grievance processing (Dalton & Todor, 1979, 1981, 1982a,b) directly address individual factors affecting stewards' behavior. First, stewards' commitment to the union was positively associated with the number of grievances filed by the steward (Dalton & Todor, 1981). Moreover, after controlling for job dissatisfaction, stewards' commitment to the union was negatively associated with settling grievances informally and with stewards counseling the grievor not to proceed with the complaint (Dalton & Todor, 1982a). Stewards' commitment to the company (after controlling for job dissatisfaction) was inversely correlated with (1) the number of grievances filed (Dalton & Todor, 1981, 1982a,b), (2) the frequency of stewards filing grievances on their own initiative, and (3) the frequency with which stewards proceeded with a grievance over the objections of the rank-and-file member (Dalton & Todor,1982). These results support early conclusions that stewards' commitment to both the union and unionism is an important determinant of the stewards' leadership style (e.g., Gouldner, 1947; Batstone et al., 1977).

In an earlier report, Dalton and Todor (1979) also addressed individual motivations associated with stewards' processing of individual grievances. The number of grievances filed by stewards was positively associated with stewards' need for achievement and need for dominance. Steward needs for autonomy, affiliation, and dominance were positively associated with stewards' reliance on informal means of grievance resolution. After controlling for the substantial correlations between stewards' needs for dominance and affiliation, and dominance and achievement, several relationships emerged. Need for dominance was positively related to the number of grievances filed and the use of informal resolution procedures. Stewards who expressed a desire to control others and the environment filed more grievances and were more likely to resolve grievances informally. Need for afliation was correlated with informal resolution of grievances (Dalton & Todor, 1979).

Thus stewards who manifested a sincere interest in the feeling of others, a desire for approval from others and a tendency to conform to the desires and norms of the group were more likely to use informal methods of grievance resolution. While not particularly illuminating in and of themselves, these findings suggest that individual differences may substantially affect steward behavior. Moreover, the studies conducted by Dalton and Todor (1979, 1981, 1982a,b) point to the central role played by shop stewards in the industrial relations process. In contrast to previous studies, which were unable to explain variation in grievance filing based on characteristics of individual rank-and-file members, Dalton and Todor (1979, 1981, 1982a,b) could account for significant and substantial amounts of variance in several aspects of grievance filing behavior.

Effects of Union Leadership

As implied at this chapter's introduction, many theorists see the shop steward as *the* rank-and-file leader (Peck, 1963). This view emerges from the consistent finding that a variety of union-relevant attitudes and behaviors are associated with union leadership. Thus the behavior of shop stewards and other union leaders has direct implications for the functioning of the union as an organization. Moreover, the preceding discussion has highlighted the role of the shop steward as a grievance processor and a mediator between individual members and both management and the union. As such, the behavior of shop stewards may reasonably be expected to influence individual members: Through the performance of his or her duties, the steward may encourage or inhibit the satisfaction of individual needs in the workplace. The shop steward's central role in union-management relations also suggests that the actions and beliefs of the steward may substantially influence the quality of union-management relations in the workplace. Finally, as illustrated by Moore (1980), the shop steward occupies a unique place in the union and in the workplace. The demands of the shop steward role place unique stress on individuals fulfilling that role and offers the opportunity for both satisfaction and distress. The effects of shop stewards on union-member relations, union-management relations, and the specific stressors experienced by shop stewards are now considered in further detail.

Union-member Relations and Shop Steward Behavior

Perhaps the most well-documented effects of shop steward behavior deal with participation in, and attitudes toward, the union. A variety of research supports the general conclusion that steward behavior has the potential to influence members' support for, satisfaction with and participation in, the union. Based on the oft-cited observation that the shop steward is the bridge between union members and the officers of the union, Gallagher and Clark (1989) note members' perceptions of the availability and skill of shop stewards as important factors in fostering positive union attitudes and active involvement in the union.

Kahn and Tannenbaum (1954) suggested that members' participation in the union is directly associated with stewards' interpersonal skills. More specifically, the stewards' ability to provide information, facilitate joint decision making, and act as a resource and support for the individual members—in short, consideration behavior—was associated with the degree of members' participation in union activities (in particular, meeting attendance). Nicholson, Ursell, and Lubbock (1981) suggest that steward performance is the link that translates individual motivation (specifically, need for involvement) into actual participation. In this context, Nicholson et al. (1981) suggest that adoption of participative styles of leadership by union officials will translate into greater membership involvement in the union. Similarly, Glick et al. (1977) report that the best predictors of members' satisfaction with the union is the perceived quality of union-member relations. Leaders' support for members' participation and involvement in decision making, and the perceptions that members are listened to and are free to voice opinions, were strong predictors of members' satisfaction with the union. These conclusions are echoed by Jarley, Kuruvilla, and Casteel (1990), who emphasize the importance of union-member relations as a determinant of members' satisfaction with the union. Keeping members informed, encouraging members to express opinions, giving members a "voice" in how the union was run, and being available to the members were all behaviors associated with members' satisfaction with the union (Jarley et al., 1990). The accessibility of stewards and union officers has also been identified as a strong predictor of members' commitment to the union (Thacker, Fields, & Barclay, 1990).

Another dimension of steward behavior relevant to the success of the union as an organization is the perceived effectiveness of steward representation. Throughout this book we identify perceptions of union instrumentality as an important if not central component of the unionization process. Members' perceptions of union instrumentality are associated with the decision to join a union (see Chapter 3), individual commitment to the union (see Chapter 4), members' participation in the union (see Chapter 5), and members' decision to vote for union decertification (see Chapter 7). In part, members' perceptions of instrumentality originate with the gains won at the bargaining table. Although influential, a more immediate, and frequent, source for instrumentality perceptions is the union's success in *administering* the collective agreement. More specifically, the union's record of representing individual members and their grievances provides a potent source of information on the instrumentality of union membership. It is not surprising that the perceived effectiveness of the steward is associated with positive union attitudes. In particular, leader effectiveness in handling grievances, supporting members, negotiating with management, and administering union funds wisely is a substantial predictor of members' satisfaction with the union (Glick et al., 1977; Jarley et al., 1990). Moreover, the members' evaluation of the *process* (but not the outcome) of grievance handling by the union, a primary responsibility of shop stewards, is related to members' commitment to the union (Clark, Gallagher, & Pavlak, 1990). As a final comment on this issue, at least some evidence suggests that the resolution of different types of grievances may exert differential effects on union-member relations. Thus, Gordon and Bowlby (1988) report that union-member relations were improved by the settlement of grievances centered around work discipline. Possibly as a result of the nature of competitive seniority rights, no such improvement was noted for grievances dealing with staffing issues (Gordon & Bowlby, 1988).

Aside from the skill and accessibility shop stewards must display for successful performance of their duties, stewards also act to encourage membership support and involvement in their role as socialization agents (Gallagher & Clark, 1989). Perhaps the most direct evidence for this suggestion comes from Fullagar, McCoy, and Shull's (1992) recent analysis of union commitment among apprentices who were new to the union. In the particular setting they studied, each apprentice was assigned to work with a journeyman. Apprentices' evaluation of their journeyman's transformational leadership characteristics were strong predictors of apprentices' subsequent union commitment and union attitudes. In this particular setting (the construction industry), journeymen introduced the new members to the union and the norms of union membership, a role more typically assigned to the union steward. Bass (1985) makes the distinction between transformational and transactional leaders. Transactional leadership relies heavily on the notion of equitable exchange in which the leader provides rewards in exchange for compliance. In the union, the use of reward power (French & Raven, 1959) is inappropriate and, consequently, transactional leadership is less relevant to unions. Rather, union leaders must place greater emphasis on the use of transformational leadership to gain strong personal identification with the goals and objectives of the union, and to encourage members to transcend their own self-interests and become more active and ideologically identified with organized labor. Transformational leadership has been associated with performance beyond expectations in settings other than the corporate one. Three factors characterize transformational leadership: (1) *charisma*, whereby the union leader instills a sense of pride in the union and transmits the unions' mission, (2) *individual consideration*, which refers to the leaders' stimulation of learning experiences and individual involvement of rank-and-file members, and (3) *intellectual stimulation*, whereby the leader is intellectually innovative and stimulating, providing union members with new ways of looking at organizational issues. Fullagar, McCoy, and Shull (1992) found that both charisma and individual consideration facilitated the socialization of new union members and helped in the development of positive union attitudes. Indirect support for the importance of early socialization also emerges from studies of union commitment that identify members' experiences in the first year of union membership as strong correlates of union commitment (e.g., Fullagar & Barling, 1987; Gordon et al., 1980) and participation in the union (Fullagar & Barling, 1989).

It is clear that the shop steward plays a vital role in building and maintaining the union (McCarthy, 1967). As a socialization agent, grievance processor, and communicator, the shop steward has the potential to influence members' attitudes toward and involvement in the union. The central role of shop stewards in fostering such attitudes and behaviors lends weight to suggestions that stewards should be provided with specific training in leadership, communication, and the duties of their role in the union (Pedler, 1974). Echoing the comments of McCarthy (1967) on the state of shop steward training, Nicholson (1976) points out that training is often haphazard at best. Neophyte stewards learn the requirements of their new role by being plunged in the deep end, reading union literature, or being mentored by a more senior steward (often the one they are replacing). This observation is consistent with Kochan's (1980) suggestion that unions often pay little attention to internal communication, and the finding that steward training is often not directed toward acquisition of the specific behavioral skills they require. While the level and quality of steward training vary widely across and within individual unions, the diverse array of organizational consequences associated with effective steward performance suggests that more systematic and needs-based training for shop stewards would be of considerable benefit to the union.

Union-management Relations and Shop Steward Behavior

As mentioned several times in this chapter, shop stewards play a central role in industrial relations at the local level. Unfortunately, the amount of research on the steward's role in industrial relations does not reflect that centrality. With the possible exception of Dalton and Todor's (1979, 1981, 1982a,b) findings that demonstrate the central role stewards play in the processing of individual grievances, little research exists on the involvement of stewards in industrial relations. The importance of stewards in industrial relations is also evident in the finding that managers would prefer to deal with stewards rather than full-time union officials, a finding attributed to stewards' greater familiarity with local conditions and norms (Clegg et al., 1961; McCarthy & Parker, 1968).

As the union representative on the shop floor, the shop steward is in a unique position to substantially influence the tone of local labor relations. Stewards engage in a variety of formal and informal negotiations with management during the administration of the collective agreement (McCarthy & Parker, 1968). For the most part, these negotiations focus on the proper interpretation of the collective agreement and the individual and collective rights of the rank-and-file members. The research findings of Dalton and Todor (1979, 1981, 1982a,b) suggest that individual factors may substantially predict this aspect of labor relations—namely, the processing of grievances. Similarly, Batstone et al. (1977) identified several outcomes related to stewards' leadership styles. For the most part these outcomes have a direct impact on local labor relations (e.g., processing grievances, setting local priorities). Individual characteristics of the steward, such as commitment, motivation (Dalton & Todor, 1979, 1981, 1982a,b), and militancy (Shirom, 1977) may substantially affect the ways in which they approach the task of administering the collective agreement. Research has not yet fully addressed the role of the steward in shaping the local industrial relations climate and its behavioral manifestations.

Steward Stress and Strain

The lack of steward training (Bluen & Barling, 1988), the volume of work assigned to shop stewards (Nicholson, 1976), the incompatibility of the steward role with family responsibilities (Gouldner, 1947), and the often conflicting expectations of members, union leaders, and management (Ginzberg, 1948) combine to make the stewards' role highly stressful. Ginzberg (1948, p. 10) quotes a labor leader who resigned his position, saying

> It's not so much the hours worked. It's the life of ever-present tension, worry, uncertainty, expectancy, the life of uncertainty. Responsible labor leadership keeps a man [sic] keyed up most of the time.

Individuals acting as shop stewards are subject to a variety of stressors. In their analysis of industrial relations stress, Bluen and Barling (1988) identified four types of stressors of particular relevance to stewards. First, stewards experience role ambiguity as a major stressor (Nicholson, 1976) attributable to the lack of clear performance guidelines (Bluen & Barling, 1988) and lack of steward training (Nicholson, 1976). Second, stewards may experience three types of role conflict. The irregular work hours required may conflict with family responsibilities resulting in inter-role conflict. As long ago as 1947, Gouldner noted that the requirements of labor leadership are often not compatible with family responsibilities, although Nicholson (1976) reports that conflicts with their family role were not important for the majority of stewards in their study.

Given that most stewards in Nicholson's (1976) study were men, the lack of reported conflict with family roles may be attributable to the different ways in which men and women experience their work and domestic roles (Barling, 1990). In particular, it has been suggested that married female stewards give priority to their family responsibilities while male stewards may be more likely to accord priority to their union responsibilities (Roby & Uttal, 1988). Stewards are also responsible to various constituencies within the union and the workplace. The conflicting expectations of rank-and-file members, representatives of management, and the union leadership result in the experience of inter-sender conflict for the steward (Bluen & Barling, 1988; Nicholson, 1976). Ironically, Driscoll (1981) reports that union leaders involved in cooperative labor-management efforts experienced high degrees of inter-sender role conflict. As these individuals were engaged in boundary spanning and innovative roles that go beyond their normal bargaining responsibilities, they experienced conflicting expectations from their constituencies, management, and the particular committees in which they were involved. Stewards are also often called upon to take actions they personally don't agree with. For example, pressures from union leaders or from the steward's constituency may result in the steward's having to call for a strike or work-action when he or she does not believe in the issues (Nicholson, 1976). Thus, person-role conflict is also an aspect of the steward role (Bluen & Barling, 1988; Nicholson, 1976).

A third major stressor for shop stewards is qualitative and quantitative role overload. Qualitative role overload results from the lack of appropriate training in the specific behavioral skills and knowledge areas that stewards require. Quantitative role overload occurs as a result of both the number and breadth of activities stewards are expected to engage in. The importance of role overload as a stressor for shop stewards is highlighted by Nicholson's (1976) report that over 75% of the stewards in his study reported moderate to severe role overload. In contrast, training increases steward's satisfaction with their role and decreases their experiences of role strain (Nicholson, 1976).

Lastly, Bluen and Barling (1988) suggest that the steward role may be inherently stressful. A primary responsibility of shop stewards is the initiation and processing of individual grievances. Thus, the initiation and handling of conflict between groups is a defining characteristic of the steward role. While the focus here is on conflict with management, it should also be noted that some grievances may also be a cause of conflict among the union members. For example, grievances dealing with competitive seniority rights may involve stewards in conflict both *with* management and *between* the rank-and-file members (Gordon & Bowlby, 1988). Stewards may also become involved in conflict with rank-and-file members if they advise them *not* to file a grievance.

In addition to the distress experienced by individual stewards, the strain of being a shop steward may also have organizational consequences. Earlier in this chapter we discussed the difficulty experienced by unions in recruiting candidates for shop steward elections. The consistent finding that individuals assume a shop steward role reluctantly or unopposed in an election suggests that the steward role is seen by rank-and-file members as somewhat negative.

In particular, the costs associated with being a shop steward (e.g., infringement on personal time, distress, potential for conflict) may exceed the benefits. Moreover, the stressors associated with being a shop steward may substantially contribute to turnover among union officials (i.e., resignation of their position in the union). Estimates of turnover rates for union officials vary from approximately 15% (Donovan, 1968; Leopold & Beaumont, 1984) to approximately 30% (Leopold & Beaumont, 1984; Winch, 1983), with Winch (1980) suggesting that a turnover rate in excess of 20% will result in a serious loss of expertise available to the union. Winch (1980) suggests that the single most important cause of turnover in the union results from the steward's being deprived of the resources to fulfill his or her responsibilities. Pressures from management, family responsibilities, and the lack of training/resources available to stewards may all contribute to turnover rate. Particularly among small unions, the lack of membership support for shop stewards is a leading cause of turnover (Winch, 1980).

Some Remaining Questions Concerning Union Leadership

Perhaps the most appropriate way to summarize our discussion of shop stewards is to restate Partridge's (1977) observation that a mountain of factual data is available regarding shop stewards but that, simultaneously, very little is known about the role of the shop steward. Throughout this discussion we have emphasized that the steward is a key link between the union and its members as well as between the union and management. As a grievance processor, communicator, disseminator of information, and negotiator, the shop steward exerts a powerful and pervasive effect on both union-member and union-management relations. Despite the centrality of the steward role, it has been largely ignored in discussions of labor relations and union governance.

Given the state of the literature on shop stewards, the most immediate need is for more theory-based investigations. A great deal of the available literature is descriptive and/or exploratory in nature. While this research provides useful information about the selection, role, performance, and effects of shop stewards, it is now time to move beyond the descriptive level of research to the testing of theory-based hypotheses. The available evidence suggests that the theories of organizational psychology can offer invaluable assistance in the formulation of hypotheses about shop steward behavior. Thus, concepts drawn from motivation theory (e.g., Dalton & Todor, 1979) and leadership theory (e.g., Fullagar, McCoy, & Shull, 1992) have already offered some insight into the industrial relations and union leadership role of shop stewards. Given the amount of psychological research and theorizing on leadership in corporate organizations, it seems likely that the organizational psychology literature provides a rich mine of information for researchers interested in union leadership. Correspondingly, the study of union leaders and their behavior offers organizational psychologists the opportunity to evaluate the generalizability of their theories and methods to other settings.

Throughout our discussion, we have repeatedly returned to the influence of individual attitudes, beliefs, and commitment on steward behavior. This is consistent with research reviewed elsewhere that identifies individual attitudes toward unions and belief systems as important elements in the unionization process. In this sense, assuming an office in the union, such as that of shop steward, may be seen as a pinnacle of union participation. Further research is required to ascertain how beliefs, values, and attitudes influence individuals to become shop stewards and how they affect individual performance in the steward role. While existing research suggests that such individual factors play an important role and substantially influence stewards' behavior, these effects must often be inferred on the basis of sketchy research findings. More systematic inquiry into factors influencing the shop steward is required. Such an inquiry should not be limited to individual factors but extended to include structural and group factors affecting steward behavior. In this regard it is important to recall Batstone et al.'s (1977) observation that the leadership function in unions is as such the property of the members as the leaders. Comparatively little research has examined the influence of constituencies on steward behavior.

As well as being subjects of the unionization process, shop stewards are also agents of the process. As role models, socialization agents, and disseminators of information, shop stewards in many senses are *the* union as far as the rank-and-file members are concerned. This highlights the need to identify the dimensions of effective union leadership as well as factors that encourage effective leadership. Although various sources provide a conceptual basis for linking steward behavior to members' commitment and participation in the union (e.g., Fullagar & Barling, 1989; Fullagar, McCoy, & Shull, 1992; Gordon et al., 1980), little information is available on exactly what stewards do that makes them effective leaders, and how stewards encourage rank-and-file support for the union. The available literature suggests that both steward effectiveness and communication skills are important dimensions of effective leadership. Future research may profitably seek to clarify the role stewards play in shaping union-member relations.

Finally, as noted earlier, there is a dearth of literature dealing with the effects of stewards on union-management relations. Theorists continually cite the steward as the key link between union and management in the workplace and empirical research confirms the potential impact of stewards on key aspects of industrial relations (e.g., Dalton & Todor, 1979, 1981, 1982a,b; McCarthy & Parker, 1968). Yet much more research is required to determine the exact nature of the steward in the practice of industrial relations.

7

Breakdowns in the
Unionization Process

In the preceding chapters, we considered the initial phases of the unionization process. We first discussed the factors that predict how individuals will vote to certify or join a union (see Chapter 3). Then we examined individuals' commitment to (see Chapter 4) and participation in (see Chapter 5) union activity. We presented next the leadership role of shop stewards in facilitating the unionization process (see Chapter 6). As argued before, any consideration of the unionization process would be incomplete without also considering why union members choose to decertify an existing bargaining unit. Decertification represents the collective decision to get rid of the existing bargaining unit. In some jurisdictions, union members can also exercise an individual right to leave the union. We now turn our attention to a consideration of these collective and individual rights, both of which constitute a final phase in the unionization process.

Decertification: When the Union Leaves the Member

There is a considerable body of literature on why individuals choose to vote for a union in certification elections. Some of the conceptual models developed to explain union voting behavior allow for a relatively exact specification of the voting decision (e.g., Brett, 1980). In contrast, far fewer studies investigate why workers choose to decertify their current bargaining unit (Lynch & Sandver, 1987). Several factors might account for this discrepancy. First, decertification elections represent a more recent phenomenon than certification elections. Decertification procedures were only formalized in the United States following the passage of the Taft-Hartley Act in 1947, whereas the certification procedure was formalized earlier with the Wagner Act of 1935. Second, there are far more certification than decertification elections, so that the proportion of studies focusing on certification and decertification generally reflects their actual occurrence. Lastly, there is an implicit assumption that the reasons why individuals choose to vote to certify a union also hold true in decertification elections. For example, if individuals certify or join unions because unions are seen as instrumental in resolving workplace dissatisfactions, perhaps individuals choose to decertify bargaining units that are no longer seen as instrumental in this regard.

At least three forms of decertification exist, and some understanding of each is important because of their different meaning, causes, and outcomes. In one type, workers attempt to decertify an existing bargaining unit but not replace it with any other. In the second, workers try to decertify their union, with the immediate or distal goal of replacing it with a different bargaining unit. In the third, if management has verifiable grounds to believe that the bargaining unit no longer represents a majority of workers (e.g., because of petitions or through resignations, layoffs, or transfers of bargaining unit members), management have the right either to apply for or to initiate a decertification election.

The first form of decertification identified above is consistent with worker disenchantment both with the union that currently represents them as well as with unions in general. As such, a vote to decertify the union in this situation could reflect a rejection of unionism. In the second form, a vote in favor of decertification represents workers' beliefs that their current bargaining units are not representing them adequately. They still seek union representation but wish to exchange their bargaining unit for one that is perceived to be more effective. In this case, the vote to decertify signifies a rejection of a particular union rather than rejection of unionism in general. (These two forms of decertification clearly illustrate the difference between general and specific union attitudes introduced in Chapters 3 and 4.) The third type of decertification (i.e., in which management initiates the decertification campaign) is consistent with attempts by management to attain a union-free environment, and this trend will be discussed further in this section. All these forms of decertification activity reflect single union elections, which remain the most frequent form of decertification (Anderson et al., 1980). Nonetheless, despite the potential importance of differentiating between these varying types of decertification, with few exceptions the research to date has focused on decertification in general.

Unions can also be decertified following a different process. It is also possible (though infrequent) for another union to challenge the existing bargaining unit. Research findings suggest that the likelihood of success for a union petitioning to oust the incumbent union is better than average (Anderson et al., 1979), possibly because the petitioning union would only commit its scarce resources to such a campaign if it believed it had a reasonable chance of succeeding in the first instance. We will not consider this process in detail, as it is more consistent with union raiding than decertification, and there is far less research on union raiding than on decertification.

The Extent of Decertification Elections

Several issues surrounding the decertification elections, such as the frequency of their occurrence, deserve comment. The most obvious issue is the degree to which decertification elections are successful, especially given considerable and continuing concern about the decreasing proportion of the workforce that is unionized in the United States. Estimates concerning the extent of decertification from different writers converge (e.g., Anderson et al., 1979, 1980; Kilgour, 1987; Yanish, 1985). First, there were relatively few decertification elections soon after the passage of the Taft-Hartley Act in 1947 (Krislov, 1954), probably because the actors in the system were unware of the Act and the process involved. It is now estimated that the number of decertifications increased fivefold between 1954 and 1976 (Dickens, Wholey, & Robinson, 1987; Krislov, 1979). More recently, it is estimated that approximately two-thirds of decertification elections result in decertification, with a relatively small range around this figure (namely, 61.4%–73.4% in any given year between 1948 and 1977; Anderson et al., 1980). Anderson et al. (1980) note, however, that while the number of successful decertifications increased during this period, the average size of the bargaining unit involved in decertification decreased. What this means is that the proportion of the workforce that is unionized is not necessarily affected by decertification.

Nonetheless, the data on which such observations are made were collected in the United States and do not necessarily generalize across different countries. For example, Keon (1988, p. 38) shows that decertification attempts are far less likely to succeed in Ontario, Canada. For the period, 1965/66 through to 1985/86, only 52.5% of decertification attempts resulted in the removal of the bargaining unit.

Several sources indicate that despite losses in membership from decertification, the overall size of the organized labor force still increases each year. For example, in Ontario, Canada, on average there has been a net annual *gain* of 20,668 employees certified between 1969/70–1976/77, and 1980/81–1985/86. However, the data from Canada may not be generalizable to other countries, because public policy in Canada is far more favorable to the presence of unions than, for example, is the case in the United States. As a result, the proportions of organized workers in Canada is more than double that of the United States, and there is a greater number of successful decertifications in the United States (Kumar, 1987). Thus, it is instructive to note that the same general *pattern* concerning the relative gain or loss occurs in the United States. Krislov (1979) estimates that the number of voters in decertification elections is still only 10% of the total number of workers involved in certification and decertification elections. This should be seen together with the fact that the absolute size of the unit involved in decertification elections is smaller than that involved in certification elections. Thus, for every one worker lost to the labor movement through a decertification, eight are gained following successful organizing drives. Sandver and Heneman (1981) showed that between 1973 to 1978, 45,519 workers in the United States were involved in certification votes, while only 3,596 participated in decertification votes. Thus, while not minimizing the possible effects of decertification on nonquantitative aspects such as morale and union revenues, in considering the meaning of any decertification to the labor movement it must be borne in mind that more members are certified in a given year than are decertified.

Predicting the Outcome of Decertification Elections

Despite the importance of understanding the decertification process, the vast majority of reviews of the unionization process focus exclusively on the predictors of certification elections and ignore the issue of decertification (e.g., Fiorito et al., 1986). We now turn our attention to an understanding of why individuals choose to decertify an existing bargaining unit. Following the structure of the chapter on certification elections, we focus on demographic, macro-level, and micro-level predictors. While the chapter on certification elections also included an assessment of the role of personality characteristics and work beliefs, there are simply no studies investigating whether these factors predict voting behavior in decertification elections.

Demographic Predictors

As noted elsewhere, several empirical studies assess whether demographic characteristics predispose individuals toward a pro-union vote. Likewise, a large body of research has addressed the issue of whether a demographic profile can be constructed of the "loyal" union member. In contrast, consistent with the paucity of research on decertification in general, very few studies have questioned whether any relationship exists between demographic characteristics and the likelihood of supporting decertification. In their sample of faculty employees within a single university, Bigoness and Tosi (1984) found that males were significantly more likely to vote to decertify the union. Consistent with findings and explanations regarding voting in certification elections, they suggest that the greater experience of discrimination by women, and the perception by women that unions can provide protection against unfair discrimination, accounts for this finding (Bigoness & Tosi, 1984). Because unions ensure equality of treatment for all their members, females might also perceive greater benefits associated with continued union representation. Even given such explanations, though, it is questionable whether any practical implications ensue from this finding, especially because other studies have found no effect of gender on decertification (Lawler & Hundley, 1983). Also, while blacks are more likely to vote to certify a union, no significant black/white differences emerge with respect to decertification (Dickens et al., 1987).

Macro-level Predictors

Most of the research on the predictors of decertification has been at the level of macro-level variables, rather than focusing on psychological or demographic predictors. Aspects such as the size of the bargaining unit, regionality, the nature of the union, industry-wide salary levels, and particularly management/union tactics have been addressed. Although the focus throughout this book is to provide a psychological understanding of the unionization process, these predictors are now discussed separately. In each case, we explicitly consider how these macro-level factors proxy individual level processes.

The possibility that the size of the bargaining unit is associated with the outcome of decertification elections was observed soon after decertification was legally permitted (Krislov, 1956). Since Krislov's observations, numerous studies have investigated whether a relationship exists between the number of workers in a given bargaining unit and the outcome of a decertification election. The findings are consistent across studies: Larger bargaining units are less likely to succumb to a decertification compaign (Ahlburg & Dworkin, 1984; Anderson et al., 1979; Chafetz & Fraser, 1979; Dickens et al., 1987; Fulmer & Gilman, 1981; Pearce & Peterson, 1987). However, unions that experience decertification among their locals tend to be larger than average (Chafetz & Fraser, 1979). Thus, small bargaining units within large unions are most likely to succumb to decertification. There is no agreement, however, as to the effects of company size on decertification. Fulmer (1978) suggests decertification is more likely in larger companies; Chafetz and Fraser (1979) suggest the opposite.

Several factors have been advanced to account for the greater likelihood for smaller bargaining units to decertify. First, unions typically have limited financial and human resources available. As a result, shop stewards often receive very little training (see Chapter 6), even though the tasks they must engage in require sophisticated skills (Bluen & Barling, 1988). Also, because small bargaining units are relatively more expensive to service than larger units because of economies of scale (Ahlburg & Dworkin, 1984), their membership may not receive the attention they deserve, or believe they deserve, from the union. Any negative effects of unions' limited financial and human resources is exacerbated in smaller bargaining units. Second, unions might be more willing to expend their limited resources to fight against decertification of larger bargaining units, because of the relatively greater impact on the union should decertification be successful (Anderson et al., 1979). Third, the fact that smaller bargaining units within larger unions are more likely to decertify is consistent with Elliott and Hawkins' (1982) findings of a "trade-off" effect: They suggested that larger unions trade off any loss of membership from decertification with increases in their membership through organizing activities. Lastly, employees who find themselves members of small locals in large units probably exert little influence over both their employer and their unions. This could heighten members' perception that the union is not responsive to their needs. This explanation will be pursued in greater detail when we consider micro-level predictors of decertification.

Considerable attention has been focused on whether decertification is more likely in certain geographical regions of the United States. In particular, because it is believed to be more difficult to organize workers in Southern regions of the United States, the question of whether decertification is more likely to occur in southern regions of the United States has frequently been raised. This belief is based on the assumption that southern states are less hospitable to unions, as is manifest through right-to-work legislation. In his early analysis, Krislov (1956) noted that a disproportionate number of decertification elections occur in "southern" regions of the United States. When zero-order correlations between region and decertification are computed, significant but weak relationships sometimes do emerge (e.g., Lynch & Sandver, 1987). However, Anderson et al. (1979) found that this tendency only held true for multi-union elections; where single union decertification elections were held, no link emerged in their analysis between region and decertification. Anderson et al. (1979) interpret this as meaning that union members in the South may be less accepting of *ineffective* representation, rather than meaning that those members reject the *concept* of unionism. This again highlights the distinction between general and specific union attitudes (see Chapter 3).

Other studies also call into question any relationship between geographical region and decertification. Pearce and Peterson (1987) and Dickens et al. (1987) investigated the relative effects of regionality together with other predictors of decertification. Both their studies paralleled findings on union voting behavior and showed that when several predictors were investigated simultaneously, the influence of regionality was negligible. Thus, based solely on zero-order correlations, the findings from Anderson et al. (1979) and Lynch and Sandver's (1981) studies may have overemphasized the influence of regional differences on decertification. A different issue raised by Fulmer and Gilman (1981) suggests that caution be exercised in linking decertification to southern regions of the United States: While there was some support for a regionality effect in their study, decertification was more prevalent in western regions of the United States.

One additional point concerning the link between geographical region and decertification warrants discussion. Pearce and Peterson (1987) call into question the practice of testing for "south" vs. "non-south" differences. As they note, this implies considerable homogeneity within and some heterogeneity between both these groups that may not reflect reality: Some non-southern states also have right-to-work legislation (e.g., Iowa, Nevada, Utah, and Kansas). Thus, a south vs. non-south approach ignores meaningful differences *within* each of these two dichotomized categories. This may have important statistical consequences and mask any meaningful between-group differences, and these methodological issues are also relevant for predicting the outcome of certification elections (see Chapter 3).

Perhaps one of the most controversial issues in both certification and decertification elections is the effectiveness of various tactics used by management. (There would appear to be very little published research focusing on the tactics used by unions to defeat decertification attempts.) Certainly, active campaigning for decertification by management is on the increase, as is evident through increases in seminars organized specifically to educate management about achieving a union-free environment (Bigoness & Peirce, 1988), and articles in management magazines directed to the same objective (e.g., Coleman, 1985; Swann, 1983). As an example of the latter, Thompson (1987) advises managers of mental health clinics that "Unions need not be forever" (p. 36), and provides specific guidelines for weakening the position of an existing union. (This is not to suggest that strategies for surviving decertification attempts do not appear in union magazines.)

The considerable financial and human resources that management often commits to winning decertification campaigns, and the strategies used (both legal and illegal) must surely be predicated on their presumed effectiveness. Yet this assumption was questioned in one of the first major studies of union voting behavior, albeit from data derived from certification elections. As noted earlier, Getman et al. (1976) concluded from their data that illegal tactics used by management during organizing drives had no effect whatsoever on converting pro-union to anti-union votes. As a consequence, they explicitly recommended that rules regarding unfair labor practices no longer be enforced. Getman et al.'s (1976) recommendation was predicated in part on the assumption that attitudes to unions are stable, and withstand the rigors of legal or illegal tactics. Hence, managerial tactics, whether legal or illegal, would presumbly not influence the voting behavior of employees who initially manifest strong pro-union or anti-union sentiments. A recent suggestion by Summers et al. (1986) may be consistent with this perspective. They posit that campaigns would exert their strongest effects on voters who are initially undecided. Many voters may not necessarily be extremely anti- or pro-union, and so tactics are important to consider. We will now consider the possible effects of management tactics on decertification elections.

First, it is generally accepted that workers who visibly display prounion support suffer adverse consequences of various degrees, including personal threats, job transfers, unattractive job postings, illegal dismissals, and threats of reporting them for withholding tax after having paid them on a cash basis (e.g., Cooke, 1985; Chafetz & Fraser, 1979; Lawler, 1990; Summers et al., 1986). Although Summers et al. (1986) note that "the example set by the discharge of employees is likely not lost on the remaining employees" (p. 650), from an empirical perspective it is difficult to measure the effects of subtle tactics that threaten existing conditions or job loss and that may stifle union campaign efforts.

Some empirical studies examine campaign tactics during decertification. While some suggest that management engages in no illegal tactics (Fulmer, 1978) implicitly challenging the importance of the issue, they only interviewed management representatives and not union leaders (as Fulmer did), probably limiting the extent to which illegal tactics would be reported. In contrast, Anderson et al. (1982) analyzed the campaign tactics used by both management and unions during decertification. The absolute number of tactics used by management or the union had no effect. One tactic did influence the likelihood of decertification, whether engaged in by management or the union. Specifically, holding meetings and discussions was the most successful (and common) tactic. Meetings were called by both management and the union; but, as with certification elections, attendance at union-sponsored meetings was poor. While management frequently identified the continued costs of unionization and the benefits of being union-free, this tactic actually increased the likelihood of the union's surviving the decertification. Although written communication was used frequently, and typically was directed at questioning the sincerity or effectiveness of the opposing party in dealing with problems, it was not related to the outcome of the decertification election.

Another tactic that may influence the outcome of a decertification election was deliberate pre-vote delays initiated by management. Findings from various studies show that a consistent correlation exists between the outcome of certification and decertification elections and the pre-election delay. Dickens et al. (1987) showed that the effect of pre-election delays is approximately the same for certification and decertification elections. In such studies, the delay is taken as an indication of management resistance. Prior to any vote in certification or decertification elections, management enjoys greater access to the workers. Increasing the delay, therefore, allows management more access, and this effect is exacerbated because worker attendance at union meetings in general (Gordon et al., 1980) and during decertification efforts (Anderson et al., 1982) is low. The number of workers voting pro-union drops approximately 3% for every doubling in pre-election time. Prosten (1978) had earlier estimated this effect to be 2.5% per month through the first six months of the delay. Thus, whatever the intention of management in extending the pre-election time period, any delay clearly works in management's interests. Lastly, decertification was less likely to succeed if management were more "enlightened" (i.e., more responsive to employees' needs), potentially obviating the necessity for union representation (Anderson et al., 1982).

Although very little research has been conducted on union campaigns to defeat decertification, it would appear that the most influential tactic used by the union was personal communication with a trusted, credible individual from the bargaining unit, presumably because such communication also allows pivotal issues to be dealt with openly and directly. In general, however, the assumption that workers are impervious to any campaign tactics because their prior union attitudes are stable (Fulmer & Gilman, 1981; Getman et al., 1976) runs counter to more recent empirical findings (Anderson et al., 1982).

One issue that has been raised is whether it is worth the effort for management to become involved in decertification campaigns. Although management certainly can influence the outcome of some decertification campaigns, some authors counsel that the likelihood of victory is not the only issue that should be considered in management's decision whether to actively fight against continued union representation (Barbash, 1985; Bigoness & Peirce, 1988; Fulmer, 1978). Instead, management is counselled also to consider the post-decertification industrial relations climate that will prevail in the organization: Whether management in successful in decertifying the union or not, its relationship with the workforce will be altered following a hard-fought decertification election. Indeed, as with certification elections, the harder (and perhaps more illegal) the fight, the more management stands to lose by a deterioration in the post-decertification industrial relations climate.

Given the attention directed at economic factors in understanding the effects of organizing drives, it is not surprising that studies have also investigated their influence on decertification elections. These studies will not be addressed in detail at this stage for two reasons. First, two of the more important studies that have considered the effects of economic factors have directly contrasted their effects on certification and decertification elections; hence they will be discussed later in this chapter. Second, it is argued that economic conditions constitute a proxy measure of the workers' perceptions of the union's effectiveness. Accordingly, such effects will be discussed in the section on micro- or individual-level predictors. Suffice it to say at this stage that, in general, decertification is more likely when workers believe that their economic conditions would be improved by returning to non-union status (Ahlburg & Dworkin, 1984; Elliott & Hawkins, 1982). Consistent with this effect, some studies show that decertification is more likely to occur if the bargaining unit had experienced a strike, irrespective of its duration (Elliott & Hawkins, 1982), presumably because of the overall financial costs incurred during a strike relative to any gains achieved. (Other studies find no influence of strike activity; Dickens et al., 1987.) Likewise, decertifications are more likely during periods of inflation when any gains achieved by the union would be relatively less valuable (Ahlburg & Dworkin, 1984).

In trying to understand macro-level predictors of decertification, three questions have been posed concerning the effects of industry type and decertification: (1) Are certain unions more likely to face decertification elections than others? (2) Are certain unions more or less likely to be decertified? (3) Is decertification activity dependent on the nature of the industry? Obviously, these issues are interrelated, given the industry-specific nature of many unions, and so these issues are discussed together. Results from different analyses show that some unions are certainly more susceptible to decertification than others. For example, the Teamsters account for a disproportionate share of all decertification, perhaps over 30% (Anderson et al., 1979; Dickens et al., 1987; Kilgour, 1987; Krislov, 1956). Whether the Teamsters lose a substantial number of the decertification elections in which they are involved is less certain. Some data suggest they do (Kilgour, 1987), other data indicate they do not (Anderson et al., 1979). In contrast, the United Automobile Workers (UAW) are involved in very few decertification elections, and there is agreement that the UAW is successful in defeating attempts at decertification when they occur (Anderson et al., 1979; Kilgour, 1987).

Several factors could account for these differences. First, the Teamsters are perhaps the largest and most active (in terms of organizing) union in the United States (Kilgour, 1987), and both these factors (i.e., size and union activity) are associated with a greater probability of decertification (e.g., Ahlburg & Dworkin, 1984; Anderson et al., 1979; Chafetz & Fraser, 1979; Dickens et al., 1987; Fulmer & Gilman, 1981; Pearce & Peterson, 1987). Second, because of their heavy emphasis on organizing, the Teamsters presumably have a greater number of recently organized bargaining units. Research has shown that decertification elections are much more likely in recently organized units. Fulmer and Gilman (1981) speculate that this occurs because the union-management relationship would not have had sufficient opportunity to become established. Lastly, as noted in previous chapters, attitudes to unionism in general, and specific unions in particular, are critical determinants of pro-union voting (e.g., Barling, Kelloway, & Bremermann, 1991; Barling, Laliberte, Fullagar, & Kelloway, 1990; Deshpande & Fiorito, 1989; Getman et al., 1976). The predominantly negative sentiment toward the Teamsters (Cook, 1983; Summers et al., 1986) might further account for the finding that the Teamsters experience the most decertification activity. This attitudinal explanation might also explain why the UAW, which does not suffer the same negative opprobrium (e.g., Ephlin, 1988), experiences very little such activity.

In summarizing the effects of macro-level predictors, several issues emerge. First, it would appear as though several of the macro-level factors discussed (size of the bargaining unit and campaign tactics) are indeed associated with decertification. From a behavioral perspective, it is important to note each of these predictors serves as a proxy for individual-level explanations, which again point to the importance of general attitudes to unions and perceived union instrumentality as predictors of voting behavior in decertification elections. Second, there are suggestions that other variables might be investigated. For example, the role of union leadership factors has frequently been mentioned (e.g., Anderson et al., 1982; Klandermans, 1986; and see Chapter 6), but not investigated directly with respect to decertification activity. Normative pressures are also held to be important (e.g., Summers et al., 1986), and this is consistent with findings showing the influence of family socialization on union attitudes and voting in certification elections (Barling, Kelloway, & Bremermann, 1991). Nonetheless, it remains for future research to investigate their effects on voting in decertification elections.

Micro-level Predictors

So far we have considered the demographic and macro-level predictors of decertification. The single demographic variable associated with voting in decertification elections, namely, gender (Bigoness & Tosi, 1984), is of limited practical and conceptual importance. Also, although several macro-level factors were shown to be significant predictors of decertification, the magnitude of their predictive effect is usually not large (Anderson et al., 1979). We now turn our attention to an understanding of the effects of individual predictors. In many instances, the variables to be examined in this context overlap with those that were examined regarding certification elections, and this will facilitate a comparison of the predictors of certification and decertification elections later in this chapter.

As was evident in the discussions concerning certification activity and outcome, perceived union instrumentality is one of the major factors that predict whether employees vote for a union. Research on union commitment (see Chapter 4) and union participation (see Chapter 5) corroborated the importance of perceived union instrumentality. There are numerous case studies (e.g., Anderson et al., 1982) and both anecdotal (e.g., Nichols, 1988) and conceptual (Summers et al., 1986) suggestions that perceived union instrumentality also predicts decertification. First, it is important to reiterate that the meaning of perceived union instrumentality differs in certification and decertification elections. When faced with an organizing drive, employees are currently non-unionized, may never have been unionized, and probably have no direct, personal experience with the particular union. Thus, for most employees, estimation of the union's instrumentality in organizing campaigns must be based on expectations and vicarious experience. In contrast, when unionized employees encounter a decertification campaign, and must consider the value of retaining their bargaining unit, their perceptions of the bargaining unit's instrumentality is based on direct, personal experience. Interestingly, social learning theory (Bandura, 1977) predicts that the effects of personal experience on behavior should be greater than that of vicarious experience.

Despite the different bases for perceptions of the union's instrumentality among unionized and non-unionized employees, the absolute accuracy of these perceptions may be of little consequence. As Premeaux, Mondy, and Bethke (1987, p. 147) note so cogently, "The debate over the accuracy of these perceptions is unimportant because if members don't believe unions are working for them, they won't support them." Their survey of respondents in large, unionized manufacturing firms in the United States suggests that union members do not necessarily believe that union leadership emphasizes the issues they hold as important. However, Premeaux et al. (1987) did not specifically assess whether this discrepancy necessarily foreshadowed a decertification vote; they merely assumed it could. It is more important to examine research findings that have focused directly on this issue. One line of support for the role of perceived union instrumentality in predicting decertification activity derives from studies investigating macro-level predictors. For example, economic data suggest that when workers believe the economic benefits of holding a nonunion job exceed those of a union job, decertification is likely (Ahlburg & Dworkin, 1984; Farber & Saks, 1980).

Other studies have assessed the link between perceived union instrumentality and decertification using survey rather than macro-economic data. In general, these studies have used different indicators of perceived union instrumentality. Anderson et al. (1982) show that the inability of the union to deal with management, as reflected in the failure to achieve a collective agreement and poor union-management relations, predicts decertification. Clearly, these variables could be taken by union members as an indication that the union cannot meet their needs. The extent to which a union is perceived as effective has also been estimated as a cost:benefit ratio. Within such an approach, the ratio of union dues to benefits derived from union membership is taken as an indication of the union's effectiveness. There are several studies showing that when members believe that such costs outweigh the benefits, decertification is more likely (Anderson et al., 1982; Chafetz & Fraser, 1979).

Whereas Chafetz and Fraser's (1979) and Anderson et al.'s (1982) interviews were conducted some time after the decertification activity, Bigoness and Tosi (1984) mailed questionnaires to people one day after they were involved in a decertification election, ensuring that the questionnaires were received within the week following the vote. This is important because any reports of voting would be less affected by problems involving retrospective recall and normative pressures of coworkers and other salient individuals. Their study again showed that perceived union instrumentality was a significant predictor of voting behavior in the decertification election. Also, because they entered all the predictors of decertification in a regression analysis, it was possible to conclude that perceived union instrumentality was a more important predictor than any of the other variables they analyzed (namely, general attitude toward unions, organizational commitment, intrinsic and extrinsic job satisfaction, and gender).

The study conducted by Angle and Perry (1984) to assess the effects of organizational experiences and job attitudes on the outcome of certification elections comes closest to a naturally occurring experiment of all those we will consider in this chapter. They contrasted job-related expectations and attitudes among members of three types of bargaining units, namely, those unions that had moved toward unionization (two employee associations that had formally unionized), away from unionization (four organized units that had decertified), and those whose status did not change (fourteen stable bargaining units). Members of the subsequently decertified bargaining units were less satisfied with their union's efforts regarding pay, job security, and their jobs in general. They also felt a lack of influence with management. In contrast, members whose employee associations were replaced with formal bargaining units were more satisfied with their association's efforts with respect to these specific job characteristics. Angle and Perry (1984) suggest that successful experimentation with the concept of collective representation may have motivated these employees to "go the rest of the way" with union certification (p. 288). It can be concluded, therefore, that not only is perceived union instrumentality important in predicting decertification, it is also at least as important if not more so than other job-related experiences.

Individuals hold general attitudes to unions well before entering the labor force (Barling, Kelloway, & Bremermann, 1991), and, as already noted, these general attitudes consistently predict voting behavior in certification elections. Summers et al. (1986) suggest such general attitudes to unions fulfill an even more important role in decertification elections, because of workers' greater direct exposure to unions than that in certification elections. Although no studies have tested Summers et al.'s (1986) specific hypothesis, Bigoness and Tosi's (1984) findings show that pro-union attitudes predict a vote to retain the union in decertification elections. This is consistent with findings showing that the Teamsters fare relatively poorly in decertification activities, presumably because of their unfavorable image (Cook, 1983; Summers et al., 1986). Thus, pro-union attitudes predict both certification and decertification. The importance of pro-union attitudes in the comprehensive unionization process becomes even more apparent when their roles in predicting union commitment and participation are acknowledged (see Chapters 4 and 5).

Because it is frequently believed that dual loyalty engenders feelings of personal discomfort or strain, it has often been assumed that simultaneous loyalty to both the union and the company would not occur. Angle and Perry (1984) investigated the relationship between dual loyalty and decertification directly. They found that workers in their decertification group were less likely to express dual loyalty to both the company and the union.

Perhaps more important than investigating the relationship between decertification and *dual* loyalty to company and union is the link between company commitment and decertification. In one study, Bigoness and Tosi (1984) found no effect of organizational commitment on decertification voting. In contrast, Angle and Perry (1984) found that members of decertified units expressed lower commitment to the organization. The seemingly discrepant findings can be reconciled, because Angle and Perry (1983) also investigated a more specific component of commitment, namely, commitment to continued membership, or what Allen and Meyer (1990) call "continuance commitment." Angle and Perry (1984) showed that members of the decertified units expressed lower levels of commitment to continued membership in the organization. This finding, therefore, is consistent with the exit-voice notion: Given their lower loyalty together with the lack of a "voice" mechanism, their lower commitment to continued membership reflects their "exit" option. These findings suggest that greater attention be paid to conceptualizing commitment in general, and organizational commitment in particular in a multidimensional framework (see Chapter 4).

Any understanding of the unionization process must consider the role of job dissatisfaction. As noted in Chapter 3, virtually all findings investigating the relationship between job dissatisfaction and voting in certification elections have shown a significant relationship (Fiorito et al., 1986). Likewise, most models of the certification process (e.g., Barling, Laliberte, Fullagar, & Kelloway, 1990; Brett, 1980; Premack & Hunter, 1988) accord a significant role to job dissatisfaction. There are significantly fewer studies investigating whether job dissatisfaction predicts decertification, and, contrary to the findings concerning certification elections, the results of these studies are somewhat inconsistent. Bigoness and Tosi (1984) found that neither intrinsic nor extrinsic job dissatisfaction predicted decertification voting, after controlling for other variables, such as perceived union instrumentality. In contrast, Angle and Perry's (1984) study showed that members of unions who were subsequently decertified expressed greater dissatisfaction with their pay, job security, and jobs in general. These higher levels of dissatisfaction were presumably a result of the failure of the bargaining unit to meet the needs of their members. However, the substantial amount of time that elapsed in Angle and Perry's (1984) study between the actual vote and the self-reporting of job dissatisfaction preclude definitive conclusions about causal effects: While it is possible that the unresolved job dissatisfaction led to decertification, there are also data indicating that the absence of a union resulted in lower job satisfaction (see Chapter 8).

Consequently, the critical role fulfilled by job dissatisfaction during organizing campaigns does not necessarily extend to decertification elections. Instead, the decision to vote to retain a union is based more on the union's perceived effectiveness than on one's current job dissatisfaction. Individuals who are dissatisfied with their jobs may vote to certify a union if they perceive it to be capable of resolving their dissatisfactions. However, dissatisfied individuals who do not perceive the union as instrumental in resolving their dissatisfactions will see little use for the union's continued existence. Accordingly, they may not vote to retain the union in a decertification election, irrespective of their dissatisfaction. Thus, decertification is more a function of the perceived lack of instrumentality of the union than current job dissatisfaction.

The effects of micro-level, or individual factors, on decertification can be summarized as follows. In general, the decision whether to vote to retain a union in the face of a decertification campaign would seem to be predicated primarily on a rational decision as to the continued benefits that would accrue from continued union representation. In addition, pro-union attitudes would appear to be important in choosing to vote to retain the bargaining unit. In contrast, job dissatisfaction does not seem to be a major factor, although further research is required.

Contrasting the Predictors of Certification and Decertification

Having considered the demographic, macro-level, and micro-level predictors of decertification, one question that arises is whether the factors that predict a pro-union vote in certification elections also predict a vote to retain the union in decertification elections. Certainly, there are suggestions that the effects of campaign strategies used do not differ (Fulmer, 1978). From the preceding discussion, both similarities and differences in the predictors of demographic, macro-level, and micro-level predictors are discernable. Briefly stated, perceived union instrumentality, general attitudes to unions, and possibly gender predict the outcome of both certification and decertification elections. In contrast, job dissatisfaction predicts pro-union voting in certification elections but the results concerning the prediction of decertification elections are not conclusive. With respect to macro-level predictors, the size of the bargaining unit and the campaign conducted by management predict the outcome of certification and decertification activity. However, most of the predictors are not shared. One conclusion is that different explanations of the certification and decertification process are required. A rival interpretation is that any such comparisons are limited because the same predictors have not necessarily been investigated within studies.

Several investigators have contrasted predictors of certification and decertification directly within the same study. The results of Lawler and Hundley (1983) and Dickens et al.'s (1987) studies strongly support the notion that the differences in the predictors of certification and decertification elections outweigh their similarities, thereby calling for different models to account for each of these two activities. Thus, based simply on the number of studies available, and the number of significant findings, it is clear that it is somewhat easier to understand and predict certification than decertification outcomes.

Decertification: Some Implications for Management and Labor

Like certification elections, the data show that decertification activity is likely if members feel they have been oversold on the benefits the union can provide relative to the costs that will be incurred (Chafetz & Fraser, 1979). As a result, it behooves unions to ensure that their members have a realistic understanding of just what benefits the union can achieve. This is a particularly important and sensitive issue. It is sensitive because unions may be sorely tempted to exaggerate their potential strengths, and ignore any shortcomings during organizing campaigns. Maintaining a delicate balance between the need to promote the union to win certification on the one hand, and impart accurate information about potential union weaknesses on the other hand, is difficult but essential. It is important because research has shown that individuals who have realistic expectations of the organization and its benefits have a lower turnover rate than their counterparts who harbor unrealistic expectations (Wanous, 1980). Unions might be well advised, therefore, to use procedures similar to realistic job previews used in organizations. Interestingly, the suggestion that unions ensure that their members have an accurate perception of what their union can accomplish highlights findings showing the importance of early socialization in the union for subsequent commitment and participation (Fullagar, McCoy, & Shull, 1992; Gordon et al., 1980).

Decertification: A Potential Threat to the Labor Movement?

A final issue that must be confronted is whether decertification activity represents a threat to the labor movement. On the one hand, we are informed that "From the union perspective, a decertification election is nothing short of an act of war" (Bigoness & Peirce, 1988, p. 52), and cautioned about "the increasing hostility of employers towards unionism, and the use of management consultants to assist firms in their efforts to return to nonunion status" (Lawler & Hundley, 1983, p. 335). Yet there are other authors whose analyses suggest that the survival of the labor movement is in no way threatened by decertification elections (e.g., Krislov, 1979; Sandver & Heneman, 1981). As Klandermans (1986) observes and we already noted in Chapter 1, "contrary to what the prophets of doom would have us believe, they (unions) will not vanish in the near future" (p. 199). We agree with Klandermans in this respect. First, from a numerical perspective, there continue to be far more certification than decertification elections, and successful decertifications are still concentrated primarily in small bargaining units. Overall, therefore, a marked increase is still occurring in the number of new union members each year. Second, one point that has been raised in the literature is that unions lose more members each year through layoffs than through decertification activity (Fulmer, 1978). If unions are to stem the tide of membership losses, this latter finding would suggest that they would be well served by directing their limited resources to focusing on the number of members lost through layoffs. Third, given the "trade-off" between successful organizing and decertification identified by Elliott and Hawkins (1982), it is obvious that some decertification activity is to be expected if unions devote their scarce resources to organizing new bargaining units. However, unions would still be well advised to ensure that current members' needs are serviced appropriately, more to promote commitment and participation than to avoid decertification.

Only focusing on the numerical consequences of decertification provides a limited understanding of their consequences, and the extent to which the survival of unions is threatened by decertification. In any analysis of this issue, Kilgour's (1987, p. 51) cogent comments should be borne in mind. It could be argued that to the extent employees no longer perceive a need for third-party representation—because of improved management practices and protective labor legislation—the development is positive. Furthermore, if employees who are dissatisfied with their union representation are exercising their right to refrain from unionization, this also must be considered a positive development. On the other hand, to the extent that decertification elections are employer-generated or encouraged, they at least violate the spirit of the National Labor Relations Act.

Quitting the Union: When the Member Leaves the Union

Decertification is not the only way that unions lose members through employee-initiated action. In jurisdictions that allow for open-shop agreements, members have the individual right to voluntarily quit the union. This process is different from decertification in several respects. First, quitting the union reflects an individual decision; decertification a collective one. Second, the very existence of the bargaining unit is threatened in a decertification, but this is not necessarily the case when individuals quit the union. Individual decisions to leave the union have no direct effect on the legal right of the union to represent the workers. However, indirect effects could occur because (1) the decision to quit probably also reflects dissatisfaction with the union's effectiveness, and may influence the attitude of the remaining members, and (2) the strength of the union depends to some extent on its size (see Chapter 2). Because unions lose fewer members through individuals quitting the union than through decertification, and because many if not most jurisdictions do not allow the individual to quit the union, there are very few studies predicting the individual decision to resign from the union.

Gordon et al. (1980) investigated the extent to which union commitment, union loyalty, job and union satisfaction, and attitudes to unions predicted whether members quit the union. Contrary to their hypothesis, none of these factors predicted whether individuals had previously resigned from their local. As Gordon et al. (1980) note, however, failure to find significant findings may have been attributable to the lack of variance in the turnover measure: Only 6.9% of the respondents had allowed their membership to lapse, limiting the likelihood that any significant relationship would be uncovered for statistical reasons.

In contrast to Gordon et al. (1980) who focused on actual turnover, Klandermans (1989) assessed predictors of the *intent* to withdraw from the union. Based on his zero-order correlations, all four dimensions of union commitment (loyalty, willingness to work for the union, belief in unions, and responsibility to union) significantly predicted the intention to resign. Furthermore, because the belief and responsibility dimensions were only moderately correlated with union turnover intentions, and the four commitment dimensions themselves were significantly intercorrelated, Klandermans (1989) also conducted a multiple regression analysis. None of the demographic factors he assessed (education, seniority, length of affiliation with the union, and age) predicted turnover intentions. After controlling for these demographic factors, loyalty to the union, willingness to work for the union, and satisfaction with the union all predicted union turnover intentions. As noted previously, satisfaction with unions is an outcome of the extent to which members perceive the union to be meeting their needs. This again emphasizes the critical role of instrumentality perceptions. Thus, Klandermans' (1989) results suggest that both union commitment and perceived union instrumentality predict whether union members voluntarily choose to resign from the union.

Thus, while it is obvious that far more research is required to obtain a comprehensive understanding of why individuals would voluntarily choose to resign from their union, some tentative conclusions can be drawn. First, the role of demographic variables is minimal and only functions as proxies. Second, individuals who are loyal to the union and satisfied with the extent to which the union meets their needs are more likely to seek to retain their membership in the union.

Conclusion

Perhaps the most salient conclusion from this chapter concerns the critical role of perceived union instrumentality. Specifically, perceived union instrumentality predicts both collective and individual action against the union. As is evident from previous chapters, perceived union instrumentality is also central to other areas of the unionization process (e.g., voting is certification elections, union commitment, union participation, and union decertification). As such, DeCotiis and LeLouarn's (1981) comment that perceived union instrumentality is the "fulcrum" in the entire unionization process cannot be underestimated.

A final comment concerning the need for further research is in order. Far more is known about the predictors of voting in certification elections and all other aspects of the unionization process than about decertification and quitting. Obviously, more research is required. Any research aimed at understanding individual voting behavior during decertification campaigns might be guided to some extent by findings on voting in certification elections. As such, research should certainly focus on general union attitudes as well as work (e.g., job satisfaction) and family socialization. In any such research, it might be particularly instructive to include those union members who abstain from voting in decertification elections.

8

Effects of Unions on
Organizational Behavior

Our most far reaching conclusion is that, in addition to well advertised effects on wages, unions alter nearly every other measurable aspect of the operation of workplaces and enterprises, from turnover to productivity to the composition of pay packages. The behavior of workers and firms and the outcomes of their interactions differ substantially between the organized and unorganized sections.

(Freeman & Medoff, 1984, p. 19)

With the resurgence of research interest in industrial relations (Brett & Hammer, 1982; Lewin & Feuille, 1982) has come numerous calls for organizational psychologists to become involved in the study of unions (e.g., Barling, 1988; Fullagar, 1984; Gordon & Burt, 1981; Gordon & Nurick, 1984; Rosen & Stagner, 1981). As the rest of this book will attest, such involvement has largely consisted of applying the theory and constructs of organizational psychology to features of the industrial relations system. The preceding chapters emphasize one side of the psychological contract between the union and its members, namely how the union can benefit from the behaviors and attitudes of its members. In this chapter we document the other side of the contract, namely, what the consequences of union membership are for the individual member.

Once individuals have joined unions and been socialized into their membership roles, the union must focus on creating work conditions and collective bargaining outcomes that will facilitate greater commitment to, and participation in, union activities. As Schein (1980) points out, "the notion of a psychological contract implies that there is an unwritten set of expectations operating at all times between every member of an organization and ... others in that organization" (p. 22). Every union member has expectations concerning the union's role in establishing salaries, working hours, working conditions, benefits, medical insurance, occupational health and safety, and so on. Indeed, many union activities are precipitated by breaches of the psychological contract that individuals have with their employing organization. Similarly, as we pointed out in Chapter 7, one of the main predictors of decertification is the violation of membership expectations by the union. The union also has expectations concerning its membership; members are expected to be loyal to the union and participate in a variety of union activities that are the basis of the union's power. Schein (1980) emphasizes the importance of the psychological contract as a determinant of behavior in organizations. Consequently, the aim of this chapter is to show how the member-union contract has an impact not only on union attachment attitudes and behaviors, but also how it affects organizational behavior, an issue largely ignored within organizational psychology.

"If union membership were (a) rare and (b) exerted no influence on behavior in organizations, avoidance of union issues by I/O psychologists would be of little consequence" (Barling, 1988, p. 103). Neither of these conditions seem to be valid. First, approximately 40% of the non-agricultural workforce in Canada (Barling, 1988) and 19% of the workforce in the United States. (Balkin, 1989) are union members. Second, in summarizing the findings of their widely cited book, *What Do Unions Do?*, Freeman and Medoff (1984) conclude that unions alter nearly every aspect of organizational behavior. Despite the empirical evidence indicating that unions can and do influence organizational behavior, research on collective bargaining outcomes has not been incorporated into the mainstream of organizational psychology research. The cost of this omission to organizational psychology may be the construction and dissemination of a truncated body of knowledge regarding organizational behavior (Barling, 1988).

In this chapter we consider how unions affect organizational behavior. First, we examine the processes through which unions may influence organizational behavior. Specifically, we focus on the suggestion that union influences on organizational behavior are indirect; they are mediated by collective bargaining gains in the "bread and butter" areas of wages, benefits, job security, and working conditions (Kochan, 1980; Kochan & Helfman, 1981). Second, we consider the nature and direction of these indirect effects on outcomes of traditional concern to organizational psychologists (e.g., turnover, absenteeism, job satisfaction, employee stress). Particular attention will be given to the implications of unions for the theory and practice of organizational psychology. Finally, we address methodological issues and identify areas for future research.

How Unions Affect Organizational Behavior

Kochan (1980, Kochan & Helfman, 1981) has suggested that unions exert effects on organizational behavior through collective bargaining and has proposed a model of collective bargaining outcomes that identifies both "primary" and "secondary" outcomes. The primary effects of collective bargaining are the gains that the union is able to realize at the bargaining table. Consistent with union members' priorities (Kochan, 1979), extrinsic benefits such as wages, benefits, job security, and working conditions have dominated the collective bargaining agenda of North American unions (Gallagher & Clark, 1989). Gains in these areas are determined primarily by the unions' ability to acquire and use power in the bargaining relationship (Kochan, 1980). For example, the union wage effect is largely dependent on the ability of the union to achieve monopoly power within an industry (Freeman & Medoff, 1984).

According to Kochan's (1980) model, union effects on organizational behavior are "secondary" outcomes that emerge through management's reaction to collective agreement provisions. Management may react to union gains in collective bargaining in at least one of two ways. Neo-classical economic theory suggests that management will react to increased labor costs (resulting from increased wages and benefits) by (1) increasing product price, (2) reducing output and labor and (3) replacing labor with capital through investment in new technology (e.g., Freeman & Medoff, 1984; Gallagher, 1983; Kochan, 1980; Kochan & Helfman, 1981). Alternatively, collective bargaining may have a shock effect on management so that it reacts by introducing more efficient management strategies (Kochan, 1980), such as the introduction of centralized and professionally managed human resource functions (Gallagher, 1983). In either case, management's adjustment to the conditions imposed by collective bargaining (and the unions' counterreaction to managerial action) will determine the nature and extent of union effects on organizational behavior.

Primary Outcomes of Collective Bargaining

Kochan's (1980; Kochan & Helfman, 1981) model of the outcomes of collective bargaining identifies the primary outcomes as being the "bread and butter" issues that have traditionally dominated union concerns (Gallaghar & Clark, 1989); that is, wages, fringe benefits, job security, and working conditions. This focus on extrinsic factors is consistent with the desires of the union membership (Kochan, 1979). The ability of unions to achieve their goals in these areas has important ramifications for organizational behavior both within the union (e.g., Kelloway, Barling, & Fullagar, 1990) and within the organization.

Compensation

Perhaps the most intensely researched of all the outcomes of collective bargaining is the effect of unions on wages (Gallaghar, 1983). While a review of this voluminous literature is beyond the scope of this chapter, it is clear that unions have a direct effect on the level, form, structure, and system of compensation plans (Balkin, 1989). Although these effects vary across industry and individuals (Freeman & Medoff, 1984), some general conclusions may be drawn.

First, and most important, unions raise wages. Estimates of the union wage effect vary but in general wage levels in unionized industries are 10 to 20% higher than wages for comparable non-unionized industries (Freeman & Medoff, 1984; Gallagher, 1983). Similarly, unions have a positive impact on employee benefits with unionized industries spending more on fringe benefits than comparable non-unionized firms (Freeman & Medoff, 1984). The magnitude of these effects varies across industries with a greater union wage effect being observed in heavily unionized industries where unions are able to acquire monopoly power (Freeman & Medoff, 1984). The magnitude of the union wage effect also varies with individuals; it is greater for men, minorities, younger workers, and junior blue-collar workers (Freeman & Medoff, 1984). In addition to the increase in wages attributable to unions there is also evidence suggesting that union wages are more secure—that union wages are less sensitive to fluctuations in the economy than wages in non-unionized industries (e.g., Mitchell, 1980).

Unions may also affect the *form* of compensation (Balkin, 1989) offered to employees. In general, non-unionized firms determine wages on the basis of local labor market conditions (Kochan, 1980). The pay preferences of younger, more mobile, and highly skilled workers assume a priority in determining compensation for non-unionized individuals. In contrast, union compensation packages are determined on the basis of a variety of concerns such as wage patterns in other union contracts, both regional and national labor market conditions, and the cost of living (Kochan, 1980). As democratic institutions, labor unions are more responsive to the needs of the membership resulting in the preferences of senior, less mobile employees assuming greater importance in determining pay policies (Freeman & Medoff, 1984). Unionized firms, for example, spend more on employee benefit plans than do non-unionized firms (Freeman, 1981). Moreover, the composition of such benefit plans is affected by unions; unionized firms spend more on deferred compensation plans such as pensions, health care, insurance, and vacation/holiday pay (Freeman, 1981; Freeman & Medoff, 1984). On the other hand, unionized firms spend correspondingly less on bonuses and profit sharing than non-unionized firms (Freeman, 1981; Freeman & Medoff, 1984). Klein (1987), for example, examined the implementation of Employee Stock Ownership Plans in thirty-seven companies. She found that while twenty-eight of the firms with stock ownership plans were non-unionized, only nine firms with such plans were unionized (Klein, 1987).

Most unions attempt to establish uniform wage rates for comparable workers within a particular organization (Balkin, 1989). Two types of policies are of particular interest. First, unions attempt to establish a single rate of pay for each job class (Slichter et al., 1960). This policy results in a wage compression effect by reducing wage disparities both within plant and within industry (Freeman & Medoff, 1984). Moreover, unions reduce the disparity between blue-collar and white-collar workers as well as between skilled and unskilled workers (Freeman, 1980; Freeman & Medoff, 1984). Second, unions attempt to gain automatic increases in wages based on seniority and/or the cost of living. In contrast to non-unionized firms, which may determine wage increases on the basis of education, experience, and performance, unions have generally opposed performance-based compensation schemes (Freeman & Medoff, 1984; Slichter et al., 1960). Wage increases based on merit were found to be almost four times as unlikely in unionized firms when compared to non-unionized firms (Freeman, 1980). Moreover, those unionized firms that have implemented *merit*-based salary increases may find that the plans often become *automatic* salary increases in practice. Because union members who have not received a merit increase can grieve and win, the merit plan often becomes an annual salary increase (Freeman & Medoff, 1984).

A final consideration in this discussion of union effects on compensation is the issue of piece-rate pay. Organizational psychologists have often cited piece-rate pay as a means of linking compensation to performance. Indeed, organizational psychology advocated the use of piece-rate pay, and time and motion study, under the rubric of scientific management. This phrase was often used by union members as a term of abuse and ridicule (Skelton & Yandle, 1982), and the practice that contributed to the estrangement of organizational psychology from the labor movement (Rosen & Stagner, 1981). Union opposition to piece-rate pay may have declined somewhat, particularly in certain industries such as the steel industry (Skelton & Yandle, 1982). Where such plans have been implemented, however, they have become part of the collective bargaining process with unions demanding the right to be involved in establishing standards and rates (Skelton & Yandle, 1982).

The effect of unions and collective bargaining on wages and fringe benefits has some important implications for the theory and practice of oranizational psychology. Employee reactions to compensation issues have largely been conceptualized in terms of pay equity (Locke, 1983). According to equity theory (Pinder, 1984), individuals evaluate their inputs and outputs relative to those of another. When the ratio of inputs and outputs is not equal to the same ratio for selected referents, a state of inequity exists (possibly resulting in dissatisfaction; see Locke, 1983). Unions have the potential to affect this equity ratio in three respects. First, by attempting to establish uniform wage rates within a job class, unions may contribute to equity perceptions by equating the outcomes received by individuals. Second, unions may affect the weighting of specific inputs for individuals. By focusing on a standard wage for a particular occupation and emphasizing seniority as the basis for certain benefits, unions act to clarify what inputs are relevant for compensation decisions. Moreover, through seniority lists employees receive an accurate picture of their standing relative to other employees. Third, unions may affect equity perceptions by influencing the choice of appropriate referents, i.e., other members of the bargaining unit or employees in the same job class and grade. Equity theorists commonly assume that job performance is the most relevant input for the equity equation (Mowday, 1983). The presence of a union in the workplace may substantially negate this assumption through the union's emphasis on seniority and opposition to merit-based pay incentives.

There is an emerging literature on the structure of compensation systems from the perspective of organizational psychology. A recent review of strategic considerations in designing compensation policies mentioned a variety of concerns (Lawler, 1987) but failed to even acknowledge the potential impact of unions and collective bargaining on the design of such systems. In particular, Lawler (1987) suggests that the objectives of compensation systems include (1) attraction and retention of employees, (2) motivation, (3) culture, (4) reinforcement and definition of organizational structure and (5) cost reduction. This set of objectives may not be shared by the union; indeed the union may have conflicting goals such as the redistribution of corporate profits to the individual. The rather simplistic assumption that organizations can design compensation plans solely to fulfill corporate objectives runs through the organizational psychology literature. The validity of this assumption in a unionized environment is questionable at best.

Job Security

Collective agreements often contain clauses that directly influence individual job security such as provisions for layoffs, job transfers, and contracting out (Slichter et al., 1960). The prevalence of such provisions indicates the high priority placed on job security by union members. Based on the *Quality of Employment Survey* data, union membership was the best predictor of whether individuals would trade a 10% increase in real wages in exchange for increased job security (Kochan, 1980).

Given this emphasis on job security, it is perhaps surprising to find that union members are more likely to be laid off than their non-unionized counterparts and unionized firms are two to four times as likely to lay off workers (Freeman & Medoff, 1984). Explanations for this anomaly include the increased susceptibility of unionized firms to cyclical business cycles and the greater reliance of unionized firms on temporary layoffs as a means of adjusting to business cycles (Freeman & Medoff, 1984). Consistent with the increased use of temporary layoffs in unionized firms, unions have sought provisions for both preserving jobs and protecting the incomes of dislocated employees (Kochan, 1980). Thus unions may negotiate "contracting out" and similar provisions that define the jobs that must be done by union members (Slichter et al., 1960). By doing so, unions increase job security by reserving certain jobs for their members.

The effect of unions on job security is not uniform within a particular union. Rather, unions improve the security of senior employees at the expense of more junior employees through the negotiation of seniority clauses in the collective agreement (Abraham & Medoff, 1984; Freeman & Medoff, 1984). Seniority is one of the guiding principles of the union movement (Leonard, 1986), and seniority provisions are frequently incorporated into collective agreements as a means of regulating promotions, layoffs, and job transfers. These provisions are referred to as competitive seniority status (Gordon & Johnson, 1982) because they provide senior workers with a competitive advantage over more junior employees in job assignments. The majority of union contracts contain such seniority provisions. Kochan (1980) reports that in a survey of collective agreements, seniority was mentioned as a factor in promotion in 90% of the manufacturing and 43% of the nonmanufacturing agreements. Seniority clauses emerge from the view that seniority confers a "property right" whereby senior employees are entitled to the most secure jobs, to have first opportunity at promotion, and have first choice of vacation schedules and time off (Kochan,

1980; for a review of the concept of property rights as applied to employment, see Gordon & Lee, 1990).

In addition to protection from job loss, Kochan (1980) points out that a major benefit of unionization is security from arbitrary treatment. Through the provision of grievance systems and development of the "just cause" principle for dismissal or discipline, unions substantially increase the security of union members (Kochan, 1980). A majority of union contracts contain provisions for a grievance system (Gordon & Miller, 1984) and handling of grievances is seen by union members as the highest priority for unions (Kochan, 1979). The institution of grievance policies may have direct effects on organizational variables other than job security. For example, the presence of grievance systems may have a positive impact on productivity by providing a channel of communication that identifies problems in the organization (Slichter et al., 1960). Moreover, the implementation of grievance systems provides employees with a "voice" mechanism (Freeman & Medoff, 1984) through which specific dissatisfactions may be redressed without the need for work stoppages (Gordon & Miller, 1984) or individual withdrawal (Freeman & Medoff, 1984).

There are several implications of union effects on job security for organizational behaviour and the management of organizations. In particular, the empirical evidence suggests that unionized workforces may be more stable than non-unionized ones. In response, unionized firms may invest considerable resources in the management of the human resource function in response to the stability of the workforce (Gallagher, 1983). Employee selection and training may assume an increased importance in such an environment. The empirical evidence confirms this suggestion. Unionized firms are more likely (1) to have a separate human resources program, (2) to exert greater care in the selection of new employees, and (3) to invest more in employee training than comparable non-unionized firms (Steele, Myles, & McIntyre, 1954).

Unions also increase the security of their members from arbitrary decision making through the provision of grievance systems. The corollary of this is that management in unionized firms may become more efficient than management in non-unionized firms. Through the implementation of grievance systems with provisions for third-party dispute resolution, unions substantially increase the costs of arbitrary management decisions. One would expect, and empirical evidence confirms (Clark, 1980), that management decision making in a unionized environment would be more regulated by formal procedures and based on objective criteria (Gallagher 1983).

Working Conditions: Occupational Safety and Health

Unions have made intensive efforts to improve occupational health and safety in the workplace through advocating for government regulations, negotiating health and safety provisions, and encouraging the formation of labor-management committees to deal with health and safety issues (Kochan, 1980). In addition to the negotiation of clauses dealing with health and safety, unions may also negotiate compensating wage differentials for workers exposed to higher risks (Kochan, 1980). By doing so, they increase the incentive for management to improve working conditions by increasing the costs of dangerous work.

Overall, unions substantially increase awareness of health and safety issues in the workplace. Kochan (1980) reports that, although there are no differences between injury rates for unionized and non-unionized individuals, union members are substantially more aware of on-the-job hazards. Kochan (1980) concludes that although unions have been successful in negotiating increased wages for dangerous work and in promoting awareness of workplace hazards, they have been less successful in actually reducing injury rates. These conclusions may be confounded, however, by data suggesting that blue-collar union members are more likely to be found in risky industries (Leigh, 1982; Worrall & Butler, 1983). Thus, the effect of unions on occupational health and safety may be at least partially offset by higher injury rates in unionized industries.

A counterintuitive finding emerged from Appleton and Baker's (1984) study of safety in bituminous coal mines. These authors compared mine injury rates between coal mines represented by the United Mine Workers of America (UMWA) and non-unionized mines. The best predictor of four indices of injury rates (i.e., numbers of total injuries, disabling injuries, no-lost-workday injuries, and intermediate injuries) was union status, suggesting that the presence of a union was associated was *higher* injury rates. One plausible explanation for this finding is a reporting bias whereby unionized mines are more likely (due to union monitoring) to report all accidents than non-unionized mines. Conversely, employees lacking the protection of the union may be less willing to report safety hazards and nondebilitating injuries. The authors dismiss this explanation, however, and conclude that union-induced work rules and differences in unionized and non-unionized workforces explain the differences in safety records. Appleton and Baker's (1984) analysis and conclusions have been criticized on several points (e.g., insufficient information about sampling methods, lack of consideration of relevant variables such as employee age and superficial analysis that failed to consider confounding effects) by both the UMWA (Weeks, 1985) and other researchers (Bennett & Passmore, 1985). While no definitive conclusions are possible, it does seem that unions have a direct effect on worker and management awareness of occupational health and safety (Kochan, 1980). Whether such awareness translates into actual reductions in injury rates remains to be determined.

In addition to safety and health issues, unions also negotiate contract provisions dealing with a variety of working conditions, for example, hours of work, scheduling of rest breaks, and, in some cases, rate of production (Slichter et al., 1960). To the extent that unions are successful in negotiating these gains, unionization may have an indirect effect on occupational health and safety. Provisions such as rest breaks, minimization of overtime, and shift scheduling may all affect the risk of on-the-job injury. Moreover, unions are increasingly focusing on the work environment itself. Identifying hazardous substances in the workplace, providing proper safeguards, and training workers in handling hazardous materials are all issues of concern to unions. The union, therefore, may be expected to have a substantial effect on workers' health and safety.

Management Reactions to Unionization

As indicated earlier, neo-classical economic theory suggests that management may react to the increased costs associated with unionization by replacing labor with capital (Freeman & Medoff, 1984; Gallagher, 1983; Kochan, 1980). An alternate theory suggests that unionization has a "shock effect" (Kochan, 1980) on management, whereby management reacts to unionization by becoming more efficient. Such increased efficiency may be evidenced by the introduction of centralized, professional human resources functions and increased reliance on formalized decision making (Gallagher, 1983). Several authors have presented evidence that supports the shock effect of unions on management, although there are differing views regarding whether this impact is good or bad. On the one hand, union involvement in the formulation of management decisions may be seen as usurping the rights of management to run the workplace. On the other hand, collective bargaining may be viewed as a way of managing the workplace rather than an abandonment of traditional management prerogatives (Peterson, 1957). In this regard, it should be noted that through their involvement in establishing work rules and organizational policies, unions may have both positive and negative effects on organizational behavior (Freeman & Medoff, 1984).

Steele, Myles, and McIntyre (1954) surveyed 600 union and non-union manufacturing plants in the southeast United States. While their findings may be somewhat dated, they did identify several differences in management decision making between unionized and non-unionized environments. With respect to hiring new employees, unionized firms were significantly more likely to use employment tests, application blanks, reference checks, and age qualifications than non-unionized plants. Consistent with suggestions made earlier in this chapter, unionized firms were less likely to use performance incentives and more likely to use performance appraisals, job evaluations, and seniority as a criteria for job transfers, promotions, and layoffs. In addition to being more likely to have a human resources department, unionized firms were more likely to sponsor safety programs, employee training programs, and to conduct personnel research.

At least two variables substantially moderated these differences. First, larger plants were more likely to engage in formalized human resource management than were smaller plants and unions were more frequently present in large plants. Second, the existence of a separate human resource department was related to the firms' use of human resources management techniques. Again, unions were more likely to be found in firms with personnel specialists. Thus it is unclear whether the differences that emerged were attributable to plant size, the presence of a personnel specialist, or unionization. After controlling for plant size and the presence of human resource specialists, however, significant differences were still observed between union and non-union plants. In general, Steele et al. (1954) comment that the effect of unionization on management decision making was more pronounced in smaller plants than in larger ones. These findings are consistent with the view that the presence of a union is *one* influence but not *the only* influence on management decision making.

A more recent investigation of organizational personnel practices also supports the hypothesis that unionization has a direct impact on human resource policies. Jackson, Schuler, and Rivero (1989) examined personnel practices in 267 organizations as a function of various organizational characteristics (i.e., unionization, size, industry sector, the pursuit of innovation as a competitive strategy, manufacturing technology, and organizational structure). Jackson et al. (1989) report that personnel practices for hourly employees did vary as a result of unionization. Fewer differences emerged for managerial employees. Specifically, hourly workers in unionized organizations were more likely to be subject to formal performance appraisals based on objective criteria. Unionized companies were more likely to use the results of performance appraisals to identify training needs and to offer training to their employees. Paradoxically, hourly workers in unionized firms were more likely to be offered bonuses based on company-wide productivity and to have compensation tied to performance. Finally, unionization had a lesser impact on the application of personnel policies to managerial employees. One of the most interesting effects that did emerge, however, was that managers in unionized companies were more likely to have a portion of their performance appraisal based on subordinate input; that is, hourly workers contributed to the evaluation of a manager's performance.

The results of Jackson et al.'s (1989) are not amenable to clear interpretation regarding unionization. First, as Jackson et al. (1989) point out, their results suggest that the organizations they surveyed enjoyed a somewhat nontraditional union-management relationship. Second, the distinction Jackson et al. (1989) make between "union" and "non-union" organizations is not related to the extent of unionization within the company. As they state, "the distinction here is between firms that do and those that do not have at least one active union. The distinction is *not* between employees who are members of unions and those who are not" (Jackson et al., 1989, p. 772). Thus it is possible that organizations classified as being union had a small percentage of employees who were actually union members. It is difficult, therefore, to determine whether the differences Jackson et al. found are attributable to unionization per se. Indeed it is possible that some differences, such as the provision of performance-based compensation, are a result of organizations trying to stop the spread of unions in the company.

Somewhat clearer findings emerged from Clark's (1980) study of unionization in the cement industry. Based on case studies of six cement plants that unionized, Clark (1980) was able to compare management functioning before and after unionization. Most relevant to the current discussion are his observations that unionization was followed by a fundamental change in work rules especially regarding entry and exit, internal mobility, and dispute resolution. In general, unionization was accompanied by the introduction of formal decision-making procedures and the decreased use of managerial judgment in making human resources decisions.

The effect of unions on managerial decision making is seen clearly in the development of personnel policies (Gallagher, 1983). It is commonly recognized that unions influence the use of seniority as a criteria for promotions and job transfers although the effect is smaller than one would anticipate (e.g., Abraham & Medoff, 1985; Freeman & Medoff, 1984). The magnitude of the effect is suppressed by the observation that seniority often plays a role in promotion decisions in non-unionized (Mills, 1985; Olson & Berger, 1983) as well as in unionized firms. Given that seniority is directly related to job experience, reliance on seniority as a criterion for promotion is to be expected. Unions may also have an effect on hiring decisions; Kalachek and Raines (1980) report that one managerial response to union wage premiums may be to raise the hiring standards of the firm and in particular to place more weight on education as a hiring criteria. As Jackson et al. (1989) suggest, the presence of a union may well result in the implementation of policies that are in the organization's best interests.

In addition to influencing the development of formal policies and procedures, the presence of a union can substantially influence the implementation of these procedures. Beyer, Trice, and Hunt (1979) examined supervisors' use of policies relating to employee alcoholism and the Equal Employment Opportunity (EEO) guidelines. Based on data from 634 supervisors in seventy-one organizations, they concluded that supervisors' awareness and use of policy was related to their perceptions of the unions' power. It is important to note that the supervisors' perception of the degree of union support for a policy was not a significant predictor. Rather, supervisors took the fact that the union had a position as an indication of union interest and a potential source of grievances. While these effects emerged for policies regarding alcohol use by employees, the effect was less clear for the use of EEO policies. The smaller effect was attributed to EEO guidelines being federally regulated (Beyer et al., 1979). Again this supports the notion that unions have an effect on organizational behavior, but that it is only one of several influences.

In summary, the available literature supports Freeman and Medoff's (1984) suggestion that the presence of a union is associated with more efficient managerial decision making. In particular, this inceased efficiency is attributable to the formalization of decision making and the substitution of policy for individual judgment as a basis for decision making. The extent and nature of these reactions may substantially determine, and be determined by, the quality of union-management relations. In turn, the quality of union-management relations may be a determinant of the secondary outcomes of collective bargaining to which we now turn our attention.

Secondary Outcomes of Collective Bargaining

As the preceding discussion indicates, unions have substantial effects on organizational behavior through the negotiation of specific provisions in the collective agreement. Additional effects also accrue during the administration of the collective agreement as management (and the union) adjusts to the new environmental conditions mandated by the collective agreement. The primary determinant of how successful the union is in negotiating specific provisions in the collective agreement is the power of the union (Kochan, 1980; Kochan & Helfman, 1981). In contrast, the effects we now discuss are determined largely by the union's success in negotiating specific provisions and the reaction of management to these provisions. In discussing the secondary effects of collective bargaining, we first consider effects on relevant organizational behaviors (i.e., productivity and performance, turnover, and absenteeism) followed by a discussion of union effects on organizational experiences and their evaluation (e.g., job satisfaction, job stress).

Productivity and Performance

In contradiction to traditional managerial views of the role of unions, Freeman and Medoff (1984) have concluded that unions substantially increase the productivity of organizations. That is, after controlling for various organizational characteristics, unionized firms are more productive than their non-unionized counterparts. It is perhaps important to note in this context that the increases in firm productivity identified by Freeman and Medoff (1984) and others (e.g., Clark, 1980) do not seem to offset the increased costs of unionization. Indeed, unionized firms are found to be less profitable than non-unionized firms.

The union impact on firm productivity is explained by two factors. First, as discussed below, unionization leads to a more stable workforce by reducing voluntary turnover (Freeman & Medoff, 1984). A direct consequence of this increased stability is the firms' investment in human resources management. As noted above, one way an organization can respond to this increased stability is to invest more resources in the selection and training of employees. Another means for companies to adjust to the increased costs of unionism is to institute more efficient management policies including formalized decision-making procedures and increased monitoring of individual productivity (Clark, 1980).

The union effect on firm productivity provides a conceptual basis for the hypothesis that unionization may have an effect on individual job performance. Although the available research literature has focused on firm productivity (a macro-level variable), the explanation for the union versus non-union differential is couched in terms that would lead one to expect similar differences in individual job performance (a micro-level variable). Through more rigorous selection, investment in employee training, and the institution of more professional management practices, an organization attempts to adjust to the costs of unionism by increasing individual job performance. While the end result of such strategies is an increase in firm productivity, the initial effect is plausibly an increase in individual job performance.

While there is a lack of research evidence to support (or disconfirm) this hypothesis, some indirect evidence indicates that unionization may affect individual job performance. Specifically, Freeman and Medoff (1984) suggest that the union effect on firm productivity is moderated by the quality of union-management relations. When the industrial relations climate is favorable, unionization is associated with higher firm productivity. Conversely, a poor quality of union-management relations is associated with decreased productivity in unionized firms. These findings are consistent with the suggestion that unionization may have an effect on individual job performance. Job performance may be conceptualized as a function of individual skill and individual motivation. By investing in employee selection, training, and professional management techniques, the organization is influencing the skill component in this equation. Presumably the quality of union-management relationships influences the motivation component. When the quality of union management relations is poor, the potential for increments in job performance may be offset by decreased individual motivation, work stoppages, and work-to-rule campaigns.

Thus while there are conceptual and empirical grounds to suspect that unionization has an effect on individual job performance, there is currently no empirical data that addresses this issue. As such, the hypothesis remains an intriguing possibility that has substantial implications for the study of organizational behavior.

Turnover

Perhaps one of the most well-documented effects of unions on organizational behavior is the reduction in voluntary employee turnover in unionized industries (e.g., Freeman, 1980; Freeman & Medoff, 1984; Gallagher, 1983; Kochan & Helfman, 1981). Consistent with Kochan's (1980) model of collective bargaining, unions reduce turnover through two basic processes. First, unions increase wages and improve working conditions. These primary union effects make unionized jobs more attractive and, conversely, reduce the likelihood of finding an equivalent job. The union effect on benefits, and particularly the increase in deferred compensation schemes that favor senior workers (Freeman, 1981), contribute to the union effect on turnover. Similarly, benefits based on seniority also act to decrease the voluntary turnover rate (Block, 1978).

Second, Freeman and Medoff (1984) argue that unions reduce turnover by providing individuals with a "voice" (Hirschman, 1970). That is, even after controlling for the reduction in turnover attributable to increased wages, unions substantially reduce voluntary employee turnover (Freeman & Medoff, 1984). Through the provision of employee grievance systems, unions provide the individual an alternative to quitting—the opportunity to redress specific dissatisfactions through the grievance system. Several lines of evidence lend credence to an "exit-voice" (Hirschman, 1970) explanation of the union effect on voluntary turnover. In his study of 111 hospitals, Spencer (1986) found that irrespective of union status, lower quit rates were associated with more voice mechanisms provided to the employees. The lack of a union effect in Spencer's study may be attributable to a spillover (Freeman & Medoff, 1984) or union-threat (Spencer, 1986) effect of unionism. In an effort to maintain their union-free status, organizations often offer employees the same benefits of unionism such as the provision of grievance systems. In either case it seems that the provision of voice mechanisms, rather than unionism *per se*, reduces voluntary turnover. Moreover, consistent with the predictions of an exit-voice model,

Blau and Kahn (1983) found that the effect of unionism on quitting is larger for older rather than younger men. Similarly, Farber (1980) found unionism exerted differential effects for younger (as opposed to more senior) employees. These effects support the exit-voice hypothesis in that younger workers have not acquired rights to the tenure-dependent benefits of unionism (Farber, 1980) so that the voice benefit of unionism accrues primarily to more senior workers. Alternatively, older workers have considerably more invested in a particular job in the form of pensions and vested benefits. The reduction in turnover among older employees that is attributed to unionization may simply reflect the fact that turnover among older employees is less than turnover among younger workers (Mowday et al., 1982).

The development of complex linkage models to predict turnover has resulted from the consistent finding that job dissatisfaction is at best moderately correlated with turnover (Mobley, 1977, 1982). While organizational psychologists have attempted to reconcile theory with empirical observation by positing increasingly complex models, the presence of unions in the workplace suggests at least one other potential explanation for the magnitude of the satisfaction-turnover correlation. Specifically, if unions reduce employee turnover, the criterion variable (turnover) may be restricted in range, thereby suppressing the magnitude of the correlation.

If unions reduce voluntary turnover, several implications for organizational psychology ensue. The organizational psychology literature typically treats turnover as a "withdrawal" behavior through which employees express dissatisfaction with the job by quitting (e.g., Mobley, 1977, 1982). The "exit-voice" (Freeman & Medoff, 1984) model of unionism suggests another alternative. Unions provide mechanisms for individuals to express their dissatisfaction and influence their working conditions. According to the exit-voice model, the provision of such mechanisms reduces the probability that an individual will voluntarily resign his or her position. Contemporary theories of voluntary turnover, therefore, might be deficient in that they fail to consider the alternative of voice as a response to job dissatisfaction. In particular, the "linkage" models of turnover (e.g., Mobley, 1977, 1982) that consider a sequence of events leading from job dissatisfaction to turnover may be incompletely specified in unionized environments where the hypothesized sequence of events may be "short-circuited" by union voice mechanisms. While this observation does not invalidate models of the turnover process, it does suggest a need to consider alternative routes for resolving dissatisfaction.

Absenteeism

If unions reduce voluntary turnover by providing voice mechanisms to individuals then these effects might be logically extended to other forms of individual withdrawal such as absenteeism. The empirical literature, however, does not support such an extension. Specifically, while unions do seem to have an impact on employee absenteeism, the relationship is positive rather than negative as for turnover; unionized firms experience higher absenteeism rates (e.g., Allen,

1984; Leigh, 1981). At least two explanations have been offered to account for this anomaly. First, Allen (1984) points out that absenteeism does not fit neatly into the exit-voice paradigm as it is applied to turnover. To the extent that absenteeism results from job dissatisfaction (Hackett, 1989), absence from work is indeed an "exit" behavior as it involves an escape from unpleasant working conditions. On the other hand, absenteeism may also be considered a voice mechanism. In this view the temporary withdrawal of services by an individual may be one means of signalling discontent to management.

Second, several authors have suggested that increased sick-leave benefits negotiated during collective bargaining are associated with higher rates of absenteeism (e.g., Leigh, 1981). For example, in their analysis of twenty-nine organizations, Dalton and Perry (1981) demonstrated significant and positive correlations between three collective bargaining provisions (wage rate, accumulation of sick-leave benefits, and lack of remuneration for unused sick-leave benefits) and absenteeism. This is consistent with a view of absenteeism that is grounded in exchange theory and suggests that absenteeism is not a withdrawal behavior *per se*. Rather, casual absenteeism is attributed to the "informal contract" between management and labor (Chadwick-Jones, 1981). In this view, absenteeism emerges as a result of the negotiation process between management and labor. While Chadwick-Jones (1981) points to the role of informal negotiations between employees and management in determining acceptable absenteeism rates, it is conceivable that the formal negotiation of a collective agreement and its subsequent administration may play a similar role.

As with turnover, organizational psychologists have consistently identified a moderate correlation between employee attitudes, such as job dissatisfaction, and employee individual absenteeism (e.g., Hackett, 1989; Porter & Steers, 1973; Muchinsky, 1977; Steers & Rhodes, 1978; Vroom, 1964). Muchinsky (1977) suggests that "of all variables that have been related to absenteeism, the most consistent results have occurred with attitudinal predictors" (p. 322). Given the modest magnitude of the obtained correlations (Hackett, 1989), this observation may be more pessimistic than optimistic. As with turnover, one potential explanation for this lack of predictive power may be the role of unions in increasing employee absenteeism. That is, the magnitude of the relationship between job dissatisfaction and absenteeism suggests that other influences play an important role (e.g., gender; see Hackett, 1989), and the available literature regarding the union effect on absenteeism suggests that unions may be one such influence.

Job Dissatisfaction

"In survey after survey of job satisfaction, unionized workers ... report themselves less satisfied with most facets of their work" (Freeman & Medoff, 1984, p. 136). As Freeman and Medoff point out, the negative effect of unions on job satisfaction has been well documented (e.g., Berger, Olson, & Boudreau, 1983; Borjas, 1979; Evans & Ondrack, 1990; Freeman, 1978; Freeman & Medoff, 1984; Kochan, 1980; Kochan & Helfman, 1981; Odewahn & Petty, 1980;

Schwochau, 1987) and has been identified as one of the paradoxes in the study of union effects (Pfeffer & Davis-Blake, 1990). The paradox emerges through the observation that unions simultaneously decrease both job satisfaction and turnover (Borjas, 1979; Freeman & Medoff, 1984). Thus unionized workers are more dissatisfied with their jobs but less likely to quit.

Perhaps the most commonly cited resolution of this paradox is in the positing of a "voice" hypothesis (e.g., Borjas, 1979; Freeman & Medoff, 1984; Pfeffer & Davis-Blake, 1990), whereby unions increase dissatisfaction by alerting members to the unpleasant aspects of their jobs (Bluen & van Zwam, 1987; Freeman & Medoff, 1984). According to the voice hypothesis, therefore, the higher levels of job dissatisfaction expressed by union members are due to the politicization of the workforce rather than dissatisfaction *per se* (this has also been referred to as the conscientizing hypothesis, see Berger et al., 1983). Support for the exit-voice hypothesis emerges from several studies of job satisfaction in unionized and non-unionized samples.

In his analysis of data from the *National Longitudinal Survey of Mature Men*, Borjas (1979) examined the impact of voice mechanisms on job satisfaction. In particular, he argued that voice mechanisms reflect the demands of more senior workers. Because younger employees are more mobile and more likely to quit their jobs when dissatisfied (and hence more likely to leave the union), union voice mechanisms must reflect the concerns of more senior workers to be effective. Consistent with this hypothesis, Borjas reports that the increase in job dissatisfaction attributable to unionism occurred primarily among the more senior employees. Borjas concludes that these more senior workers have become more politicized and as a result, *express* a higher level of dissatisfaction.

In their review of union effects on job satisfaction, Freeman and Medoff (1984) cite several lines of evidence to support the exit-voice hypothesis. First, they summarize findings from five national probability surveys. In all five surveys union members reported lower intentions to quit. In four of the surveys union members had a lower actual quit rate (data was not available for the fifth study, namely, the *Quality of Employment Survey*, 1977). Paradoxically, union members reported lower job satisfaction in four surveys (*Panel Study of Income Dynamics*, 1972–1973; *Older Men, National Longitudinal Study*, 1969–1971; *Younger Men, National Longitudinal Study*, 1969–1971; *Quality of Employment Survey*, 1977). In the remaining survey (*Quality of Employment Survey*, 1973) there was no difference in reported job satisfaction between union and non-union workers. Freeman and Medoff (1984) conclude that these findings require the differentiation between "true" and "voiced" job dissatisfaction. Specifically, the suggestion here is that the lower job satisfaction reported by union members may be attributable to the union's making members more aware of, and providing an outlet to voice dissatisfaction with, working conditions. This explanation is comparable to Kochan and Helfman's (1981) comments regarding occupational health and safety. Recall that although no differences existed between union and non-union workers in terms of *actual* job injuries, union members *report* more awareness of on-the-job hazards than do non-union workers.

The evidence for a union voice effect with respect to job satisfaction must also consider the specific facets of satisfaction (Pfeffer & Davis-Blake, 1990). While studies of overall job satisfaction have suggested a negative effect of unionization (e.g., Borjas, 1979; Freeman, 1978; Freeman & Medoff, 1984), studies of facet satisfactions require more complex interpretation. First, several studies suggest that unions may have a positive rather than a negative impact on specific facet satisfactions. For example, Bluen and van Zwam (1987) obtained data on the Job Descriptive Index (JDI, Smith, Kendall, & Hulin, 1969). The JDI measures satisfaction with the work itself, pay, supervision, coworkers, and opportunities for promotion. Only one significant main effect emerged from this analysis: satisfaction with promotion was higher among union members than for non-union members. Satisfaction with the work itself was moderated by race and sex such that satisfaction was higher for black non-unionized females than for white non-unionized females. Also, unionized males were more satisfied with their coworkers than unionized females; the opposite effect emerged for non-unionized workers. Schwochau (1987) found that union members reported lower levels of satisfaction with four job facets (satisfaction with supervision, coworkers, job content, and resource adequacy), but higher satisfaction with pay than non-unionized respondents.

The fact that different facets of job satisfaction are differentially correlated with unionism is dependent on whether the specific job facet is under the control of the union (Hammer, 1978). Specifically, based on responses from 277 members of a building construction union, Hammer (1978) reports a significant correlation of .52 between perceived union strength and pay satisfaction. Correlations with other facet satisfactions were not significant. Pfeffer and Davis-Blake (1990) re-analyzed the 1977 *Quality of Employment Survey* data (also used by Freeman & Medoff, 1984, and Kochan & Helfman, 1981) and suggested that characteristics of the job environment (such as autonomy, conflict, quality of supervision, and work pacing) were correlated with both unionization and satisfaction. After controlling for the effects of these job characteristics, the negative relationship between unionization and overall job satisfaction became positive. In further analyses, Pfeffer and Davis-Blake (1990) found that the positive effect of unionization on satisfaction was positive for members of craft and white-collar unions, for which the presence of a union increased individual control in the workplace. Finally, Gomez-Mejia and Balkin (1984) analyzed job and pay satisfaction among high school teachers, approximately half of whom were unionized. They report that unionization did not have an effect on satisfaction with promotions, supervision, job content, job context, or resource adequacy. Unionzation was significantly related to pay satisfaction in that unionized teachers were more satisfied with their pay (Gomez-Mejia & Balkin, 1984). Moreover, union status moderated the relationship between gender and pay satisfaction such that unionized women were more satisfied with their pay than were unionized men; no such differences emerged for the non-unionized samples. Gomez-Mejia and Balkin (1984) attribute this finding to the effect of unions on reducing pay differentials between men and women.

These findings are consistent with Kochan's (1980; Kochan & Helfman,

1981) model of the effects of collective bargaining on organizational variables. Specifically, when taken together, the research evidence suggests that the effects of unions on job satisfaction is indirect rather than direct; the magnitude and direction of such effects depends upon union success in achieving their goals in collective bargaining and management reactions to the environment created by the collective agreement. Three recent studies have specifically addressed the indirect effect of unions on job satisfaction. First, Berger et al. (1983) analyzed data from the 1973 *Quality of Employment Survey*. Based on Locke's (1983) theory of job satisfaction, Berger et al. proposed indirect models for each of five facet satisfactions (i.e., pay, coworkers, promotion, supervision, work itself) measured by the JDI (Smith et al., 1969), as well as a measure of satisfaction with "resource adequacy." Specifically, they suggested that the effect of unions on facet satisfactions is indirect, being mediated by the effect of unions on (1) work values and (2) outcomes. For each of the five models estimated unions exerted the hypothesized indirect effects on facet satisfaction.

> Unions had a positive indirect affect [sic] on pay satisfaction by increasing values toward pay outcomes, as well as by increasing hourly wages and the probability of receiving several fringe benefits. Unions had negative effect on satisfaction with both supervision and co-worker by altering perceived supervisory behavior. Unions decrease satisfaction with work itself through decreased task scope perceptions. Finally, unions decrease promotion satisfaction through negative effects on promotion values (Berger et al., 1983, p. 318).

Berger et al. (1983) further conclude that unions exert more powerful effects on work outcomes (i.e., pay, benefits, job scope) than on work values and that unions emphasize traditional bread-and-butter areas at the expense of concern for job design and career development. Berger et al.'s (1983) conclusions are strengthened by two studies that either replicate or confirm their findings. First, Kirmeyer and Shirom (1986) re-examined data from the 1977 *Quality of Employment Survey* and found that unionized individuals reported less autonomy than non-unionized workers. This finding is consistent with the formalization of decision making in unionized environments (e.g., Gallagher, 1983). Second, Evans and Ondrack (1990) have reported on a replication of Berger et al.'s (1983) analysis for two facet satisfactions: satisfaction with pay and satisfaction with the work itself. Based on data from a random survey of 1193 male, blue-collar workers, Evans and Ondrack (1990) found that the effect of unions on satisfaction with work is mediated by the union effect on job complexity. Specifically, union members report that their jobs have less autonomy, task identity, skill variety, task significance, and feedback than non-unionized workers. Second, unionization had a significant positive impact on satisfaction with pay. Although this effect was not mediated by actual pay or pay-need strength, the authors point out that they did not measure the full set of compensation outcomes addressed by Berger et al. (1983). Specifically, Evans and Ondrack (1990) were unable to determine the effect of unions on fringe benefits as a mediator of the unionization-pay satisfaction relationship.

Job satisfaction is probably the single most studied variable in organizational psychology (Locke, 1983). Despite the extensive empirical work focusing on the measurement, causes, correlates, and consequences of job satisfaction, the effect of unions and collective bargaining on job satisfaction has been largely overlooked by organizational psychologists. It is in this sense that Barling (1988) warned about constructing a truncated body of literature. Theories of job satisfaction that do not consider the role of unions may not be relevant to unionized environments. Alternately, to the extent that organizational psychologists identify job satisfaction as a cause of absenteeism or turnover, unionization may be an unmeasured third variable that substantially affects the posited relationship.

Consistent with Kochan's (1980) model of collective bargaining outcomes, studies of the unionization-job satisfaction relationship have suggested that the effect of unions on job satisfaction is mediated by the relationship between unions and working conditions. Specifically, unionization is associated with lower autonomy, task complexity, task significance, and feedback. At least one unanswered question is the direction of this relationship. While unionization is associated with less satisfying working conditions, it is unclear whether such dissatisfaction is a result of a union voice effect (e.g., Freeman & Medoff, 1984), or of management reacting to unionization by the development of narrow job descriptions and increased reliance on routinization in the workplace. Alternately, job dissatisfaction has been identified as a precursor to unionization (e.g., Barling, Laliberte, Fullagar, & Kelloway, 1990; Brett, 1980; Premack & Hunter, 1988). Accordingly, the relationship between union membership status and job satisfaction may reflect the unions' success or failure in redressing the specific dissatisfactions that led to unionization.

Stressors, Stress, and Strain

While not widely researched, there are conceptual reasons to suggest that unions and the practice of industrial relations have consequences in terms of individual stress and strain. First, unions negotiate contract provisions that directly affect working conditions (Slichter et al., 1960). Management may react by implementing more formal policies and standardized job descriptions (Gallagher, 1983). The result of such increased formalization may be experienced as a reduction in role ambiguity and increase in role conflict, two components of role stress (Kahn, Wolfe, Quinn, Snoek, & Rosenthal, 1964). Empirical support for these suggestions emerged from Odewhan and Petty's (1980) study of 178 hospitals aides. In their initial analysis, union members reported higher job tension and anxiety, higher role conflict, and decreased perceptions of personal competence when compared to non-unionized employees. No significant differences emerged for role ambiguity. Unfortunately, there is no clear interpretation of these findings as the initial differences became nonsignificant after controlling for demographic variables (education, organizational tenure, and position tenure). The differences, however, were still in the hypothesized directions (Odewhan & Petty, 1980). Shirom and Kirmeyer (1988) found that union members experienced more inter-role conflict and more role ambiguity than nonmembers. Moreover, union membership moderated the relationship between role stressors and strain (somatic complaints), with members who saw the union as being effective reporting lower levels of both stress and strain (Shirom & Kirmeyer, 1988).

Aside from the effect of unions on working conditions, the practice of industrial relations, which involves elements of both conflict and change, may be inherently stressful (Bluen & Barling, 1987, 1988). Empirical evidence suggests that the conflict and uncertainty surrounding strikes (Barling & Milligan, 1987; MacBride, Lancee, & Freeman, 1981) and collective bargaining (Bluen & Jubiler-Lurie, 1990) produces psychological distress. In both cases the psychological distress was still evident three months (Bluen & Jubiler-Lurie, 1990) and six months (Barling & Milligan, 1987; MacBride et al., 1981) later. Similarly, involvement in cooperative union-management ventures may be stressful for the individuals involved (Driscoll, 1981). That is, union leaders who engaged in cooperative ventures report that their cooperation with management conflicts with the adversarial stance expected of them by their members.

The effect of industrial relations on individual strain may be substantially determined by the individual's position in the union and the stage of the unionization process. As discussed earlier (see Chapter 6), Nicholson (1976) reports that a majority of shop stewards experienced moderate to severe role overload in addition to other role stressors. Bluen and Barling (1988) have extended this analysis and identified stressors relevant to union leaders, shop stewards, rank-and-file union members, upper management, supervisors, and industrial relations managers. Across these roles, different stressors may emerge during the establishment of a union-management relationship, administration of a collective agreement, as well as during breakdowns in the union-management relation. While the theory of industrial relations stressors is comparatively well developed (e.g., Bluen & Barling, 1987, 1988) there is a need for research that examines the propositions of the theory in contexts other than those of strikes and negotiations.

Job Security

Earlier we reviewed suggestions that unions increase job security for their members by the negotiation of seniority benefit clauses and the provision of grievance systems (Kochan, 1980; Kochan & Helfman, 1981). These lines of evidence suggest that unions increase *objective* job security. Yet from the standpoint of organizational psychology, job security is a *perception* (Johnson, Bobko, & Hartenian, 1986). In particular, job insecurity is a perception that arises through the severity of the threat to one's job and the powerlessness to counteract this threat (Ashford, Lee, & Bobko, 1987; Greenhalgh & Rosenblatt, 1984). It is perceptions of the valence (importance) and likelihood of job loss that define a threat (Ashford et al., 1989) and the perception of powerlessness that defines job insecurity. Given that unions influence objective job security, how might they influence perceptions of it?

Johnson et al. (1988) have examined this question in their survey of union members representing twenty-six unions who were attending a labor school. Based on their analysis, job insecurity was negatively associated with satisfaction with the union and membership in an industrial rather than a craft union. (Women and married individuals reported more job insecurity than men and single respondents.) In contradiction to Kochan's (1980) suggestions, the perceived power of the union and specific contract provisions negotiated by the union (i.e., provisions for advance notice of layoffs, restricted competition through regulation of contracting out, job protection, and financial assistance) had no significant effect on respondents' perceptions of job insecurity. Thus, although provisions dealing with advance notice of layoffs, restricted competition, and supplemental unemployment benefits correlated with perceptions of job insecurity, only respondents' knowledge of supplemental unemployment benefit provisions emerged as a significant predictor of job insecurity in the regression analyses. Interpretation of these findings is limited by the lack of data presented that would allow for assessment of collinearity among the predictor variables chosen. However, these results do suggest that although unions may reduce perceptions of job insecurity through negotiation of contract provisions, the effect is not large.

Johnson et al. (1988) suggest that unions may influence job insecurity more directly by the unions' short-term behavior in countering specific threats. Thus the union effect may not emerge through the negotiation of contract provisions *per se* (which are long term and typically not directed at an immediate threat) but rather through the enforcement of existing contract provisions. Research focusing on survivor reactions to layoffs (e.g., Brockner, 1988) offers some indirect support for this hypothesis. In particular, this line of research suggests that the stress experienced by survivors of layoffs may be occasioned by (1) job insecurity, (2) perceived injustice and (3) anger and guilt (Brockner, 1988). By enforcing provisions regarding layoffs and seniorities, unions may act to substantially reduce perceptions of inequity. Moreover, the union may play a "watchdog" role which ensures that union members see the layoffs and/or management to be legitimate. Thus, unions may reduce both job insecurity and the stress associated with job insecurity.

The preceding discussion has expanded on Freeman and Medoff's (1984) conclusion that the effect of unions is pervasive, affecting almost all aspects of organizational functioning. Consistent with Kochan's (1980) model, we have suggested that unions have primary effects in the areas of wages, benefits, working conditions, and job security. Managerial reactions to the increased costs associated with unionization substantially determine the nature and strength of the secondary outcomes of turnover, absenteeism, and individual attitudes and satisfactions. The implications of these conclusions for organizational psychology are clear. Although the role of unions in shaping organizational behavior is often overlooked, the findings presented here suggest that unions may serve as a determinant of behaviors and attitudes of interest to organizational psychology. Moreover, because unions may affect multiple behaviors, the presence of a union may be an unmeasured third variable in organizational research. Failure to consider the role of unions in shaping organizational behavior may lead to the promulgation of misspecified models and the development of a knowledge base not directly applicable to unionized environments.

Methodological Issues in Studying the Effects of Unions on Organizational Behavior

Most of the literature dealing with union influences on organizational behavior is based on an economic research tradition of union impact research. Gallagher (1983) has identified several methodological issues that substantially limit the conclusions that we may draw from union impact research. The direction of causal relationships, the reliance on dichotomous measures of unionization as proxy measures, the existence of spillover effects, and the limited amount of available data all act to limit the interpretation of the research findings reviewed here.

First, it is not clear whether unionization is a cause or a consequence of organizational behavior, or both. As Gallagher (1983) points out, the higher wages, decreased turnover, and improved working conditions associated with unionism may be either a result of collective bargaining as suggested by Kochan (1980), or a reflection of the fact that unions tend to concentrate their organizational efforts in stable, high-wage industries. Similarly, it is unclear whether job satisfaction is a cause or a result of unionization or both. Studies of individual unionization decisions (e.g., Brett, 1980; Premack & Hunter, 1988) treat job dissatisfaction as a *causal* factor in the decision to unionize, while union impact studies (e.g., Freeman & Medoff, 1984; Kochan & Helfman, 1981) treat job satisfaction as a *result* of union activities. Perhaps the resolution of this issue is found in considering the maturity of the bargaining relationship. For example, in long-established bargaining relationships it is unlikely that current job dissatisfaction can be treated as a cause of unionization activities that occurred some time previously. It should be recognized in this context that most union members do not actually vote for a union but rather join pre-existing unions as a condition of employment. It is unlikely, therefore, that job dissatisfaction can be treated as a cause of unionization for members of long-established bargaining relationships. For such members, job dissatisfaction may properly be viewed as an outcome of collective bargaining.

Most of the studies reviewed here have treated unionization as a simple dichotomous variable (i.e., union member vs. nonmember). This practice has several limitations. First, as Gallagher (1983) notes, the practice of treating unionization as a dichotomous variable obscures differences between newly organized and well-established unions. Yet newly organized unions and well-established ones have substantially different goals, with the latter's goals and objectives being influenced by their collective bargaining history in a particular firm. In particular, the politicization of the workforce cited as a cause of decreased job satisfaction in union members is a plausible explanation for new but not for well-established unions. New unions may raise individual awareness of specific dissatisfactions as a means of gaining recognition and negotiating a first collective agreement. For more established unions, such a strategy may backfire in drawing attention to the failure or inability of the union to redress specific dissatisfactions through previous rounds of collective bargaining.

A second problem with the use of a dichotomous classification arises from the observation that union effects do not accrue equally to all union members. At one level, unions are more responsive to the needs of the more senior union members (Kochan, 1980). One would expect, therefore, that senior and junior employees may experience differential union effects. Similarly, many explanations advanced for union effects rely on the exit-voice paradigm (Hirschman, 1970). For example, the reduction in voluntary turnover associated with unionization is often attributed to the provision of union-voice mechanisms such as grievance systems (e.g., Freeman & Medoff, 1984). The voice explanation presupposes that the presence of a voice mechanism is synonymous with its use. Yet disaffected union members may not trust or use such mechanisms. The consistent finding that union commitment is a correlate and precursor of participation in union activities (e.g., Fullagar & Barling, 1989; Kelloway et al., 1990) suggests that non committed union members are less likely to participate in the activities of the union, including use of the grievance procedure (Kelloway & Catano, 1989). This observation is particularly relevant given that most union members never have the opportunity of deciding whether to vote for a union. They join a union as a condition of employment. Enforced membership may not generate the same commitment (and indeed may generate precisely the opposite attitudes) as voluntary choice of union membership. Accordingly, a focus on membership status may obscure individual differences that substantially moderate the hypothesized effects.

The reliance on a dichotomous variable to represent unionization has grown out of an economic research tradition that relies on macro-level data and is encouraged by the re-analysis of large micro-level data sets that contain information on membership status. A more psychologically sound approach to the study of union effects would focus on individual perceptions of union power (e.g., Hammer, 1978), union instrumentality (e.g., Fullagar & Barling, 1989; Kelloway et al., 1990), and individual attachment/loyalty to the union (Gordon et al., 1980).

The same economic tradition that has led to a reliance on the use of union membership data has resulted in a research base largely focused on inter-firm or inter-industry comparisons. Such comparisons are made more difficult by the existence of "spillover" effects whereby non-unionized firms attempt to provide the same benefits as unionized firms in attempts to stave off unionization campaigns. The existence of such spillover effects reduces the magnitude of empirically derived union effects. A related problem stemming from the reliance on establishment level data is that intra-firm influences are not identified. It is to be hoped that the recognition of potential union effects will lead to the publication of more studies that can identify salient intra-firm and individual characteristics that moderate or mediate the influence of unions on organizational psychology.

Finally, many of the effects reviewed above have limited empirical support. There has simply not been enough research interest in the influence of unions on organizational behavior to fully understand these effects. This problem is compounded by the re-analysis of large data sets at the expense of collecting new data. Even when union influences are identified, the generalizability of the effects remains in question. The limited literature available suggests clearly that unionization does have an effect on organizational behavior. The strength, direction, and moderating influences of these effects have not been adequately addressed in the existing literature and remain as a challenge for future research.

Some Implications of Unionization for Organizational Psychology

There are at least two major implications of unionization for organizational psychology. First, research and practice in the more traditional areas of organizational psychology should be conducted with an awareness of the potential impact of unions on relevant variables. Second, the existence of unions provides organizational psychologists with a host of new research questions that further the understanding of organizational behavior. Both implications are predicated on the integration of collective bargaining and organizational psychology research.

As the preceding discussion indicates, the collective bargaining relationship has a variety of effects on variables relevant to the study of organizational psychology. Absenteeism, turnover, job satisfaction, role stress, and job security have all been identified as outcomes of collective bargaining. Given these findings, it behooves researchers to be aware of, and report, the union status of their samples (Barling, 1988). Identification of data collected in unionized and non-unionized environments would allow for assessments of both the generalizability of the research findings and the potential moderating effects of union membership. This suggestion assumes increasing importance when both the predictor and the criterion that are the focus of the research effort are both affected by union membership (e.g., the job satisfaction-turnover or job satisfaction-absenteeism relationship). Given the identification of research settings as unionized or non-unionized, meta-analytic techniques (e.g., Hunter, Schmidt, & Jackson, 1982) could profitably be used to ascertain the moderating effect of unions on such relationships. Alternately, individual studies could include measures of perceived union power or perceived union instrumentality and examine the impact of such perceptions on organizational behavior (e.g., Hammer, 1978).

An alternate and complementary approach is to focus on the host of research questions that arise as a consequence of unionization. What is the impact of unionization on management decision making or on supervisory behavior? What features of the collective bargaining relationship lead to consequences in terms of organizational behavior? What role do union leaders and shop stewards play in the organization? In addition to the impact of unionization on organizational behavior, the presence of a union in the workplace allows for new forms of organizational behavior such as grievance filing. In contrast to the more traditional areas of inquiry, however, the operation and consequences of grievance filing are poorly understood (Gordon & Johnson, 1982). Recognizing the conceptual implications of unionization for organizational behavior presents both new ways of looking at traditional research topics and new research questions that to date have gone unanswered.

Conclusion

Finally, Kochan and Helfman (1980) point out that identification of union–non-union differentials is only the starting point in understanding the implications of unionization and collective bargaining.

> The key information that is needed to guide public policy and private practice is not the average union effect but what causes variations in the performance of unions and employers under collective bargaining.

Providing this information is a task well suited to organizational psychology.

9

Concluding Thoughts
and Challenges

As we have indicated, our primary aim in writing this book was to illustrate how a knowledge of organizational psychology and unions could be enhanced by an understanding of each other. It is appropriate at this stage to examine the extent to which this aim was realized.

The Process of Unionization

We started off with the premise that the practice of equating unionization with voting for a union, or joining a union, is both inaccurate and counter productive. Based on available data within organizational psychology, we argued that voting for, or joining a union, was neither the first nor the final phase of the unionization process. Instead, from a psychological perspective, the understanding of why people would vote for or join a union would be strengthened by considering prior determinants such as early family socialization experiences. Likewise, the process of unionization extends well past the initial decision to vote for, or join, a union. The influence of structural characteristics and union leadership on members' attitudes and behaviors was also considered. After becoming a union member, the individual then decides whether to offer his or her loyalty to the union, whether or not to participate in union activities, and the extent of that participation. Ultimately, under certain conditions, individuals can collectively decertify their bargaining unit or individually resign their membership. Just as the influence of family socialization early in the unionization process is acknowledged, the role of union leadership is emphasized once the individual has joined the union. Thus, even Klandermans' (1986) description of participation as "joining, acting, quitting" (p. 189) fails to capture critical components of the unionization process such as commitment and leadership.

Each of these phases of the total unionization process was examined sequentially throughout this book. In doing so, we found that there were some remarkably common themes that dominate the various phases of unionization. An examination of these themes or similarities is important in the extent to which they can advance an understanding of unionization as a continuous process.

Whether considering the individual decision to vote for or against a union in certification (Chapter 3) or decertification elections (Chapter 7), to offer one's commitment and loyalty to the union (Chapter 4), or to participate actively in union activities (Chapter 5), the data are unequivocal: Individuals are far more likely to manifest pro-union attitudes and engage in pro-union behaviors if they believe that an improvement in their own general working conditions will result. From a conceptual perspective, therefore, the notions of instrumentality and rationality are strongly supported. At this stage, we echo DeCotiis and LeLouarn's (1981) conclusion that perceived union instrumentality is the "fulcrum" of the unionization process.

Deshpande and Fiorito (1989) introduced a useful conceptual distinction when they differentiated between "specific" and "general" union attitudes. Specific union attitudes concern the attitudes and beliefs about a particular union; as such, we argue that they are similar to beliefs about the instrumentality of the particular union. In contrast, "general" union attitudes involve attitudes and beliefs about organized labor. General and specific union attitudes are not necessarily correlated. However, research shows consistently that general union attitudes also fulfill a vital role in the unionization process. Certainly, general union attitudes are a major predictor of the decision to vote for or against a union (Getman et al., 1976). Likewise, general union attitudes are implicated in the development of commitment to, and participation in the union.

Two conclusions are appropriate in comparing the effects of specific and general union attitudes. First, specific union attitudes exert direct effects on the unionization process. In contrast, general union attitudes tend to exert indirect effects, often through their effects on specific union attitudes (i.e., instrumentality beliefs; see Barling, Laliberte, Fullagar, & Kelloway, 1990). Second, the effects of specific union attitudes are somewhat stronger than those of general union beliefs.

Increasingly, union leaders are becoming concerned over both membership attitudes toward unions and the deteriorating public image of labor (Craft & Abboushi, 1983). Negative attitudes toward unions are believed to affect crucial union activities and, more specifically, the process of attachment to labor unions. Many union leaders believe that the image of labor affects not only organizing efforts, but also bargaining effectiveness and political activity (Craft & Abboushi, 1983). Several labor organizations (e.g., the AFL-CIO) have undertaken activities and developed programs to redress the negative image of labor. However, both specific (i.e., instrumentality perceptions) and general (i.e., "big labor" image) union attitudes have always been treated as predictor or antecedent variables. Extensive research now needs to be undertaken to ascertain the causes of specific and general attitudes to unions, to broaden our conceptual understanding, and to provide labor organizations with some guidance regarding the focus of any programs aimed at improving the image of labor. Recent research, for example, has indicated that pre-employment union socialization influences (Barling, Kelloway, & Bremermann, 1991), and early union socialization experiences (Fullagar, McCoy, & Shull, 1992) are important determinants of individual attitudes toward unions. Unions can have little impact on pre-union socialization experiences, but can exert considerable control over the socialization experiences of new members.

In attempting to understand all aspects of the unionization process, job dissatisfaction has probably attracted more theoretical attention and empirical scrutiny than any other variable. Unlike general and specific union attitudes, whose effects across the unionization process are consistent, job dissatisfaction fulfills several different roles in the unionization process. Job dissatisfaction is a necessary but insufficient cause of the decision to vote for a union in a certification election. In contrast, job dissatisfaction is neither a necessary nor a sufficient factor in the decision to vote in favor of the bargaining unit in a decertification election. Both these findings can be explained in terms of the instrumentality and rationality of the decision to seek and retain union representation. When individuals are dissatisfied with their jobs, they will vote for, or join, a union that is perceived as being capable of resolving that dissatisfaction. However, regardless of the level of job dissatisfaction, unionized members are unlikely to vote to retain the bargaining unit in a decertification election if it is perceived to be ineffective.

In contrast to the findings relating general and specific union attitudes to commitment and participation, the findings are not as consistent as those relating job dissatisfaction to certification and decertification elections. Certainly, studies show that job dissatisfaction (Fullagar & Barling, 1989) and job satisfaction (Joseph & Dharmangadan, 1987) predict union commitment, and that there is no relationship (e.g., Barling, Wade, & Fullagar, 1990). The most plausible explanation for the latter two findings is that the union was not perceived as capable of resolving the particular facets of dissatisfaction that were considered salient to the individual members.

Throughout the unionization literature, there has been a tendency for researchers to be seduced by demographic correlates of the unionization process. We see these as epiphenomenal effects, in that they are indicators of more fundamental, underlying processes that have been alluded to in the research but seldom focused on and never empirically confirmed. As one case in point, there are differences between blacks and whites in the propensity to unionize (see Chapter 3) and in the development of union loyalty (see Chapter 4). We argued consistently throughout the book and elsewhere (Fullagar & Barling, 1989), however, that such findings are not a function of racial differences *per se*. Instead, racial discrimination continues, and results in blacks and whites experiencing different workplace conditions. Hence, any racial differences are not attributable to demographic characteristics, but rather to the experience of social and workplace discrimination by black individuals.

Let us also look at the research that has emphasized gender differences in unionization levels, and union attitudes and beliefs. Several studies have established that there are fewer female union members than males, and various factors have been hypothesized to explain this difference: discrimination in the workplace, lower levels of commitment to full-time work, less employment in male-dominated and traditionally unionized industries, conflict between union and family responsibilities, and gender-based differences in desire for union representation (see Fiorito & Greer, 1982). Yet inferring an effect of gender on union-related variables is confounded by the association of gender with other determinants of unionism such as occupational effects and job-related issues. Kochan (1979) found that when these factors were controlled, traditional gender differences in union preference were no longer evident, and that women were as willing to join unions as men. A similar finding was derived by Fiorito and Greer (1986, pp. 161–162) who conclude that

> Gender differences in union membership and other unionism measures can be attributed to factors other than gender per se ... In other words, explanations for gender-related variation in unionism measures can be found in terms of labor force attachment, industrial and occupational distributions, exposure to or experiences with unions, different levels of satisfaction and particular job facets, and similar factors that may vary with gender. One implication of these findings is that gender differences in unionism measures will diminish as occupational and industrial distributions become more gender-neutral.

As a result, and as noted throughout, we question whether continuing to investigate whether demographic characteristics can provide any useful information for understanding the unionization process. Furthermore, we believe that attempts to identify a "union type" are not only fruitless, but also ethically questionable.

Unlike previous considerations of the unionization process (e.g., Fiorito et al., 1986), we explicitly included the role of union leadership due to its influence on members' union attitudes and behavior. Undoubtedly, union leadership, and in particular the behavior of shop stewards, affects union members in areas considered critical for union functioning, such as the filing of grievances and the socialization of new members. Nonetheless, the influence of union leadership on micro-level variables, such as grievance filing, and union attitudes remains one of the least researched components of the unionization process (together with decertification and union quitting). Future research should certainly focus in greater detail on both leadership and decertification. In any such research, it would be useful to address the relative contribution of the different predictors of unionization. As one example, Barling, Kelloway, Bremermann (1991) showed that early family socialization influences were twice as great as those of work beliefs. Such information has both conceptual and pragmatic appeal.

Thus, it is clear that a knowledge of organizational psychology can advance our conceptual understanding of the process of unionization. In addition, this expanded awareness of the total unionization process could also be of practical benefit to those whose aim is to enhance workplace democracy and improve working conditions. While we argue that this psychological perspective is both an important and necessary one, by itself it is insufficient. We warn against an exclusive and restrictive psychological approach that would view union members as existing in isolation from the social context in which the union system occurs. Such an approach does an injustice to the extent to which an understanding of industrial relations has benefited from economic and legal analyses, as well as the extent to which psychologists in general emphasize the role of environmental factors in understanding individual behavior. Any comprehensive understanding of the unionization process will only be achieved through a multi-disciplinary focus. Accordingly, throughout this book, we adopted a broader focus by concentrating both on an individual level of analysis together with a macro-level analysis that included the effects of group and structural factors.

At the outset, we also suggested that the belief that we could obtain a comprehensive understanding of organizational behavior without simultaneously considering the unionization process was simplistic. The evidence offered in Chapter 8 and elsewhere (e.g., Freeman & Medoff, 1984; Katz et al., 1985) is consistent in illustrating the effects of unions on organizational functioning and behavior, and the impact of industrial relations systems on organizational effectiveness. Research that attempts to integrate organizational and union functioning, therefore, can be of both theoretical and methodological benefit to both fields. We have gone further and argued that an understanding of organizational psychology is inadequate if it ignores the impact of labor unions on employees' attitudes and behaviors.

Some Remaining Challenges

Accepting that the unionization process extends well beyond voting for or joining a union, and that individuals' attitudes and behavior influence the unionization process and vice versa, we can identify several conceptual, practical, and methodological challenges for the future.

Conceptual Challenges

Throughout this text, we have limited our focus to unions vis-à-vis their role regarding workplace conditions. Such a perspective, however, does not do justice to the full range of issues to which unions address their attention. Although they are a prominent focus of American unions, workplace conditions reflect only one issue unions have applied themselves to. Specifically, unions have also expanded their bargaining agendas to include social issues. By the begining of the 1990s, for example, the Canadian Automobile Workers and the United Steelworkers of America had each negotiated provisions in many collective agreements whereby employers contribute an amount per worker per hour that goes into the union's social fund. These monies are then used for activities as diverse as supporting child-care centers, soup kitchens, and anti-poverty programs in third-world countries. However, their focus remains primarily directed at "business" issues.

In contrast, consistent with a "radical" perspective (Bluen, 1986), many unions have fundamental societal change as their major bargaining issue. Dramatic recent examples of this "social unionism" include the union movement in Poland and South Africa. The extent to which "social unionism" transcends traditional workplace issues can be understood from a statement by the National Union of Mineworkers (NUM), one of the three largest unions in South Africa (Barrett & Mullins, 1990):

> There can be no justice, no decent life, for South African mineworkers except under a people's government. . . . The trade union struggle cannot be seen in isolation from the political struggle. . . . The strategy of the NUM is based on an understanding of all these factors. It sees itself as part of the struggle for liberation (Middleton, 1990, p. 14).

One important conceptual question that emerges is whether the knowledge base gained from investigating "business unionism" is generalizable to "social unionism." Although the data available from which to answer this question are scarce, we argue that specific and general union beliefs would predict the unionization process, irrespective of the union's aims. Indeed, one reason for the current popularity of black trade unions in South Africa is the extent to which they make socio-political issues, such as the abolition of apartheid, their priority, and the successes they have achieved (Middleton, 1990). Certainly, Fiorito (1987) documented how pro-union voting intentions were increased when workers perceive the union as high in political instrumentality. In addition, Fullagar and Barling (1989) found that when black union members were disadvantaged with respect to social and political conditions, life dissatisfaction predicted union loyalty if the union was perceived as instrumental in resolving these non-workplace issues.

Research Challenges

The argument that unionization is not synonymous with union membership has important consequences for theory and research. From a theoretical perspective, we have argued consistently that after joining a union, the level of members' commitment and participation varies. This also has critical research implications for the design and conduct of research on the unionization process. To date, the vast body of research focusing on the effects of unionization has invariably contrasted union members and nonmembers. Such an approach, however, totally ignores the considerable variability in attitudes and behaviors of union members (e.g., Freeman & Medoff, 1984). This omission is potentially serious, because it can be argued that any effects of union membership may be *underestimated* by ignoring the variability in union members' attitudes and behaviors. In trying to understand the causes and consequences of union membership and unionization, a different research strategy may be required. Instead of taking a between-group approach and contrasting union members and nonmembers, it may be more profitable to utilize a within-group approach that directly focuses on the effects of variations in commitment and participation on organizational outcomes.

Another research priority concerns the conceptualization and operationalization of perceived union instrumentality. In our analysis of individual attachment to labor organizations, we have emphasized the critical role of perceived union instrumentality. Fiorito (1987) has suggested the utility of broadening the concept of union instrumentality by including perceptions of the union's instrumentality: "Union instrumentality is multifaceted: It has economic and noneconomic facets, workplace-level and political facets" (pp. 285–286). The results of Fiorito's (1987) study show that worker' perceptions of high union political instrumentality have a significant and positive impact on pro-union voting intention. Given that labor organizations are extending their functions and activities not only to include economic, bread-and-butter issues, but also non-economic (e.g., child care and family benefits) and political activity, broadening the conceptualization and operationalization of union instrumentality has implications for the way we perceive unions and the reasons why individuals become attached to them.

One area of considerable debate among social psychologists that is particularly relevant in understanding individual attachment to unions is the relationship between attitudes and behavior. We have attempted to show that both instrumental and general attitudes toward unions affect all stages of the unionization process and that there is a growing body of research to indicate this. However, if union attitudes play such a prominent role in determining the process of unionization, then further research is required that ascertains the causes and predictors of such attitudes. Furthermore, Krahn and Lowe (1984) point out that research on union attitudes has low external validity because (1) research is focused on unionized employees of single organizations in a specific sector of the economy, and (2) most research has been focused on American and, to a lesser degree British, workers. Consequently, future research needs to assess the extent of cross-national differences in union attitudes and how they relate to variations in industrial relations.

Practical Challenges

Needless to say, several practical challenges will have to be confronted in the years ahead. We suggested in Chapter 4 that perceptions of union-management relationship play an important role in determining both commitment to the union and the company. There are indications that the nature of the relationship between labor unions and management is undergoing a fundamental change, as are the issues that rank-and-file union members want to see form part of the bargaining agenda. The 1980s were witness to a trend in collective bargaining toward concession bargaining and an increase in labor-management cooperation and quality of working life (QWL) programs. (By QWL, we mean cooperative attempts by management and labor to increase employee participation at all levels of organizational decision making.) Forecasts suggest that such trends will continue in the 1990s (Katz, 1985). The process of collective bargaining has also changed. Katz (1985) reports that in the United States economic pressures have produced a decentralization of bargaining (especially in the auto, rubber, and steel industries). As a result, issues are being resolved at a company- or plant-level, rather than at a national or industry level to a greater extent.

At the same time a change has occurred in labor-management relations to enhance union-management cooperation and for both parties to define problems and examine new approaches to these problems by sharing relevant information. This is very different from the centralized, distributive, and pattern bargaining of the postwar period. Katz (1985) also notes that the structure of management has also changed in that the industrial relations function in many organizations has become subsumed under more general human resources management. This obviously has a direct impact on industrial/organizational psychologists whose major professional and vocational outlet is in human resources departments. More and more, such departments are having to deal with industrial relations and labor issues. Consequently, there is an increasing pressure to consider labor unions in the training and education of I/O psychologists, where previously this has been an area of neglect.

Communication between management and labor also became more direct in an attempt to change the expectations of workers (Katz, 1985). Furthermore, the outcomes of collective bargaining also altered toward a greater emphasis on profit-sharing schemes and other forms of contingent compensation, greater job security and plant-closing moratoriums, and efforts at labor-management cooperation. Obviously, such changes in the process and outcomes of collective bargaining have an impact on the roles of the actors involved, and affect the behaviors and attitudes of both workers and management. As Kochan, Katz, and Mower (1985, p. 271) point out;

> The growth of quality-of-work-life (QWL) programs, related forms of worker participation, and experiments with new forms of work organization have posed both challenges and opportunities to the American labor movement. On the one hand, these informal mechanisms require union leaders and managers to modify their traditional roles and relationships in significant ways. On the other hand, they open new channels for direct worker involvement, and, possibly, for greater worker and union influence.

In a survey of more than 900 rank-and-file members from five local unions, Kochan et al. (1985) found that there was considerable interest among workers in QWL issues, even when compared to interest expressed in bread-and-butter and strategic issues. This represents a fundamental change. A decade earlier, union members ranked job enrichment and other quality of worklife attempts as being of very low priority (Giles & Holley, 1978). Adapting to new demands from rank-and-files will present something of a challenge both for union leadership as well as management.

Importantly, union participation in QWL programs did not have a negative impact on membership perceptions of the union. In fact, member's perceptions of their union's performance improved when (1) the union was seen as a joint partner in the QWL process, (2) QWL was perceived as improving work organization, enhancing job security, and increasing organizational performance, (3) QWL issues were linked to other collective bargaining agendas, and (4) the union was still seen as protecting its membership's bread-and-butter concerns. What this study emphasizes, therefore, is that participation in QWL programs by unions has an impact on member attitudes and that, again, perceptions of union instrumentality are important predictors of the effectiveness of such programs. Organizational psychologists could make a valuable contribution by detailing under what circumstances QWL programs work for the union and exactly what the impact of such programs is on the organizational performance, union attitudes, and union participation of members and nonmembers.

These QWL programs also present a challenge to unions inasmuch as they require different leadership skills and training for local labor leaders in such areas as group dynamics, problem solving, and team building. However, exactly which leadership characteristics and styles facilitate worker participation and the success of QWL programs has yet to be determined. The QWL efforts usually entail work reorganization and a change from the traditional job control that U.S. workers are used to. As Kochan et al. (1985) note, this impacts on all parties because it "implies a movement toward a more proactive form of labor-management relations based around joint research and analysis, planning, and consultation" (p. 303). For the worker, this work redesign usually means greater job variety, responsibility, autonomy, and opportunities for skill enhancement and acquisition. The union is required to exchange some of its traditional sources of power for greater influence over a broader range of issues. For its part, management has to concede some of its control and become more flexible in its human resources management and redesign its role.

As we noted in Chapter 8, unions have an effect on an organization's pay level, form, structure, and system (see also Balkin, 1989). This effect has been traditionally applied through distributive collective bargaining based on an adversarial union-management relationship. However, the decline in union membership has caused some U.S. unions to alter their adversarial posture and engage in cooperative efforts with management to establish innovative pay policies in order to adjust to an environment that is legally and economically uncertain. Examples of these pay policies include *skill-based pay*, where employees are rewarded for acquiring new job skills; *two-tiered pay plans*, whereby workers already employed by the company have a higher pay rate than those who are newly hired; and *comparable worth* pay policies that are based on pay equity and established through processes of job evaluation and analysis. Balkin (1989) has indicated that research is needed to ascertain the affect of unions on the adoption of innovative pay policies. We recommend that research also investigates the impact of such pay schemes on unions and member attachment to labor organizations.

The extent to which the unionization processes can be understood from the perspective of organizational psychology is illustrated in the preceding chapters. Accepting the necessity of additional basic psychological research for an understanding of the unionization process, we contend that a more meaningful test for organizational psychology exists. Specifically, it is now up to organizational psychology to demonstrate that its knowledge base and its interventions can be used to advance the functional efficiency of unions as organizations. In addition, knowledge from organizational psychology should also be used to enhance the unionization process, thereby benefiting both the union and the individual member. Technically, organizational psychology is well suited to this task. Its focus has traditionally been on maximizing the functional efficiency of organizations and the attitudes and behaviors of its members. It is now time for organizational psychology to include unions in its focus on organizations.

Appendix

Extent to Which Union-related Issues Are Covered in Leading Organizational Psychology Textbooks

Authors	Title and Year	Total	Union
Baron	*Behavior in Organizations*, 1983	567	2
Bass/Barrett	*People, Work, Organizations* (2nd ed.), 1981	657	3
Beck	*Applying Psychology: Understanding People* 1982	461	0
Beer/Spector/Lawrence Mills/Walton	*Human Resource Management: A General Manager's Perspective*, 1985	782	18
Bowditch/Buono	*A Primer on Organizational Behavior* (2nd ed.), 1990	373	1
Cascio	*Applied Psychology in Personnel Management*, 1978	373	5
Cohen/Fink/Gadon/ Willits	*Effective Behavior in Organizations*, 1980	713	0
Cohen/Fink/Gadon Willits	*Effective Behavior in Organizations* (4th ed.), 1988	943	0
Daft	*Organization Theory and Design* (2nd ed.), 1986	571	0
Daft/Steers	*Organizations: A Micro/Macro Approach*, 1986	598	3
Davis/Newstrom	*Human Behavior at Work: Organizational Behavior* (7th ed.), 1985	552	64
Davis/Newstrom	*Organizational Behavior: Readings and Exercises* (7th ed.), 1985	552	0
Dessler	*Organizational Theory: Integrating Structure and Behavior* (2nd ed.), 1986	472	0
Donnelly/Gibson/ Ivancevich	*Fundamentals of Management* (5th ed.), 1984	780	0
DuBrin	*Foundations of Organizational Behavior An Applied Perspective*	476	1
Feldman/Arnold	*Managing Individual and Group Behavior in Organizations*, 1983	595	11
Gerloff	*Organizational Theory and Design*, 1985	367	0
Gibson/Ivancevich/ Donnelly	*Organizations: Behavior, Structures and Processes* (6th ed.), 1988	807	2
Gray/Starke	*Organizational Behavior: Concepts and Applications* (4th ed.), 1988	703	14

Authors	Title and Year	Total	Union
Hall	*Organizations: Structures, Processes Outcomes* (4th ed.), 1987	314	1
von Haller Gilmer	*Applied Psychology: Adjustments in Life and Work* (2nd ed.), 1975	426	4
von Haller Gilmer/ Deci	*Industrial and Organizational Psychology* (4th ed.), 1977	453	18
Hampton/Summer/ Webber	*Organizational Behavior and the Practice of Management* (5th ed.), 1987	853	6
Hellriegel/Slocum	*Organizational Behavior* (2nd ed.), 1979	687	3
Hellriegel/Slocum/ Woodman	*Organizational Behavior* (4th ed.), 1986	631	0
Hellriegel/Slocum/ Woodman	*Organizational Behavior* (5th ed.), 1989	609	5
Hersey/Blanchard	*Management of Organizational Behavior: Utilizing Human Resources* (3rd ed.), 1977	324	2
Hersey/Blanchard	*Management of Organizational Behavior: Utilizing Human Resources* (5th ed.), 1988	449	3
Howell/Dipboye	*Essentials of Industrial Organizational Psychology* (3rd ed.), 1986	414	0
Ivancevich/Matteson	*Organizational Behavior and Management*, 1987	752	7
Ivancevich/Matteson	*Organizational Behavior and Management* (2nd ed.), 1990	650	26
Ivancevich/Szilagyi/ Wallace	*Organizational Behavior and Performance*, 1977	553	0
Jackson/Morgan/ Paolillo	*Organizational Theory: A Macro Perspective for Management* (3rd ed.), 1986	372	0
Jewell	*Contemporary Industrial/Organizational Psychology*, 1985	478	3
Jewell/Siegall	*Contemporary Industrial/Organizational Psychology* (2nd ed.), 1990	529	5
Johns	*Organizational Behavior: Understanding Life at Work*, 1983	516	8
Johns	*Organizational Behavior: Understanding Life at Work* (2nd ed.), 1988	653	4
Klein/Ritti	*Understanding Organizational Behavior* (2nd ed.), 1984	677	10
Korman	*Organizational Behavior*, 1977	397	0
Landy	*Psychology of Work and Behavior* (3rd ed.), 1985	622	0
Landy	*Psychology of Work and Behavior* (4th ed.), 1989	715	0
Larwood	*Organizational Behavior and Management* 1984	515	11
Luthans	*Organizational Behavior* (4th ed.), 1985	672	5
Luthans	*Organizational Behavior* (5th ed.), 1989	624	2

Authors	Title and Year	Total	Union
Maier/Verser	*Psychology in Industrial Organizations* (5th ed.), 1982	623	20
McCormick/Ilgen	*Industrial and Organizational Psychology* (8th ed.), 1988	437	0
Middlemist/Hitt	*Organizational Behavior: Managerial Strategies for Performance*, 1988	577	2
Miner	*Organizational Behavior: Performance and Productivity*, 1988	658	34
Mitchell	*People in Organizations: Understanding Their Behavior*, 1978	466	0
Moorhead/Griffin	*Organizational Behavior* (2nd ed.), 1989	772	12
Muchinsky	*Psychology Applied to Work* (2nd ed.), 1987	707	34
Muchinsky	*Psychology Applied to Work* (3rd ed.), 1990	557	33
Organ/Bateman	*Organizational Behavior: An Applied Psychological Approach* (3rd ed.), 1986	687	5
Quinn/Faerman/ Thompson/McGrath	*Becoming a Manager: A Competency Framework*, 1990	333	0
Porter/Lawler/ Hackman	*Behavior in Organizations*, 1975	523	2
Rambo	*Work and Organizational Behavior*, 1982	485	29
Rashid/Archer	*Organizational Behavior*, 1983	421	1
Reitz	*Behavior in Organizations* (3rd ed.), 1987	619	5
Riggio	*Introduction to Industrial/Organizational Psychology*, 1990	437	0
Robbins	*Essentials of Organizational Behavior* (2nd ed.), 1988	233	0
Robbins	*Organizational Behavior* (4th ed.), 1989	556	5
Robey	*Designing Organizations* (2nd ed.), 1986	635	21
Saal/Knight	*Industrial/Organization Psychology: Science and Practice*, 1988	521	41
Schermerhorn/Hunt/ Osborn	*Managing Organizational Behavior* (3rd ed.), 1988	608	3
Schultz	*Psychology and Industry Today* (3rd ed.), 1982	498	8
Schultz/Schultz	*Psychology and Industry Today* (4th ed.), 1986	548	14
Schultz/Schultz	*Psychology and Industry Today* (5th ed.), 1990	624	9
Smither	*The Psychology of Work and Human Performance*, 1988	408	0
Starling	*The Changing Environment of Business* (2nd ed.), 1984	596	11
Steers	*Introduction to Organizational Behavior* (2nd ed.), 1984	550	1
Szilagyi/Wallace	*Organizational Behavior and Performance* (3rd ed.), 1983	602	9

Authors	Title and Year	Total	Union
Tossi/Rizzo/Carroll	*Managing Organizational Behavior* (2nd ed.), 1990	726	8
Umstot	*Understanding Organizational Behavior,* (2nd ed.), 1988	501	4
Wexley/Yukl	*Organizational Behavior and Personnel Psychology,* 1984	548	14
Wickens	*Engineering Psychology and Human Performance,* 1984	499	0

References

Abraham, K. G., & Medoff, J. L. (1984). Length of service and layoffs in union and nonunion work groups. *Industrial and Labor Relations Review, 38*, 87–97.

Abraham, K. G., & Medoff, J. L. (1985). Length of service and promotions in union and nonunion work groups. *Industrial and Labor Relations Review, 38*, 408–419.

Ackerman, J. A. (1979). The impact of the coal strike of 1977–1978. *Industrial and Labor Relations Revie, 32*, 175–188.

Adams, A., & Krislov, J. (1974). New union organizing: A test of the Ashenfelter-Pencavel model of trade union growth. *Quarterly Journal of Economics, 88*, 304–311.

Adams, E. F., Laker, D. R., & Hulin, C. L. (1977). An investigation of the influence of job level and functional specialty on job attitudes and perceptions. *Journal of Applied Psychology, 62*, 335–343.

Ahlburg, D. A., & Dworkin, J. B. (1984). The influence of macroeconomic variables on the probability of union decertication. *Journal of Labor Research, 5*, 13–28.

Allen, R. E., & Keaveny, T. J. (1981). Correlates of university faculty interest in unionization: A replication and extension. *Journal of Applied Psychology, 66*, 582–588.

Allen, R. E., & Keaveny, T. J. (1983). *Contemporary labor relations.* Reading, MA: Addison-Wesley.

Allen, N. J., & Meyer, J. (1990). The measurement and antecedents of affective, continuance and normative commitment to the organization. *Journal of Occupational Psychology, 63*, 1–18.

Allen, S. G. (1984). Trade unions, absenteeism and exit-voice. *Industrial and Labor Relations Review, 37*, 331–345.

Alutto, J. A., & Belasco, J. A. (1974). Determinants of attitudinal militancy among nurses and teachers. *Industrial and Labor Relations Review, 32*, 175–188.

American Psychologist (1984). The psychologist and organized labor, *39*, 428–445.

Anderson, J. C. (1978). A comparative analysis of local union democracy. *Industrial Relations, 17*, 278–295.

Anderson, J. C. (1979). Local union participation: A reexamination. *Industrial Relations, 18*, 18–31.

Anderson, J. C. (1979a). Determinants of bargaining outcomes in the Federal Government of Canada. *Industrial and Labor Relations Review, 32*, 224–241.

Anderson, J. C. (1979b). Bargaining outcomes: An IR systems approach. *Industrial Relations, 18*, 127–143.

Anderson, J. C., Busman, G., & O'Reilly, C. A. (1979). What factors influence the outcome of decertication elections? *Monthly Labor Review, 102(11)*, 32–36.

Anderson, J. C., Busman, G., & O'Reilly, C. A. (1982). The decertication process: Evidence from California. *Industrial Relations, 21*, 178–195.

Anderson, J. C., O'Reilly, C. A., & Busman, G. (1980). Union decertication in the U.S.: 1947–1977. *Industrial Relations, 19,* 100–107.

Angle, H. L., & Perry, J. L. (1984). Union member attitudes and bargaining unit stability in urban transit. In B. D. Dennis (Ed.), *Proceedings of the 36th Annual Meeting of the Industrial Relations Research Association* (pp. 284–290). Madison, WI: Industrial Relations Research Association.

Angle, H. L., & Perry, J. L. (1988). Dual Commitment and labor management relationship climates. *Academy of Management Journal, 29,* 31–50.

Appleton, W. C., & Baker, J. G. (1984). The effect of unionization on safety in bituminous coal mines. *Journal of Labor Research, 5,* 139–147.

Argyris, C. (1964). *Integrating the individual and the organization.* New York: Wiley.

Arrowsmith, D., & Courchene, M. (1989). *The current industrial relations scene in Canada, 1989: Collective bargaining reference tables.* Kingston, Ontario: Industrial Relations Centre, Queen's University.

Arvey, R. D., Bouchard, T. J., Segal, N. L., & Abraham, L. M. (1989). Job satisfaction: Environmental and genetic components. *Journal of Applied Psychology, 74,* 187–192.

Ashenfelter, O., & Pencavel, J. H. (1969). American trade union growth: 1900–1960. *Quarterly Journal of Economics, 83,* 434–448.

Ashford, S. J., Lee, C., & Bobko, P. (1989). Content, causes, and consequences of job insecurity: A theory-based measure and substantive test. *Academy of Management Journal, 32,* 803–829.

Bacharach, B. B., & Aiken, M. (1977). Communication in administrative bureaucracies. *Academy of Management Journal, 20,* 365–377.

Bain, G. S., & Elsheikh, F. (1976). *Union growth and the business cycle: An econometric analysis.* Oxford: Basil Blackwell.

Bain, G. S., & Clegg, H. A. (1974). A strategy for industrial relations research in Great Britain. *British Journal of Industrial Relations, 12,* 91–113.

Bain, G. S., & Price, R. J. (1972). Union growth and employment trends in the United Kingdom, 1964–1970. *British Journal of Industrial Relations, 10,* 366–381.

Bakke, E. W. (1945). To join or not to join. *Personnel, 22,* 2–11.

Balkin, D. B. (1989). Union influences on pay policy. *Journal of Labor Research, 10,* 299–310.

Bandura, A. (1977). *Social learning theory.* Englewood Cliffs, NJ: Prentice-Hall.

Barbash, J. (1969). Rationalization in the American union. In G. G. Somers (Ed.), *Essays in Industrial Relations Theory* (pp. 147–162). Ames: Iowa State University Press.

Barbash, J. (1985). Do we really want labor on the ropes? *Harvard Business Review, 63,* 3–8.

Barling, J. (1988). Industrial relations—a "blind spot" in the teaching, research and practice of industrial/organizational psychology. *Canadian Psychology, 29,* 103–108.

Barling, J. (1990). *Employment, stress and family functioning.* Chichester: John Wiley.

Barling, J., & Fullagar, C. (1990). *Perceived union instrumentality: Development of a scale.* Unpublished manuscript.

Barling, J., & Milligan, J. (1987). Some psychological consequences of striking: A six-month longitudinal study. *Journal of Occupational Behaviour, 8,* 127–138.

Barling, J., Fullagar, C., McElvie, L., & Kelloway, E. K. (1992). Union loyalty and strike propensity. *Journal of Social Psychology,* in press.

Barling, J., Kelloway, E. K., & Bremermann, E. H. (1991). Pre-employment predictors of union attitudes: The role of family socialization and work beliefs. *Journal of Applied Psychology, 76,* 725–731.

Barling, J., Laliberte, M., Fullagar, C., & Kelloway, E. K. (1990). *Work and personal predictors of the intent to unionize.* Manuscript submitted for publication.

Barling, J., Wade, B., & Fullagar, C. (1990). Predicting employee commitment to company and union: Divergent models. *Journal of Occupational Psychology, 63,* 49–61.

Baron, R. A. (1983). *Behavior in organizations.* Newton, MA: Allyn & Bacon Inc.

Barrett, J. T., & Mullins, A. F. (1990). South African trade unions: a historical account, 1970–90. *Monthly Labor Review,* October, 25–31.

Bass, B. M. (1985). *Leadership and performance beyond expectations.* New York: Free Press.

Bass, B. M., & Barrett, G. V. (1981). *People, work, organizations* (2nd ed.). Newton, MA: Allyn & Bacon Inc.

Bass, B. M., & Mitchell, C. W. (1976). Influence on the felt need for collective bargaining by business and science professionals. *Journal of Applied Psychology, 61,* 770–773.

Batstone, E., Boraston, I., & Frenkel, S. (1977). *Shop stewards in action:The organization of workplace conflict and accommodation.* Oxford: Blackwell.

Batstone, E., Boraston, I., & Frenkel, S. (1978). *The social organization of strikes.* Blackwell: Oxford.

Beaumont, P. (1981). The nature of the relationship between safety representatives and their workforce constituencies. *Industrial Relations Journal, 12,* 53–60.

Beck, R. C. (1982). *Applying psychology: Understanding people.* Englewood Cliffs, NJ: Prentice-Hall.

Becker, B. E., & Miller, R. U. (1981). Patterns and determinants of union growth in the hospital industry. *Journal of Labor Research, 2,* 309–328.

Becker, B. E., & Olson, C. A. (1986). The impact of strikes on shareholder equity. *Industrial and Labor Relations Review, 39,* 425–438.

Becker, H. S. (1960). Notes on the conceptualization of commitment. *American Journal of Sociology, 66,* 32–42.

Beer, M., Spector, B., Lawrence, P. R., Mills, D. Q., & Walton, R. E. (1985). *Human resource management: A general manager's perspective.* New York: The Free Press.

Begin, J. P. (1979). Faculty bargaining and reward systems. In D. R. Lewis & W. E. Becker (Eds.), *Academic rewards in higher education.* Cambridge, MA: Ballinger.

Bennett, J. D., & Passmore, D. L. (1985). Unions and coal mine safety: Comment. *Journal of Labor Research, 6,* 211–215.

Bennis, W. (1969). Organizational development and the fate of bureaucracy. In L. L. Cummings & W. E. Scott (Eds.), *Organizational behavior and human performance.* Homewood, IL: Irwin-Dorsey.

Bennis, W. (1973). *Beyond democracy: Essays on the development and evolution of human organizations.* New York: McGraw-Hill.

Benson, J. (1989). *Understanding shop steward behavior at the workplace: A framework for analysis.* Working paper No. 45, Labour Studies Programme, University of Melbourne.

Benson, J., & Griffin, G. (1988). Gender differences in union attitudes, participation and priorities. *The Journal of Industrial Relations, 30,* 203–214.

Berger, C. J., & Cummings, L. L. (1979). Organizational structure, attitudes and behavior. In B. M. Staw (Ed.), *Research in organizational behavior* (vol. 1) (pp. 169–208). Greenwich, CT: JAI Press.

Berger, C. J., Olson, C. A., & Boudreau, J. W. (1983). Effects of unions on job satisfaction: The role of work-related and perceived rewards. *Organizational Behavior and Human Performance, 32*, 289–324.

Beutell, N. J., & Biggs, D. L. (1984). Behavioral intentions to join a union: Instrumentality × valence, locus of control and strike attitudes. *Psychological Reports, 55*, 215–222.

Beyer, J. M., & Trice, W. M. (1979). A reexamination of the relations between size and various components of organizational complexity. *Administrative Science Quarterly, 24*, 48–64.

Beyer, J. M., Trice, H. M., & Hunt, R. E. (1979). The impact of federal sector unions on supervisors use of personnel policies. *Industrial and Labor Relations Review, 33*, 212–231.

Bigoness, W. J. (1978). Correlates of faculty attitudes toward collective bargaining. *Journal of Applied Psychology, 63*, 228–233.

Bigoness, W. J., & Peirce, E. R. (1988). Responding to union decertification elections. *Personnel Administrator, 33(8)*, 49–53.

Bigoness, W. J., & Tosi, H. L. (1984). Correlates of voting behavior in a union decertification election. *Academy of Management Journal, 27*. 654–659.

Black, A. W. (1983). Some factors influencing attitudes toward militancy, membership, solidarity, and sanctions in a teachers' union. *Human Relations, 36*, 973–986.

Blake, R. R., & Mouton, J. (1968). *Corporate excellence through grid organizational development.* Houston, TX: Gulf Corporation.

Blau, F. D., & Kahn, L. M. (1983). Unionism, seniority and turnover. *Industrial Relations, 22*, 362–373.

Blauner, R. (1964). *Alienation and freedom.* Chicago: University of Chicago Press.

Block, R. N. (1978). The impact of seniority provisions on the manufacturing quit rate. *Industrial and Labor Relations Review, 31*, 474–488.

Block, R. N., & Premack, S. L. (1983). The unionization process: A review of the literature. In D. B. Lipsky & J. M. Douglas (Eds.), *Advances in industrial and labor relations* (Vol. 1) (pp. 31–70). Greenwich, CT: JAI Press.

Block, R. N., & Roomkin, M. (1982). A preliminary analysis of the participation rate and margin of victory in NLRB elections. In B. Dennis (Ed.), *Proceedings of the thirty-fourth annual meeting of the Industrial Relations Research Association* (pp. 220–226). Madison: Industrial Relations Research Association.

Bluen, S. D. (1986). Industrial relations: Approaches and ideologies. In J. Barling, C. Fullagar, & S. D. Bluen (Eds.), *Behavior in Organizations: South African perspectives* (pp. 673–708). Johannesburg, South Africa: Lexicon.

Bluen, S. D., & Barling, J. (1987). Stress and the industrial relations process: Development of the Industrial Relations Events Scale. *South African Journal of Psychology, 17*, 150–159.

Bluen, S. D., & Barling, J. (1988). Psychological stressors associated with industrial relations. In C. L. Cooper and R. Payne (Eds.), *Causes, coping and consequences of stress at work* (pp. 175–205). London: John Wiley & Sons.

Bluen, S. D., & Donald, C. (1991). The nature and measurement of in-company industrial relations climate. *South African Journal of Psychology, 21*, 12–20.

Bluen, S. D., & Jubiler-Lurie, V. G. (1990). Some consequences of labor-management negotiations: Laboratory and field studies. *Journal of Organizational Behavior, 11*, 105–118.

Bluen, S. D., & van Zwam, C. (1987). Trade union membership and job satisfaction. *South African Journal of Psychology, 17*, 160–164.

Blyton, P. (1981). Research note: The influence of job grade differences in white-collar shop steward committee meetings. *Industrial Relations Journal, 12*, 72–74.

Blyton, P., Nicholson, N., & Ursell, G. (1981). Job status and white-collar members' union activity. *Journal of Occupational Psychology, 54*, 33–45.

Bok, D. C., & Dunlop, J. T. (1970). *Labor and the American community.* New York: Simon & Schuster.

Borjas, G. J. (1979). Job satisfaction, wages, and unions. *The Journal of Human Resources, 14*, 21–39.

Bornheimer, D. G. (1985). Conditions influencing faculty voting in collective bargaining elections. *Research in Higher Education, 22*, 291–305.

Bowditch, J. L., & Buono, A. F. (1990). *A primer on organizational behavior* (2nd ed.). New York: John Wiley.

Bowen, P., & Shaw, M. (1972). Patterns of white collar unionization in the steel industry. *Industrial Relations Journal, 3*, 8–34.

Brett, J. M. (1980). Why employees want unions. *Organizational Dynamics, 8*, 47–59.

Brett, J. M., & Goldberg, S. B. (1979). Wildcat strikes in bitumous coal mining. *Industrial and Labor Relations Review, 32*, 465–483.

Brett, J. M., & Hammer, T. H. (1982). Organizational behavior and industrial relations. In T. A. Kochan, D. J. Mitchell, & L. Dyer (Eds.), *Industrial relations research in the 1970's: Review and appraisal* (pp. 221–281): Madison, WI: Industrial Relations Research Association.

Brief, A. P., & Rude, D. E. (1981). Voting in union certification elections: A conceptual analysis. *Academy of Management Review, 6*, 261–267.

Brief, A. P., Aldag, R. J., & Wallden, R. A. (1976). Correlates of supervisory style among policemen. *Criminal Justice and Behavior, 3*, 263–271.

Broad, G. (1983). Shop steward leadership and the dynamics of workplace industrial relations. *Industrial Relations Journal, 14*, 59–67.

Brockner, J. (1988). The effects of work layoffs on survivors: Research, theory and practice. In L. L. Cummings and B. M. Staw (Eds.), *Research in organizational behavior* (Vol. 10) (pp. 213–255). Greenwich, CT: JAI Press.

Brooke, P. P., Russell, D. W., & Price, J. L. (1988). Discriminant validation of measures of job satisfaction, job involvement and organizational commitment. *Journal of Applied Psychology, 73*, 139–145.

Buchanan, B. (1974). Building organizational commitment: The socialization of managers in work organizations. *Administrative Science Quarterly, 19*, 533–546.

Buchholz, R. A. (1978). The work ethic reconsidered. *Industrial and Labor Relations Review, 31*, 450–459.

Buchholz, R. A. (1979). An empirical study of contemporary beliefs about work in American society. *Journal of Applied Psychology, 63*, 219–227.

Butler, R. J. (1976). Relative deprivation and power: A switched replication design using time series data of strike rates in American and British coal mining. *Human Relations*, 623–641.

Campbell, J. R., & Pritchard, R. D. (1983). Motivation theory in industrial and organizational psychology. In M. D. Dunnette (Ed.), *Handbook of industrial and organizational psychology* (pp. 63–130). Chicago: Rand McNally.

Campbell, J. P., Daft, R. L., & Hulin, C. L. (1982). *What to study: Generating and developing research questions.* Beverly Hills, CA: Sage.

Cascio, W. (1978). *Applied psychology in personnel management.* Preston, VI: Prentice-Hall.

Catano, V. M., & Rodger, R. (1986). *A faculty strike: An analysis of voting behavior and strike activity.* Paper presented at the Canadian Psychological Association Annual Conference, Toronto, Ontario.

Chacko, T. I. (1985). Member participation in union activities: Perceptions of union priorities, performance, and satisfaction. *Journal of Labor Research, 4,* 363–373.

Chadwick-Jones, J. K. (1981). Renegotiating absence levels. *Journal of Occupational Behavior, 2,* 255–266.

Chafetz, I., & Fraser. C. R. P. (1979). Union decertification: An exploratory analysis. *Industrial Relations, 18,* 59–69.

Chaison, G. N., & Andiappan, P. (1989). An analysis of the barriers to women becoming local union officers. *Journal of Labor Research, 10,* 149–162.

Chalykoff, J., & Cappelli, P. (1986). "Union avoidance": Management's new industrial relations strategy. *Monthly Labor Review, 109,* 45–46.

Chamberlain, E. N. (1935). What labor is thinking. *Personnel Journal, 14,* 118–123.

Chermesh, R. (1979). Strikes: The issue of social responsibility. *British Journal of Industrial Relations, 17,* 337–346.

Child, J. (1973). Predicting and understanding organizational structure. *Administrative Science Quarterly, 18,* 168–175.

Child, J., Loveridge, R., & Warner, M. (1973). Towards an organizational study of trade unions. *Sociology, 7,* 71–91.

Chusmir, L. H. (1982). Job commitment and organizational woman. *Academy of Management Review, 7,* 595–602.

Clark, K. (1980). The impact of unionization on productivity: A case study. *Industrial and Labor Relations Review, 33,* 451–469.

Clark, P. F., & Gallaghar, D. G. (1988). Membership perceptions on the value and effect of grievance procedures. *Proceedings of the 40th annual meeting of the Industrial Relations Research Association,* pp. 406–414.

Clark, P. F., Gallagher, D. G., & Pavlak, T. J. (1990). Member commitment in an American union: The role of the grievance procedure. *Industrial Relations Journal, 21,* 147–157.

Clegg, H. A. (1976). *Trade unionism under collective bargaining.* Blackwell: Oxford.

Clegg, H. A., Killick, A. J., & Adams, R. (1961). *Trade union officers: A study of full-time officers, branch secretaries and shop stewards in British trade unions.* Oxford: Basil Blackwell.

Coates, M. L., Arrowsmith, D., & Courchene, M. (1989). *The Current Industrial Relations Scene in Canada, 1989: The labor movement and trade unionism reference tables.* Industrial Relations Centre, Queen's University, Kingston, Ontario.

Cohen, A. R., Fink, S. L., Gadon, H., & Willits, R. D. (1980). *Effective behavior in organizations.* Homewood, IL: Richard D. Irwin.

Cohen, A. R., Fink, S. L., Gadon, H., & Willits, R. D. (1988). *Effective behavior in organizations* (4th ed.). Homewood, IL: Richard D. Irwin.

Cole, G. D. H. (1920). *Guild socialism restated.* London: Leonard Parsons.

Coleman, F. T. (1985). Not always a union. *Personnel Journal, 64(3),* 42–45.

Conlon, E. J., & Gallagher, D. G. (1987). Commitment to employer and union: Effects of membership status. *Academy of Management Journal, 30,* 151–162.

Cook, A. H. (1963). *Union democracy: Practice and ideal.* Ithaca, NY: New York School of Industrial and Labor Relations, Cornell University.

Cook, F. G., Clark, S. C. Roberts, K., & Semeonoff, E. (1975). White and blue-collar workers' attitudes to trade unionism and social class. *Industrial Relations Journal, 6,* 47–58.

Cook, J. (1983). Brother Cunningham and the guards. *Forbes Magazine*, February, 107–112.

Cook, T. D., & Campbell, D. T. (1979). *Quasi-experimentation: Design and analysis issues for field settings*. New York: Houghton Mifflin.

Cooke, W. N. (1983). Determinants of the outcomes of union certification elections. *Industrial and Labor Relations Review, 36*, 402–414.

Cooke, W. N. (1985). The rising toll of discrimination against union activists. *Industrial Relations, 24*, 421–441.

Cornfield, D. B. (1986). Declining union membership in the post World War II era: The United Furniture Workers, 1939–1982. *American Journal of Sociology, 91*, 506–520.

Cornfield, D. B., Filho, H. B. C., & Chun, B. J. (1990). Household, work and labor activism: Gender differences in the determinants of union membership participation. *Work and Occupations, 17*, 131–151.

Craft, J. A., & Abboushi, S. (1983). The union image: Concept, programs and analysis. *Journal of Labor Research, 4*, 299–314.

Cregan, C., & Johnston, S. (1990). An industrial relations approach to the free rider problem: Young people and trade union membership in the UK. *British Journal of Industrial Relations, 28*, 84–104.

Cummings, L. L. (1982). Organizational behavior. *Annual Review of Psychology, 33*, 541–579.

Daft, R. L. (1986). *Organization theory and design* (2nd ed.). St. Paul, MN: West Publishing.

Daft, R. L. & Bradshaw, P. J. (1980). The process of horizontal differentiation: Two models. *Administrative Science Quarterly, 25*, 441–450.

Daft, R. L., & Steers, R. M. (1986). *Organizations: A micro/macro approach*. Glenview, IL: Scott Foresman & Co.

Dalton, D. R., & Perry, J. L. (1981). Absenteeism and the collective bargaining agreement: An empirical test. *Academy of Management Journal, 24*, 425–431.

Dalton, D. R., & Todor, W. D. (1979). Manifest needs of stewards: Propensity to file a grievance. *Journal of Applied Psychology, 64*, 654–659.

Dalton, D. R., & Todor, W. D. (1981). Grievances filed and the role of the union steward vs. the rank and file member: An empirical test. *International Review of Applied Psychology, 30*, 199–207.

Dalton, D. R., & Todor, W. D. (1982a). Antecedents of grievance filing behavior: Attitude/behavioral consistency and the union steward. *Academy of Management Journal, 25*, 158–169.

Dalton, D. R., & Todor, W. D. (1982b). Union steward locus of control, job, union involvement, and grievance behavior. *Journal of Business Research, 10*, 85–101.

Dalton, D. R., Todor, W. D., Spendolini, M. J., Felding, G. J., & Porter, L. W. (1980). Organizations, structure, and performance: A critical reviews. *Academy of Management Review, 5*, 49–64.

Dastmalchian, A., Blyton, F., & Abdollahyan, M. R. (1982). Industrial relations climate and company effectiveness. *Personnel Review, 11*, 35–39.

Dastmalchian, A., Blyton, P., & Adamson, R. (1989). Industrial relations climate: Testing a construct. *Journal of Occupational Psychology, 62*, 21–32.

Davis, E. (1980). *Shop stewards in Australia: Some impressions*. Department of Industrial Relations, University of New South Wales, Kensington, New South Wales.

Davis, K., & Newstrom, J. W. (1985). *Organizational behavior: Readings and exercises* (7th ed.). New York: McGraw-Hill.

Dean, L. R. (1954). Union activity and dual loyalty. *Industrial and Labor Relations Review, 12*, 526–536.

Dean, L. R. (1958). Interaction, reported and observed: The case of one local union. *Human Organization, 18*, 36–44.

DeCotiis, T. A., & LeLouarn, J. (1981). A predictive study of voting behavior in a representation election using union instrumentality and work perceptions. *Organizational Behavior and Human Performance, 27*, 103–118.

Delaney, J. T., Fiorito, J., & Masters, M. F. (1988). The effects of union, organizational and environmental characteristics on union political action. *American Journal of Political Science, 32*, 616–642.

Derber, M. (1969). "Industrial democracy" as an organizing concept for a theory of industrial relations. In G. G. Somers (Ed.), *Essays in Industrial Relations Throry* (pp. 177–190). Ames: Iowa State University Press.

Deshpande, S. P., & Fiorito, J. (1989). Specific and general beliefs in union voting models. *Academy of Management Journal, 32*, 883–897.

Dessler, G. (1986). *Organizational theory: Integrating structure and behavior* (2nd ed.). Englewood-Cliffs, NJ: Prentice-Hall.

Dewar, R., & Werbel, J. (1979). Universalistic and contingency predictions of employee satisfaction and conflict. *Administrative Science Quarterly, 24*, 426–448.

Dickens, W. T. (1983). The effect of company campaigns on certification elections: Law and reality once again. *Industrial and Labor Relations Review, 36*, 560–575.

Dickens, W. T., & Leonard, J. S. (1985). Accounting for the decline in union membership, 1950–1980. *Industrial and Labor Relations Review, 38*, 323–334.

Dickens, W. T., Wholey, D. R., & Robinson, J. C. (1987). Correlates of union support in NLRB elections. *Industrial Relations, 26*, 240–252.

Dollard, J., Doob, L., Miller, N., Mowrer, O., & Seers, R. (1939). *Frustration and aggression*. New Haven: Yale University Press.

Donaldson, L., & Warner, M. (1974). Bureaucratic and electoral control in occupational interest associations. *Sociology, 8*, 47–58.

Donnelly, J. H., Gibson, J. L., & Ivancevich, J. M. (1984). *Fundamentals of management* (5th ed.). Plano, TX: Business Publications.

Donovan, T. N. (1968). *Royal commission on trade unions and employers' associations 1965—1968: Report*. London: Her Majesty's Stationery Office.

Driscoll, J. W. (1981). Coping with role conflict: An exploratory field study of union-management cooperation. *International Review of Applied Psychology. 30*, 177–198.

Dubey, B. L., Chawla, A. S., & Verma, S. K. (1984). A personality study of striking and non-striking employees. *Journal of Psychological Researches, 28*, 114–118.

Dubey, B. L., Uppal, K. K., & Verma, S. K. (1983). Some psychological correlates of striking and non-striking employees. *Indian Journal of Clinical Psychology, 10*, 337–342.

Dubin, R. (1960). A theory of conflict and power in union-management relations. *Industrial and Labor Relations Review, 13*, 501–518.

Dubin, R. (1973). Work and non-work: Institutional perspectives. In M. D. Dunnette (Ed.), *Work and Non-Work in the Year 2001* (pp. 53–68). Monterey, CA: Brooks/Cole.

DuBrin, A. J. (1984). *Foundations of organizational behavior: An applied perspective*. Englewood Cliffs NJ: Prentice-Hall.

Duncan, G. J., & Stafford, F. P. (1980). Do union members receive compensating wage differentials? *American Economic Review, 70*, 355–371.

Dunlop, J. T. (1958). *Industrial relations systems.* New York: Holt-Rinehart.

Edelstein, J. D., & Warner, M. (1975). *Comparative union democracy: Organization and opposition in British and American unions.* NY: Halsted Press.

Elliot, R., & Hawkins, B. M. (1982). Do union organizing activities affect decertification? *Journal of Labor Research, 3,* 153–161.

England, G. W. (1960). Dual allegiance to company and union. *Personnel Administration, 23,* 20–25.

Ephlin, D. F. (1988). Revolution by evolution: The changing relationship between GM and UAW. *Academy of Management Executive, 11,* 63–66.

Ethical Standards for Psychologists (2nd rev.). (1977). Washington, D. C.: American Psychological Association.

Etzioni, A. (1961). *A comparative analysis of complex organizations.* New York: Free Press.

Evans, M. G., & Ondrack, D. A. (1990). The role of job outcomes and values in understanding the union's impact on job satisfaction: A replication *Human Relations, 43,* 401–418.

Farber, H. S. (1980). Unionism, labor turnover, and wages of young men. In R. C. Ehrenderg (Ed.), *Research in labor economics* (Vol. 3), (pp. 33–53). Greenwich, CT: JAI Press.

Farber, H. S., & Saks, D. H. (1980). Why workers want unions: The role of relative wages and job characteristics. *Journal of Political Economy, 88,* 349–369.

Feather, N. (1982). *Expectations and actions: Expectancy-value models in psychology.* Hillsdale, NJ: Erlbaum.

Feldman, D. C. (1976). A contingency theory of socialization. *Administrative Science Quarterly, 21,* 433–452.

Feldman, D. C. & Arnold, H. J. (1983). *Managing individual and group behavior in organizations.* New York: McGraw-Hill.

Ferris, K. R., & Aranya, N. (1983). A comparison of two organizational commitment scales. *Personnel Psychology, 36,* 87–98.

Festinger, L. (1957). *A theory of cognitive dissonance.* Evanston, IL: Row, Peterson.

Feuille, P., & Blandin, J. (1974). Faculty job satisfaction and bargaining sentiments: A case study. *Academy of Management Journal, 17,* 678–692.

Feuille, P., Hendricks, W. E., & Kahn, L. M. (1981). Wage and nonwage outcomes in collective bargaining: Determinants and tradeoffs. *Journal of Labor Research, 2,* 39–53.

Fiedler, F. E. (1967). *A theory of leadership effectiveness.* New York: McGraw-Hill.

Fields, M. W., Masters, M. F., & Thacker, J. W. (1987). Union commitment and membership support for political action: An exploratory analysis. *Journal of Labor Research, 8,* 143–157.

Fiorito, J. (1982). Models of union growth: A test of the Bain-Elsheikh model for the U.S. *Industrial Relations, 21,* 123–127.

Fiorito, J. (1987). Political instrumentality perceptions and desire for union representation. *Journal of Labor Research, 8,* 272–289.

Fiorito, J., & Gallagher, D. G. (1986). Job content, job status, and unionism. In D. B. Lipsky & D. Lewin (Eds.), *Advances in industrial and labor relations* (Vol. 3), (pp. 261–316). Greenwich, CT: JAI Press.

Fiorito, J., & Greer, C. R. (1982). Determinants of U.S. unionism: Past research and future needs. *Industrial Relations, 21,* 1–32.

Fiorito, J., & Greer, C. R. (1986). Gender differences in union membership, preferences and beliefs. *Journal of Labor Research, 7,* 145–164.

Fiorito, J., & Hendricks, W. E. (1987a). The characteristics of national unions. In D. Lewin, D. Lipsky, & D. Sockell (Eds.), *Advances in Industrial and Labor Relations* (Vol. 4), (pp. 1–42). Greenwich, CT: JAI Press.

Fiorito, J., & Hendricks, W. E. (1987b). Union characteristics and bargaining outcomes. *Industrial and Labor Relations Review, 40,* 569–584.

Fiorito, J., Gallagher, D. G., & Greer, C. R. (1986). Determinants of unionism: A review of the literature. *Research in Personnel and Human Resources Management, 4,* 269–306.

Fiorito, J., Gramm, C., & Hendricks, W. (1990). *Environmental determinants of centralization of the collective bargaining function in American unions.* Unpublished manuscript, Department of Industrial Relations and Human Resources, University of Iowa.

Fishbein, M., & Ajzen, I. (1975). *Belief, attitude, intention and behavior: An introduction to theory and research.* Reading, MA: Addison-Wesley.

Fisher, C. D., & Gitelson, R. (1983). A meta analysis of the correlates of role conflict and ambiguity. *Journal of Applied Psychology, 68,* 320–333.

Fisher, L. H., & McConnell, G. (1954). Internal conflict and labor-union solidarity. In A. Kornhauser, R. Dubin, & A. M. Ross (Eds.), *Industrial conflict* (pp. 132—143). New York: McGraw-Hill.

Flanders, A. (1985). *Industrial relations: What is wrong with the system.* London: Faber & Faber.

Ford, J. D., & Slocum, J. W. (1977). Size, technology, environment and the structure of organizations. *Academy of Management Review, 2,* 561–575.

Form, W. H. (1976). *Blue-collar stratification: Auto-workers in four countries.* Princeton, NJ: Princeton University Press.

Form, W. H., & Dansereau, H. K. (1957). Union member orientation and patterns of social integration. *Industrial and Labor Relations Review, 11,* 3–12.

Fosh, P. (1981). *The active trade unionist: A study of motivation and participation at the branch level.* Cambridge: Cambridge University Press.

Fox, A. (1966). Research papers 3. Industrial sociology and industrial relations. *Royal Commission on Trade Unions and Employers' Associations.* London: Her Majesty's Stationery Office.

Fox, A. (1971). *A sociology of work in industry.* London: Collier-MacMillan.

Fox, W. S., & Wince, M. H. (1976). The structure and determinants of occupational militancy among school teachers. *Industrial and Labor Relations Review, 30,* 47–58.

Freeman, R. B. (1976). Individual mobility and union voice in the labor market. *American Economic Review, 66,* 361–368.

Freeman, R. B. (1978). Job satisfaction as an economic variable. *American Economic Review, 68,* 135–141.

Freeman, R. B. (1980). Unionism and the dispersion of wages. *Industrial and Labor Relations Review, 34,* 3–23.

Freeman, R. B. (1980). The effect of unionism on worker attachment to firms. *Journal of Labor Research, 1,* 29–61.

Freeman, R. B. (1981). The effect of unionism on fringe benefits. *Industrial and Labor Relations Review, 34,* 489–509.

Freeman, R. B. (1985). Why are unions faring so poorly in NLRB representation elections? In T. A. Kochan (Ed.), *Challenges and choices facing American labor* (pp. 45–64). Cambridge, MA: MIT Press.

Freeman, R. B., & Medoff, J. L. (1984). *What do unions do?* New York: Basic Books.

French, J. R., & Raven, B. (1959). The bases of social power. In D. Cartwright (Ed.),

Studies in social power. Ann Arbor: University of Michigan, Institute for Social Research.

Friedman, D. (1983). Why workers strike: Individual decisions and structural constraints. In M. Hechter (Ed.), *The microfoundations of macrosociology*. Philadelphia: Temple University Press.

Friedman, L., & Harvey, R. J. (1986). Factors of union commitment: The case for lower dimensionality. *Journal of Applied Psychology, 71*, 371–376.

Fryer, R. H., Fairclough, A. J., & Manson, T. B. (1978). Facilities for female shop stewards: The employment protection act and collective agreements. *British Journal of Industrial Relations, 16*, 160–174.

Fukami, C. V., & Larson, E. W. (1984). Commitment to company and union: Parallel models. *Journal of Applied Psychology, 69*, 367–371.

Fullagar, C. (1984). Psychology and labor: A relationship of neglect. *South African Journal of Psychology, 14*, 95–100.

Fullagar, C. (1986). A factor analytic study on the validity of a union commitment scale. *Journal of Applied Psychology, 71*, 129–137.

Fullagar, C., & Barling, J. (1987). Toward a model of union commitment. *Advances in Industrial and Labor Relations, 4*, 43–78.

Fullagar, C., & Barling, J. (1989). A longitudinal test of a model of the antecedents and consequences of union loyalty. *Journal of Applied Psychology, 74*, 213–227.

Fullagar, C., & Barling, J. (1991). Predictors and outcomes of different patterns of organizational and union loyalty. *Journal of Occupational Psychology, 64*, 129–143.

Fullagar, C., & Howland, K. (1990). *Unionization: A social psychological approach*. Manuscript under preparation. Department of Psychology, Kansas State University.

Fullagar, C., Barling, J., & Christie, P. (1991). Dual commitment in aggressive and protective unions. *Applied Psychology: An International Review, 39*, 93–104.

Fullagar, C., McCoy, D., & Shull, C. (1992). The socialization of union loyalty. *Journal of Organizational Behavior, 13*, 13–26.

Fulmer, W. E. (1978). When employees want to oust their union. *Harvard Business Review, 56*, 163–170.

Fulmer, W. E., & Gilman, T. A. (1981). Why do workers vote for union decertification? *Personnel, 58*, 28–35.

Gallagher, D. G. (1983). Integrating collective bargaining and human resources management research. In G. R. Ferris and K. M. Rowland (Eds.), *Research in personnel and human resources management, A research annual* (Vol. 1), pp. 235–268. Greenwich, CT: JAI Press.

Gallagher, D. G. (1984). The relationship between organizational and union commitment among federal government employees. *Proceedings of the Academy of Management* (pp. 319–323). Madison, WT: Industrial Relations Research Association.

Gallagher, D. G., & Clark, P. F. (1989). Research on union commitment: Implications for labor. *Labor Studies Journal, 14*, 53–71.

Gallagher, D. G., & Jeong, Y. (1989). *Methodological concerns with behavioral studies of union membership*. Presented at the Tenth Annual Southern Regional Industrial Relations Academic Seminar, West Virginia University, Morgantown.

Gallagher, D. C., & Wetzel, K. W. (1990). *The union membership roster as a source of possible sample bias in the study of union commitment*. Presented at the Fifth Annual Conference of the Society for Industrial and Organizational Psychology, April 20–22, Miami Beach, Florida.

Gamm, S. (1979). The election base of national union executive boards. *Industrial and Labor Relations Review, 32*, 295–311.

Garbarino, J. W. (1975). *Faculty bargaining, change and conflict.* New York: McGrow-Hill.

Garbarino, J. W. (1980). Faculty unionization: The Pre-Yeshiva years, 1966–1979. *Industrial Relations, 19*, 221–230.

Garson, B. (1981). *All the live long day: The meaning and demeaning of everyday work.* New York: Penguin.

Geare, A. J., Herd, J. J., & Howells, J. H. (1979). *Women in trade unions: A case study of participation in New Zealand.* Wellington: Victoria University of Wellington.

Gennard, J. (1981). The effects of strike activity on households. *The British Journal of Industrial Relations, 19*, 327–344.

Gennard, J. (1982). The financial costs and returns of strikes. *The British Journal of Industrial Relations, 20*, 247–256.

Gerloff, E. A. (1985). *Organizational theory and design: A strategic approach for management.* New York: McGraw-Hill.

Getman, J. G., Goldberg, S. B., & Herman, J. B. (1976). *Union representation elections: Law and reality.* New York: Russell Sage Foundation.

Gibson, J. L., Ivancevich, J. M. & Donnelly, J. H. (1988). *Organizations: Behavior, structures and processes* (6th ed.). Plano, TX: Business Publications.

Giles, W. F., & Holley, W. H. (1978). Job enrichment versus traditional issues at the bargaining table: What union workers want. *Academy of Management Journal, 21*, 725–730.

Ginsburg, W. L. (1970). Review of literature on union growth, government and structure. In W. L. Ginsburg, E. R. Livernash, H. S. Parnes, & G. Strauss (Eds.), *A review of industrial relations research* (pp. 207–258). Madison, WI: Industrial Relations Research Association.

Ginzberg, E. (1948). *The labor leader: An exploratory study.* New York: The Macmillan Company.

Glick, W., Mirvis, P., & Harder, D. (1977). Union satisfaction and participation. *Industrial Relations, 16*, 145–151.

Goldthorpe, J. H., Lockwood, C., Bechhofer, F., & Platt, J. (1968). *The affluent worker: Industrial attitudes and behavior.* Cambridge: Cambridge University Press.

Gomberg, W. (1973). Job satisfaction: Sorting out the nonsense. *The American Federationist, 80*, 14–19.

Gomez-Mejia, L. R., & Balkin, D. B. (1984). Faculty satisfaction with pay and other job dimensions under union and nonunion conditions. *Academy of Management Journal, 27*, 591–602.

Gordon, M. E., Beauvais, L. L., & Ladd, R. T. (1984). The job satisfaction and union commitment of unionized engineers. *Industrial and Labor Relations Review, 37*, 359–370.

Gordon, M. E., & Bowlby, R. L. (1988). Propositions about grievance settlements: Finally, consultation with grievants. *Personnel Psychology, 41*, 107–123.

Gordon, M. E., & Burt, R. E. (1981). A history of industrial psychology's relationship with American unions: Lessons from the past and directions for the future. *International Review of Applied Psychology, 30*, 137–156.

Gordon, M. E., & Fryxell, G. E. (1989). Voluntariness of association as a moderator of the importance of procedural and distributive justice. *Journal of Applied Social Psychology, 19*, 993–1009.

Gordon, M. E., & Johnson, W. A. (1982). Seniority: A review of its legal and scientific standing. *Personnel Psychology*, *35*, 255–280.

Gordon, M. E., & Ladd, R. T. (1990). Dual allegiance: Renewal, reconsideration, and recantation. *Personnel Psychology*, *43*, 37–69.

Gordon, M. E., & Lee, B. (1990). Property rights in jobs: Workforce, behavioral and legal perspectives. In G. R. Ferris and K. M. Rowland (Eds.), *Research in personnel and human resources management: A research annual* (Vol. 8), pp. 303–348. Greenwich, CT: JAI Press.

Gordon, M. E., & Long, L. N. (1981). Demographic and attitudinal correlates of union joining. *Industrial Relations*, *20, 306–*311.

Gordon, M. E., & Miller, S. J. (1984). Grievances: A review of research and practice. *Personnel Psychology*, *37*, 117–146.

Gordon, M. E., & Nurick, A. J. (1981). Psychological approaches to the study of unions and union-management relations. *Psychological Bulletin*, *90*, 293–306.

Gordon, M. E., Philpot, J. W., Burt, R. E., Thompson, C. A., & Spiller, W. E. (1980). Commitment to the union: Development of a measure and an examination of its correlates. *Journal of Applied Psychology*, *65*, 474–499.

Gottlieb, B., & Kerr, W. A. (1950). An experiment in industrial harmony. *Personnel Psychology*, *3*, 445–453.

Gouldner, A. W. (1947). Attitudes of "progressive" trade union leaders. *American Journal of Sociology*, *52*, 389–393.

Gray, J. L., & Starke, F. A. (1988). *Organizational behavior: Concepts and applications* (4th ed.). Columbus, OH: Merrill Publishing Co.

Greenhalgh, L., & Rosenblatt, Z. (1984). Job insecurity: Towards conceptual clarity. *Academy of Management Review*, *9*, 438–448.

Grusky, O. (1966). Measuring role conflict. *American Journal of Sociology*, *61*, 299–303.

Guest, D. E., & Dewe, P. (1988). Why do workers belong to a trade union? A social psychological study in the UK electronics industry. *British Journal of Industrial Relations*, *26*, 178–193.

Hackett, R. D. (1989). Work attitudes and employee absenteeism: A synthesis of the literature. *Journal of Occupational Psychology*, *62*, 235–248.

Hackman, J. R., & Oldham, G. E. (1975). Development of the Job Diagnostic Survey. *Journal of Applied Psychology*, *60*, 159–170.

Hagburg, E. C. (1966). Correlates of organizational participation: An examination of factors affecting union membership activity. *Pacific Sociological Review*, *9*, 15–21.

Hall, D. T. (1972). A model of coping with role conflict: The role behavior of college educated women. *Administrative Science Quarterly*, *17, 471–*486.

Hall, R. D. (1962). Intraorganizational structure variation: Application of the bureaucratic model. *Administrative Science Quarterly*, *7*, 295–308.

Hall, R. H. (1987). *Organizations: Structures, processes and outcomes* (4th ed.). Englewood Cliffs, NJ: Prentice-Hall.

Hammer, T. H. (1978). Relationships between local union characteristics and worker behavior and attitudes. *Academy of Management Journal*, *21*, 560–577.

Hammer, T. H., & Berman, M. (1981). The role of noneconomic factors in faculty union voting. *Journal of Applied Psychology*, *66*, 415–421.

Hamner, W. C., & Smith, F. J. (1978). Work attitudes as predictors of unionization activity. *Journal of Applied Psychology*, *63*, 415–421.

Hampton, D. R., Summer, C. E., & Webber, R. A. (1987). *Organizational behavior and the practice of management* (5th ed.). Glenview, IL: Scott, Foresmen & Co.

Hardman, J. B. S. (1972). *Labor at the rubicon.* New York: New York University Press.

Harman, H. H. (1967). *Modern factor analysis* (2nd ed.). Chicago: University of Chicago Press.

Harris, P., Reichman, W., & Jacobs, A. (1983). College faculty's attitudes toward its union under conditions of adversity. *Psychological Reports, 53,* 335–338.

Hartley, J. (1984). Industrial relations psychology. In M. Gruneberg & T. Wall (Eds.), *Social psychology and organizational behavior* (pp. 149–181). Chichester: Wiley.

Hartley, J., & Kelly, J. (1986). Psychology and industrial relations: From conflict to cooperation? *Journal of Occupational Psychology, 59,* 161–176.

Harter, J. J., & Bass, B. M. (1988). Superiors' evaluations and subordinates' perceptions of transformational and transactional leadership. *Journal of Applied Psychology, 73,* 695–702.

Haywood, L., & Taylor, E. (1981). Strikes and support systems: What happened in Sudbury. *Canada's Mental Health, March,* 18–33.

Heery, E., & Kelly, J. (1989). "A cracking job for a woman"—a profile of women trade union officers. *Industrial Relations Journal, 20,* 192–202.

Hellriegel, D., & Slocum, J. W. (1979). *Organizational behavior* (2nd ed.). St. Paul, MN: West Publishing Co.

Hellriegel, D., Slocum, J. W., & Woodman, R. W. (1986). *Organizational behavior* (4th ed.). St. Paul, MN: West Publishing Co.

Hellriegel, D., Slocum, J. W., & Woodman, R. W. (1989). *Organizational behavior* (5th ed.). St. Paul, MN: West Publishing Co.

Heneman, H. G., & Sandver, M. H. (1983). Predicting the outcome of union certification elections: A review of the literature. *Industrial and Labor Relations Review, 36,* 537–559.

Heneman, H. G. & Sandver, M. H. (1989). Union characteristics and organizing success. *Journal of Labor Research, 10,* 377–389.

Herberg, W. (1943). Bureaucracy and democracy in labor unions. *Antioch Review, 3,* 405–417.

Herman, J. B. (1973). Are situational contingencies limiting job attitude-job performance relationships? *Organizational Behavior and Human Performance, 10,* 208–224.

Hersey, P., & Blanchard, K. H. (1977). *Management of organizational behavior: Utilizing human resources* (3rd ed.). Englewood Cliffs, NJ: Prentice-Hall.

Hersey, P., & Blanchard, K. H. (1988). *Management of organizational behavior: Utilizing human resources* (5th ed.). Englewood Cliffs, NJ: Prentice-Hall.

Hills, S. M. (1985). The attitudes of union and nonunion male workers toward union representation. *Industrial and Labor Relations Review, 38,* 179–194.

Hindman, H. D. (1988). *Determinants of union representation election outcomes: Evidence from the public sector.* Presented at the forty-first annual meeting of the Industrial Relations Research Association, New York.

Hirschman, A. O. (1970). *Exit, voice and loyalty: Responses to decline in firms, organizations, and states.* Cambridge, MA: Harvard University Press.

Hochner, A., Koziara, K., & Schmidt, S. (1980). Thinking about democracy and participation in unions. *Proceedings of the thirty-second Annual Meeting of the Industrial Relations Research Association* (pp. 12–19). Atlanta, December, 28–30, IRRA.

Hogan, J. A. (1948/9). The meaning of the union shop elections. *Industrial and Labor Relations Review, 19,* 319–334.

Holley, W. H., & Jennings, K. M. (1983). *The labor relations process* (2nd ed.). Hinsdale, IL: Dryden Press.

Howe, I., & Widick, B. J. (1949). *The UAW and Walter Reuther*, New York: Random House.

Howell, W., & Dipboye, R. (1986). *Essentials of industrial organizational psychology* (3rd ed.). Chicago: Dorsey Press.

Hoxie, R. F. (1921). *Trade unionism in the United States*. New York: Appleton.

Hoyman, M. M., & Stallworth, L. (1987). Participation in local unions: A comparison of black and white members. *Industrial and Labor Relations Review, 40*, 323–335.

Hrebiniak, L. G. (1975). Effects of job level and participation on employee attitudes and approaches to the prediction of turnover. *Academy of Management Journal, 17*, 649–662.

Hrebiniak, L. G. & Alutto, J. A. (1972). Personal and role-related factors in the development of organizational commitment. *Administrative Science Quarterly, 17*, 555–572.

Hunt, J. W. (1979). *Employer's guide to labor relations*. Washington, D. C.: BNA.

Hunter, J. E., Schmidt, F. L., & Jackson, G. B. (1982). *Meta-analysis: Cumulating research findings across studies*. Beverly Hills, CA: Sage.

Huszczo, G. E. (1983). Attitudinal and behavioral variables related to participation in union activities. *Journal of Labor Research, 4*, 289–297.

Huszczo, G. E., Wiggins, J. G., & Currie, J. S. (1984). The relationship between psychology and organized labor: Past, present and future. *American Psychologist, 39*, 432–440.

Hyman, R. (1975). *Industrial relations: A Marxist introduction*. London: MacMillan.

Hyman, R. (1984). *Industrial relations: A Marxist introduction* (2nd ed.). London: MacMillan.

Imberman, W. (1979). Strikes cost you more than you think. *Harvard Business Review, 57*, 133–138.

International Review of Applied Psychology, 1981.

Ivancevich, J. M., & Matteson, M. T. (1987). *Organizational behavior and management*. Plano, TX: Business Publications.

Ivancevich, J. M., & Matteson, M. T. (1990). *Organizational behavior and management* (2nd ed.). Homewood, IL: Richard D. Irwin.

Izraeli, D. N. (1985). Sex differences in self-reported influence among union officers. *Journal of Applied Psychology, 70*, 148–156.

Jackson, J. H., Morgan, C. P., & Paolillo, J. G. (1986). *Organization theory: A macro perspective for management* (3rd ed.). Englewood Cliffs, NJ: Prentice-Hall.

Jackson, M. P. (1977). *Industrial relations*. London: Croom Helm.

Jackson, S. E., Schuler, R. S., & Rivero, J. C. (1989). Organizational characteristics as predictors of personnel practices. *Personnel Psychology, 42*, 727–786.

Jago, A. G., & Vroom, V. H. (1977). Hierarchical level and leadership style. *Organizational Behavior and Human Performance, 18*, 131–145.

James, L. R. & Jones, A. P. (1976). Organizational structure: A review of structural dimensions and their conceptual relationships with individual attitudes and behavior. *Organizational Behavior and Human Performance, 16*, 74–113.

Jarley, P., Kuruvilla, S., & Casteel, D. (1990). Member-union relations and union satisfaction. *Industrial Relations, 29*, 128–134.

Jewell, L. N. (1985). *Contemporary industrial/organizational psychology*. St. Paul, MN: West Publishing Co.

Jewell, L. N., & Siegall, M. (1990). *Contemporary industrial/organizational psychology* (2nd ed.). St. Paul, MN: West Publishing Co.

Johns, G. (1983). *Organizational behavior: Understanding life at work*. Glenview, IL: Scott, Foresman & Co.

Johns, G. (1988). *Organizational behavior: Understanding life at work* (2nd ed.). Glenview, IL: Scott, Foresman & Co.

Johnson, N. B., Bobko, P., & Hartenian, L. (1986). *Union members' perceptions of job insecurity*. Paper presented at the forty-first annual meeting of the Industrial Relations Research Association, New York.

Joseph, M. I., & Dharmangadan, B. (1987). Union commitment among white collar employees: An examination of certain correlates. *Psychological Studies, 32,* 104–110.

Journal of Occupational Psychology, 1986.

Kahn, R. L., & Tannenbaum, A. S. (1954). Union leadership and member participation. *Personnel Psychology, 10,* 277–292.

Kahn, R. L., Wolfe, D. M., Quinn, R. P., Snoek, J. D., & Rosenthal, R. A. (1964). *Organizational stress: Studies in role conflict and ambiguity*. New York: Wiley.

Kalachek, E., & Raines, F. (1980). Trade unions and hiring standards. *Journal of Labor Research, 1,* 63–75.

Kanter, R. M. (1968). Commitment and social organization: A study of commitment mechanisms in utopian communities. *American Sociological Review, 33,* 449–517.

Kanungo, R. (1982). *Work alienation: An integrative approach*. New York: Wiley.

Kanungo, R. (1979). The concept of alienation and involvement revisited. *Psychological Bulletin, 86,* 119–138.

Karsh, B., & London, J. (1954). The coal miners: A study of union control. *The Quarterly Journal of Economics, 68,* 415–436.

Katz, D. (1964). The motivational basis of organizational behavior. *Behavioral Science, 9,* 131–146.

Katz, D., & Kahn, R. E. (1978). *The social psychology of organizations* (2nd ed.). New York: Wiley.

Katz, H. C. (1985). Collective bargaining and the 1982 bargaining round. In T. A. Kochan (Ed.), *Challenges and choices facing American Labor* (pp. 213–226). Cambridge, MA: MIT Press.

Katz, H. C., Kochan, T. A., & Weber, M. R. (1985). Assessing the effects of industrial relations systems on efforts to improve the quality of working life on organizational effectiveness. *Academy of Management Journal, 28,* 509–526.

Keaveny, T. J., Rose, J., & Fossum, J. (1988). *Predicting support for unionization: Part time versus full time workers and professional/technical blue collar workers*. Presented at the annual conference of the Industrial Relations Research Association, December, New York.

Keith, S. N. (1984). Collective bargaining and strikes among physicians. *Journal of the National Medical Association, 76,* 1117–1121.

Kelloway, E. K., & Catano, V. M. (1989). *Membership participation in union activities: A multivariate analysis*. Paper presented at the annual meeting of the Canadian Psychological Association, Montreal.

Kelloway, E. K., Barling, J., & Fullagar, C. (1990). *Extending a model of union commitment: The roles of union and work attitudes*. Manuscript submitted for publication.

Kelly, J., & Nicholson, N. (1980a). Strikes and other forms of industrial action. *Industrial Relations Journal, 11,* 20–31.

Kelly, J., & Nicholson, N. (1980b). The causation of strikes: A review of theoretical approaches and the potential contribution of social psychology, *Human Relations, 33.* 853–883.

Kemerer, F. R., & Baldridge, J. V. (1975). *Unions on campus*. San Francisco, CA: Jossey-Bass.

Keon, D. (1988). *Union organizing activity in Ontario, 1970–1986*. School of Industrial Relations Research Essay Series No. 16. Kingston, ON: Industrial Relations Centre, Queen's University.

Kerr, C., & Siegel, A. (1954). The interindustry propensity to strike: An international comparison. In A. Kornhauser (Ed.). *Industrial Conflict* (pp. 189–212). New York: McGraw-Hill.

Kessler, I. (1986). Shop stewards in local government revisited. *British Journal of Industrial Relations, 24*, 419–441.

Kidron, A. (1978). Work values and organizational commitment. *Academy of Management Journal, 21*, 239–247.

Kilgour, J. C. (1987). Decertifying a union: A matter of choice. *Personnel Administrator, 32(7)*, 42–51.

Kim, J., & Mueller, C. W. (1978). *Factor analysis: Statistical methods and practical issues*. New York: Sage.

Kirmeyer, S. L., & Shirom, A. (1986). Perceived job autonomy in the manufacturing sector: Effects of unions, gender, and substantive complexity. *Academy of Management Journal, 29*, 832–840.

Klandermans, P. G. (1984a). Mobilization and participation: Social-psychological expansions of resource mobilization theory. *American Sociological Review, 49*, 583–600.

Klandermans, P. G. (1984b). Mobilization and participation in trade union action: An expectancy-value approach. *Journal of Occupational Psychology, 57*, 107–120.

Klandermans, B. (1986). Psychology and trade union participation: Joining, acting, quitting. *Journal of Occupational Psychology, 59*, 189–204.

Klandermans, B. (1989). Union commitment: Replications and tests in the Dutch context. *Journal of Applied Psychology, 74*, 869–875.

Klein, K. J. (1987). Employee stock ownership and employee attitudes: A test of three models. *Journal of Applied Psychology, 72*, 319–332.

Klein, S. M., & Ritti, R. R. (1984). *Understanding organizational behavior* (2nd ed.). Belmont, CA: Wadsworth.

Kochan, T. A. (1978). *Contemporary views of American workers toward trade unions*. Washington, D. C.: U.S. Department of Labor.

Kochan, T. A. (1979). How American workers view labor unions. *Monthly Labor Review, 102*, 23–31.

Kochan, T. A. (1980). *Collective bargaining and industrial relations: From theory to policy and practice*. Homewood, IL: Richard D. Irwin.

Kochan, T. A., & Block, R. N. (1977). An interindustry analysis of bargaining outcomes: Preliminary evidence from two-digit industries. *Quarterly Journal of Economics, 91*, 431–452.

Kochan, T. A., & Helfman, D. E. (1981). The effects of collective bargaining on economic and behavioral job outcomes. In R. C. Ehrenberg (Ed.), *Research in Labor Economics* (Vol. 4), (pp. 321–365). Greenwich, CT. JAI Press.

Kochan, T. A., & Wheeler, H. N. (1975). Municipal collective bargaining: A model and analysis of bargaining outcomes. *Industrial and Labor Relations Review, 29*, 46–66.

Kochan, T. A., Katz, H. C., & McKersie, R. B. (1986). *The transformation of American industrial relations*. New York: Basic Books.

Kochan, T. A., Katz, H. C. & Mowrer, N. R. (1985). Worker participation in American unions. In T. A. Kochan (Ed.), *Challenges and choices facing American labor* (pp. 271–306). Cambridge, MA: MIT Press.

Kochan, T. A., McKersie, R. B., & Chalykoff, J. (1986). The effects of corporate strategy and workplace innovations on union representation. *Industrial and Labor Relations Review, 39,* 487–501.

Kolchin, M. G., & Hyclak, T. (1984). Participation in union activities: A multivariate analysis. *Journal of Labor Research, 5,* 255–261.

Konvitz, M. R. (1970). Labor movement, labor organization, or labor establishment. In J. Seidman (Ed.), *Trade union government and collective bargaining* (pp. 13–36). New York: Praeger.

Korman, A. K. (1977). *Organizational behavior.* Englewood Cliffs, NJ: Prentice-Hall.

Krahn, H., & Lowe, G. S. (1984). Community influences on attitudes to unions. *Relations Industrielles/Industrial Relations, 39,* 93–113.

Krislov, J. (1956). Raiding among the "legitimate" unions. *Industrial and Labor Relations Review, 8,* 19–29.

Krislov, J. (1979). Decertification elections increase but remain no major burden to unions. *Monthly Labor Review, 102(11),* 30–31.

Krislov, J. (1985). Union decertification. *Industrial and Labor Relations Review, 37,* 589–594.

Kryl, I. P. (1990). *Union participation: A review of the literature.* Paper presented at the First European Congress of Psychology.

Kumar, P., Coates, M. L. & Arrowsmith, D. (1987). *The current industrial relations scene in Canada.* Kingston, ON: Industrial Relations Centre, Queen's University.

Kuruvilla, S., Gallagher, D. G., Fiorito, J., & Wakabayashi, M. (1990). Union participation in Japan: Do Western theories apply? *Industrial and Labor Relations Review, 43,* 374–389.

Kyllonen, T. E. (1951). Social characteristics of active unionists. *American Journal of Sociology, 56,* 528–533.

Ladd, R. T., & Lipset, S. M. (1973). *Professors, unions and American higher education.* Berkeley, CA: Carnegie Commission on Higher Education.

Ladd, R. T., Gordon, M. E., Beauvais, L. L., & Morgan, R. L. (1982). Union commitment: Replication and extension. *Journal of Applied Psychology, 67,* 640–644.

Lahne, H. J. (1970). Union constitutions and collective bargaining procedures. In J. Seidman (Ed.), *Trade union government and collective bargaining* (pp. 167–195). New York: Praeger.

Landy, F. J. (1985). *Psychology of work and behavior* (3rd ed.). Homewood, IL: Dorsey.

Landy, F. J. (1989). *Psychology of work and behavior* (4th ed.). Pacific Grove, CA: Brooks/Cole.

Larson, E. W., & Fukami, C. V. (1984). *Union commitment as a moderator of the relationship between company commitment and worker behaviors.* Presented at the Academy of Management meetings, Boston.

Larwood, L. (1984). *Organizational behavior and management.* Boston: Wadsworth.

Lawler, E. E. (1987). The strategic designs of reward systems. In R. M. Steers and L. W. Porter (Eds), *Motivation and work behavior* (pp. 210–227). New York: McGraw-Hill.

Lawler, J. J. (1984). The influence of management consultants on the outcome of union certification elections. *Industrial and Labor Relations Review, 38,* 38–51.

Lawler, J. J. (1986). Union growth and decline: The impact of employer and union tactics. *Journal of Occupational Psychology, 59,* 217–230.

Lawler, J. J. (1988). A typology of employer counter-organizing tactics. In A. M.

Glassman, N. B. Davidson, and T. G. Cummings (Eds.), *Labor relations: Reports from the firing line* (pp. 176–184). Plano, TX: Business Publications.

Lawler, J. J. (1990). *Unionization and deunionization: Strategy, tactics, and outcomes.* Columbia: University of South Carolina Press.

Lawler, J. J., & Hundley, G. (1983). Determinants of certification and decertification activity. *Industrial Relations, 22,* 335–348.

Lawler, J. J., & Walker, J. M. (1984). Representation elections in higher education: Occurrence and outcomes. *Journal of Labor Research, 5,* 63–80.

Lawler, J. J., & West, R. (1985). Impact of union-avoidance strategy in representation elections. *Industrial Relations, 24,* 406–420.

Lawler, J. J., Kuleck, W., Rhode, J., & Sorenson, J. (1975). Job choice and post decision dissonance. *Organizational Behavior and Human Performance, 13,* 133–145.

Leigh, D. E. (1981). The effect of unionism on workers' valuation of future pensions benefits. *Industrial and Labor Relations Review, 34,* 510–521.

Leigh, D. E. (1986). Union preferences, job satisfaction and the union-voice hypothesis. *Industrial and Labor Relations Review, 25,* 65–71.

Leigh, J. P. (1982). Are unionized blue collar jobs more hazardous than nonunionized blue collar jobs? *Journal of Labor Research, 3,* 349–357.

LeLouarn, J. Y. (1979). Predicting union vote from worker attitudes and perceptions. *Proceedings of the Thirty-second Annual Meeting of the Industrial Relations Research Association,* (pp. 72–82). Madison, WI: Industrial Relations Research Association.

Leonard, J. S. (1986). Unions, turnover and employment variation. In D. Lewin, D. B. Lipsky, and D. Sockwell (Eds.), *Advances in industrial and labor relations* (Vol. 3), (pp. 119–151). Greenwich, CT: JAI Press.

Leopold, J., & Beaumont, P. (1984). The turnover and continuity of safety representatives. *Industrial Relations Journal, 15,* 74–82.

Lester, R. (1958). *As unions mature.* Princeton, NJ: Princeton University Press.

Lewin, D., & Feuille, P. (1982). Behavioral research in industrial relations. *Industrial and Labor Relations Review, 36,* 341–360.

Likert, R. (1967). *The human organization: Its management and value.* New York: McGraw-Hill.

Lipset, S. M. (1960). *Political man.* New York: Doubleday.

Lipset, S. M. (1986). Labor unions in the public mind. In S. M. Lipset (Ed.), *Unions in transition: Entering the second century* (pp. 287–321). San Francisco: ICS Press.

Lipset, S. M., Trow, M. A., & Coleman, J. B. (1956). *Union democracy: The internal politics of the International Typographical Union.* Glencoe, Ill: The Free Press.

Locke, E. A. (1983). The nature and causes of job satisfaction. In M. D. Dunnette (Ed.). *Handbook of industrial and organizational psychology* (pp. 1297–1350). New York: Wiley.

Lodahl, T. M., & Kejner, M. (1965). The definition and measurement of job involvement. *Journal of Applied Psychology, 49,* 24–33.

Lowe, G. S., & Krahn, H. (1989). Recent trends in public support for unions in Canada. *Journal of Labor Research, 10,* 391–410.

Lund, R. (1963). Some aspects of the Danish shop steward system. *British Journal of Industrial Relations, 1,* 370–382.

Luthans, F. (1985). *Organizational behavior* (fourth ed.). New York: McGraw-Hill.

Luthans, F. (1989). *Organizational behavior* (fifth ed.). New York: McGraw-Hill.

Lynch, L. M., & Sandver, M. H. (1987). Determinants of the decertification process. Evidence from employer-initiated elections. *Journal of Labor Research, 8,* 85–91.

MacBride, A., Lancee, W., & Freeman, S. J. J. (1981). The psychosocial impact of a labor dispute. *Journal of Occupational Psychology, 54*, 125–133.

Magenau, J. M., Martin, J. E., & Peterson, M. M. (1988). Dual and unilateral commitment among stewards and rank-and-file union members. *Academy of Management Journal, 31*, 359–376.

Mahoney, T. A. (1979). Organizational hierarchy and position worth. *Academy of Management Journal, 22*, 726–737.

Maier, N. R. F., & Verser, G. C. (1982). *Psychology in industrial organizations* (5th ed.). Boston: Houghton Mifflin.

Mancke, R. B. (1971). American trade union growth, 1900–1960: A comment. *Quarterly Journal of Economics, 85*, 187–193.

Maranto, C. I., & Fiorito, J. (1987). The effect of union characteristics on the outcome of NLRB certification elections. *Industrial and Labor Relations Review, 40*, 225–240.

Marchington, M. (1983). Typologies of shop stewards: A reconsideration. *Industrial Relations Journal, 14*, 34–48.

Martin, J. E. (1981). Dual allegiance in public sector unionism. *International Review of Applied Psychology, 30*, 245–259.

Martin, J. E. (1984). A method for predicting contested union representation elections. *Journal of Collective Negotiations, 13*, 327–338.

Martin, J. E. (1985). Employee characteristics and representation election outcomes. *Industrial and Labor Relations Review, 38*, 365–376.

Martin, J. E. (1986). Predictors of individual propensity to strike. *Industrial and Labor Relations Review, 39*, 214–227.

Maxey, C., & Mohrman, S. A. (1980). Worker attitudes toward unions: A study integrating industrial relations and organizational behavior perspectives. In B. D. Dennis (Ed.), *Proceedings of the Thirty-third Annual Meeting, December 28–30* (pp. 326–333). Madison, WI: Industrial Relations Research Association.

McCarthy, W. E. J. (1967). *Research papers 1. The role of shop stewards in British industrial relations: A survey of existing information and research.* London: Royal Commission on Trade Unions and Employers' Associations.

McCarthy, W. E. J., & Parker, S. R. (1968). *Research papers 10. Shop stewards and workshop relations: The results of a study undertaken by the Government Social Survey for the Royal Commission on Trade Unions and Employers' Associations.* London: Royal Commission on Trade Unions and Employers' Associations.

McCormick, E. J., & Ilgen, D. R. (1988). *Industrial and organizational psychology* (8th ed.). Englewood Cliffs, NJ: Prentice-Hall.

McGregor, D. (1960). *The human side of the enterprise.* New York: McGraw-Hill.

McShane, S. L. (1986a). The multidimensionality of union participation. *Journal of Occupational Psychology, 59*, 177–187.

McShane, S. L. (1986b). A path analysis of participation in union administration. *Industrial Relations, 25*, 72–80.

Medoff, J. (1979). Layoffs and alternatives under trade unions in U.S. manufacturing. *American Economic Review, 69*, 380–395.

Meissner, M. (1971). The long arm of the job: A study of work and leisure. *Industrial Relations, 10*, 239–260.

Mellor, S. (1990). The relationship between membership decline and union commitment: A field study of local unions in crisis. *Journal of Applied Psychology, 75*, 258–267.

Mercer, D. E., & Weir, D. T. (1972). Attitudes to work and trade unionism among white-collar workers. *Industrial Relations Journal, 3*, 49–60.

Messick, D. M. (1973). To join or not to join: An approach to the unionization decision. *Organizational Behavior and Human Performance, 10*, 145–156.

Messick, D. M. (1974). When a little "group interest" goes a long way: A note on social motives and union joining. *Organizational Behavior and Human Performance, 12*, 331–334.

Michels, R. (1959). *Political parties*. Glencoe, Ill: Free Press.

Middlemist, R. D., & Hitt, M. A. (1988). *Organizational behavior: Managerial strategies for performance*. Sr. Paul, MN: West Publishing Co.

Middleton, J. (1990). National Union of Mineworkers campaign for racial equality. *Sechaba, 24(7)*, 11–21.

Miller, G. W., & Young, J. F. (1955). Membership participation in the trade union local. *American Journal of Economics and Sociology, 15*, 36–43.

Miller, R. W., Zeiller, F. A., & Miller, G. W. (1965). *The practice of local union leadership: A study of five union locals*. Columbus: Ohio State University Press.

Mills, C. W. (1956). *White collar*. New York: Oxford University Press.

Mills, D. Q. (1985). Seniority versus ability in promotion decisions. *Industrial and Labor Relations Review, 39*, 421–425.

Minar, J. B. (1988). *Organizational behavior: Performance and productivity*. New York: Random House.

Mitchell, D. J. B. (1980). Unions and wages: What we've learned since the '50's. *California Management Review, 22*, 56–64.

Mitchell, T. R. (1978). *People in organizations: Understanding their behavior*. New York: McGraw-Hill.

Mobley, W. H. (1977). Intermediate linkages in the relationship between job satisfaction and employee turnover. *Journal of Applied Psychology, 62*, 237–240.

Mobley, W. H. (1982). *Employee turnover: Causes, consequences and control*. Reading, MA: Addison-Wesley.

Montgomery, B. R. (1989). The influence of attitudes and normative pressures on voting decisions in a union certification election. *Industrial and Labor Relations Review, 42*, 262–279.

Moore, R. J. (1980). The motivation to become a shop steward. *British Journal of Industrial Relations, 18*, 90–98.

Moore, W. J., & Pearce, D. K. (1976). Union growth: A test of the Ahenfelter-Pencavel model. *Industrial Relations, 15*, 244–247.

Moorhead, G., & Griffin, R. W. (1989). *Organizational behavior* (2nd ed.). Boston: Houghton/Mifflin.

Morgan, C. A. (1988). The union shop deauthorization poll. *Industrial and Labor Relations Review, 12*, 79–85.

Morris, W. J., & Sherman, J. D. (1981). Generalizability of organizational commitment model. *Academy of Management Journal, 24*, 512–526.

Morris, W. J., & Steers, R. M. (1980). Structural influences on organizational commitment. *Journal of Vocational Behavior, 17*, 50–57.

Mowday, R. T. (1983). Equity theory predictions of behavior in organizations. In R. M. Steers and L. W. Porter (Eds.), *Motivation and work behavior* (pp. 91–113). New York: McGraw-Hill.

Mowday R. T., Porter, L. W., & Steers, R. M. (1982). *Employee-organization linkages: The psychology of commitment, absenteeism and turnover*. New York: Academic Press.

Muchinsky, P. M. (1977). Employee absenteeism: A review of the literature. *Journal of Vocational Behavior, 10*, 316–340.

Muchinsky, P. M. (1987). *Psychology applied to work* (2nd ed.). Chicago: Dorsey.

Muchinsky, P. M. (1990). *Psychology applied to work* (3rd ed.). Pacific Grove, CA: Brooks/Cole.

Nash, A. (1984). British and American union stewards: A comparative analysis. *Labor Studies Journal, 9*, 46–65.

Nichols, D. (1988). Pepsi and its unions: Confrontation goes flat. *Management Review, 77(2)*, 40–42.

Nicholson, N. (1976). The role of the shop steward: An empirical case study. *Industrial Relations Journal, 7*, 15–26.

Nicholson, N. (1979). Industrial relations climate: A case study approach. *Personnel Review, 8*, 20–25.

Nicholson, N., & Kelly, J. (1980). The psychology of strikes. *Journal of Occupational Behavior, 1*, 275–284.

Nicholson, N., Ursell, G., & Blyton, P. (1980). Social background, attitudes and behavior of white collar shop stewards. *British Journal of Industrial Relations, 18*, 231–238.

Nicholson, N., Ursell, G., & Blyton, P. (1981). *The dynamics of white collar unionism: A study of local union participation.* London: Academic Press.

Nicholson, N., Ursell, G., & Lubbock, J. (1981). Membership participation in a white-collar union. *Industrial Relations, 20*, 162–178.

Odewahn, C. A., & Petty, M. M. (1980). A comparison of levels of job satisfaction, role stress, and personal competence between union members and nonmembers. *Academy of Management Journal, 23*, 150–155.

Olson, A. (1982). *Union organizational characteristics and bargaining outcomes.* M. A. Tutorial. Champaign: University of Illinois.

Olson, C. A., & Berger, C. J. (1983). The relationship between seniority, ability, and the promotion of union and nonunion workers. In D. Lewin, D. B. Lipsky and D. Sockell (Eds.), *Advances in industrial and labor relations* (Vol. 1), (pp. 91–129). Greenwich, CT: JAI Press.

Organ, D. W., & Bateman, T. (1986). *Organizational behavior: An applied psychological approach* (3rd ed.). Plano, TX: Business Publications.

Partridge, B. (1977). The activities of shop stewards. *Industrial Relations Journal, 8*, 28–42.

Pateman, C. (1970). *Participation and democratic theory.* London: Cambridge University Press.

Pearce, T. G., & Peterson, R. B. (1987). Regionality in NLRB decertification cases. *Journal of Labor Research, 8*, 253–269.

Peck, S. M. (1963). *The rank-and-file leader.* New Haven, CT: College and University Press.

Pedler, M. J. (1973). Shop stewards as leaders. *Industrial Relations Journal, 4*, 43–60.

Pedler, M. J. (1974). The training implications of the shop stewards' leadership role. *Industrial Relations Journal, 5*, 57–69.

Perline, M. M., & Lorenz, V. R. (1970). Factors influencing member participation in trade union activities. *American Journal of Economics and Sociology, 29,* 425–437.

Perrow, C. (1972). *Complex organization: A critical essay.* Glenview, Ill: Scott Freeman.

Pestonjee, D. M., Singh, A. P., & Singh, S. P. (1981). Attitude towards union as related to morale and job involvement. *Inernational Review of Applied Psychology, 30*, 209–216.

Peterson, F. (1957). Management efficiency and collective bargaining. *Industrial and Labor Relations Review, 1*, 29–49.

Pettman, B. O. (1971). *A bibliography on strikes.* Bradford: Institute of Scientific Business.

Pfeffer, J., & Davis-Blake, A. (1990). Unions and job satisfaction: An alternative view. *Work and Occupations, 17,* 259–283.

Pinder, C. C. (1984). *Work motivation: Theory, issues and applications.* Glenview, IL: Scott, Foresman & Co.

Porter, L. W., & Lawler, E. E. (1965). Properties of organization structure in relation to job attitudes and job behavior. *Psychological Bulletin, 64,* 23–51.

Porter, L. W., Lawler, E. E., & Hackman, J. R. (1975). *Behavior in organizations.* New York: McGraw-Hill.

Porter, L. W., & Smith, F. J. (1970). *The etiology of organizational commitment,* photocopy. Irvine: University of California.

Porter, L. W., & Steers, R. M. (1973). Organizational, work and personal factors in employee turnover and absenteeism. *Psychological Bulletin, 80,* 151–176.

Portwood, J., Pierson, D., & Schmidt, S. (1981). When less is more: A study of the participation/satisfaction relationship in unions. *Preceedings of the Forty-First Annual Meeting of the Academy of Management.* San Diego, CA: Academy of Management.

Premack, S. L., & Hunter, J. E. (1988). Individual unionization decisions. *Psychological Bulletin, 103,* 223–234.

Premeaux, S. R., Mondy, W., & Bethke, A. (1987). Decertification: Fulfilling unions' destiny? *Personnel Journal, 66(6),* 144–148.

Prien, E. P., & Ronan, W. W. (1971). An analysis of organizational characteristics. *Organizational Behavior and Human Performance, 6,* 215–234.

Prosten, R. (1978). The longest season: Union organizing in the last decade, a/k/a How come one team has to play with its shoelaces tied together? *Proceedings of the Thirty First Annual Meeting* (pp. 240–249). Madison, WI: Industrial Relations Research Association.

Pugh, D. S., Hickson, D. J., Hinings, C. R., & Turner, C. (1968). Dimensions of organizational structure. *Administrative Science Quarterly, 13,* 65–105.

Purcell, T. V. (1953). *The worker speaks his mind on company and union.* Cambridge: Harvard University Press.

Purcell, T. V. (1960). *Blue collar man.* Cambridge, MA: Harvard University Press.

Quinn, R. E., Faerman, S. R., Thompson, M. P., & McGrath, M. R. (1990). *Becoming a manager: A competency framework.* New York: Wiley.

Quinn, R. P., & Staines, G. L. (1977). *The 1977 Quality of Employment Survey: Descriptive Statistics with Comparison Data from the 1969–1970 and 1972–1973 Surveys.* Ann Arbor: Institute for Social Research, The University of Michigan.

Robinowitz, S., & Hall, D. (1977). Organizational research on job involvement. *Psychological Bulletin, 84,* 245–258.

Ramaswamy, E. A. (1977). The participatory dimension of trade union democracy: A comparative sociological view. *Sociology, 11,* 465–480.

Rambo, W. W. (1982). *Work and organizational behavior.* New York: Holt, Rinehart & Winston.

Rashid, S. A., & Archer, M. (1983). *Organizational behavior.* Toronto: Methuen.

Reitz, H. J. (1987). *Behavior in organizations* (3rd ed.). Homewood, IL: Richard D. Irwin.

Rhodes, S. R., & Steers, R. M. (1981). Conventional vs. worker-owned organizations. *Human Relations, 34,* 1013–1035.

Riddell, W. C. (1986). Canadian labor relations: An overview. In W. C. Riddell (Ed.), *Canadian labor relations.* Toronto: University of Toronto Press.

Riggio, R. E. (1990). *Introduction to industrial/organizational psychology*. Glenview, IL: Scott, Foresman & Co.

Robbins, S. P. (1988). *Essentials of organizational behavior* (3rd ed.). Englewood Cliffs, NJ: Prentice-Hall.

Robbins, S. P. (1989). *Essentials of organizational behavior* (4th ed.). Englewood Cliffs, NJ: Prentice-Hall.

Robertson, N., & Sams, K. I. (1978). Research note: On the work pattern of union officers. *Industrial Relations Journal, 9*, 61–64.

Robey, D. (1986). *Designing organizations* (2nd ed.). Homewood, IL: Richard D. Irwin.

Robinson, J. G., & McIlwee, J. S. (1989). Obstacles to unionization in high-tech industries. *Work and Occupations, 16*, 115–136.

Roby, P., & Uttal, L. (1988). Trade union stewards: Handling union, family and employment responsibilities. In B. A. Gutek, A. H. Stromberg, & L. Larwood (Eds.), *Women and work: An annual review* (Vol. 3), (pp. 215–248). Beverly Hills: Sage.

Rogow, R. (1967). Membership participation and centralized control. *Industrial Relations, 7*, 132–145.

Roomkin, M. (1976). Union structure, internal control and strike activity. *Industrial and Labor Relations Review, 29*, 198–217.

Roomkin, M., & Block, R. (1981). Case processing time and the outcome of represen-.tative elections: Some empirical evidence. *University of Illinois Law Review, 1*, 75–97.

Roomkin, M., & Juris, H. A. (1978). Unions in the traditional sectors: The mid-life passage of the labor movement. In B. D. Dennis (Ed.), *Proceedings of the Thirty-First Annual Meeting* (pp. 212–223). Madison, WI: Industrial Relations Research Association.

Rose, E. (1974). On the nature of work and union involvement: A study of London busmen. *Industrial Relations Journal, 5*, 27–35.

Rosen, H., & Rosen, R. (1955). *The union member speaks*. Englewood Cliffs, NJ: Prentice-Hall.

Rosen, H., & Stagner, R. (1981). Industrial/organizational psychology and unions: A viable relationship? *Professional Psychology, 11*, 477–483.

Rosier, N., & Little, T. (1986). Public opinion, trade unions and industrial relations. *Journal of Occupational Psychology, 59*, 259–272.

Rotter, J. B. (1966). Generalized expectancies for internal versus external control of reinforcement. *Psychological Monographs, 80* (1, Whole No. 609).

Saal, F. E., & Knight, P. A. (1988). *Industrial/organization psychology: Science and practice*. Belmont, CA: Wadsworth.

Salancik, G. R. (1977). Commitment and the control of organizational behavior and belief. In B. M. Staw & G. R. Salancik (Eds.), *New directions in organizational behavior* (pp. 1–54). Chicago: St. Clair Press.

Sandver, M. H. (1980). Predictors of outcomes in NLRB Certification elections. *Preceedings of the Twenty-Third Annual Meeting of the Midwest Academy of Management* (pp. 174–181). Cincinnati Ohio.

Sandver, M. H. (1982). South-non South differentials in the National Labor Relations Board certification elections. *Journal of Labor Research, 3*, 13–20.

Sandver, M. H., & Heneman, H. G. (1981). Union growth through the election process. *Industrial Relations, 20*, 109–116.

Sayles, L. R., & Strauss, G. (1953). *The local union*. Chicago: Harcourt, Brace and World.

Sayles, L. R., & Strauss, G. (1967). *The local union*. New York: Harcourt.

Schein, E. H. (1980). *Organizational psychology* (3rd ed.). Englewood Cliffs, NJ: Prentice-Hall.

Schermerhorn, J. R., Hunt, J. G., & Osborn, R. N. (1988). *Managing organizational behavior* (3rd ed.). New York: Wiley.

Schneider, B. (1985). Organizational behavior. *Annual Review of Psychology, 36,* 573–611.

Schriesheim, C. A. (1978). Job satisfaction, attitudes toward unions and voting in a union representation election. *Journal of Applied Psychology, 63,* 548–552.

Schuller, T., & Robertson, D. (1983). How representatives allocate their time: Shop steward activity and membership contact. *British Journal of Industrial Relations, 21,* 330–342.

Schultz, D. P. (1982). *Psychology and industry today* (3rd ed.). New York: Macmillan.

Schultz, D. P., & Schultz, S. E. (1986). *Psychology and industry today* (4th ed.). New York: Macmillan.

Schultz, D. P., & Schultz, S. E. (1990). *Psychology and industry today* (5th ed.). New York: Macmillan.

Schutt, R. K. (1982). Models of militancy: Support for strikes and work actions among public sector employees. *Industrial and Labor Relations Review, 35,* 406–422.

Schwochau, S. (1987). Union effects on job attitudes. *Industrial and Labor Relations Review, 10, 209–224.

Scoville, J. G. (1973). Some determinants of the structure of labor movements. In A. Sturmthal & J. G. Scoville (Eds.), *The international labor movement in transition* (pp. 58–78). Urbana: University of Illinois Press.

Seeman, M. (1959). On the meaning of alienation. *American Sociological Review, 24,* 783–791.

Seeman, M. (1984). A legacy of protest: The "Events of May" in retrospect. *Political Psychology, 5,* 437–464.

Seidman, J. (1953). Democracy in labor unions. *Journal of Political Economy, 61,* 223.

Seidman, J., & Tagliacozzo, B. L. (1960). Union government and union leadership. In N. W. Chamberlain, F. C. Pierson, & T. Wolfson (Eds.), *A decade of industrial relations research: 1946–1956* (pp. 69–91). New York: Harper & Bros.

Seidman, J., London, J., & Karsh, B. (1950). Leadership in a local union. *American Journal of Sociology, 56,* 229–237.

Seidman, J., London, J., Karsh, B., & Tagliacozzo, D. L. (1958). *The worker views his union.* Chicago: University of Chicago Press.

Shalev, M. (1983). Strikes and the crisis: Industrial conflict and unemployment in the Western nations. *Economic and industrial Democracy, 4,* 417–460.

Sheflin, N., Troy, L., & Koeller, T. (1981). Structural stability in models of American trade union growth. *Quarterly Journal of Economics, 85,* 77–88.

Sherer, P. D., & Morishima, M. (1989). Roads and roadblocks to dual commitment: Similar and dissimilar antecedents of union and company commitment. *Journal of Labor Research, 10,* 311–330.

Shirom, A. (1977). Union militancy: Structural and personal determinants. *Industrial Relations, 16,* 152–162.

Shirom, A. (1985). The labor relations system: A proposed conceptual framework. *Relations Industrielles/Industrial Relations, 40,* 303–323.

Shirom, A., & Kirmeyer, S. L. (1988). The effects of unions on blue collar role stresses and somatic strain. *Journal of Organizational Behavior, 9,* 29–42.

Shorter, E., & Tilly, C. (1974). *Strikes in France, 1830–1968.* London: Cambridge University Press.

Shostak, A. B. (1964). Industrial psychology and the trade unions: A matter of mutual indifference. In G. Fisk (Ed.), *The frontiers management psychology*. New York: Harper.

Shostak, A. B. (1985). Union efforts to relieve blue collar stress. In C. L. Cooper & M. J. Smith (Eds.). *Job stress and blue collar work* (pp. 195–205). New York: Wiley.

Simpson, D. B., & Peterson, R. B. (1972). Leadership behavior, need satisfactions, and role perceptions of labor leaders: A behavioral analysis, *Personnel Psychology, 25*, 673–686.

Skelton, B. R., & Yandle, B. (1982). Piece rate pay. *Journal of Labor Research, 3*, 201–209.

Slichter, S. H. (1947). The government of trade union. In *The challenge of industrial relations: Trade unions, management, and the public interest* (pp. 132–143). Ithaca: Cornell University.

Slichter, S. H., Healy, J. J., & Livernash, E. R. (1960). *The impact of collective bargaining on management*. Washington, D. C.: Brookings Institution.

Smith, P. C., Kendall, L. M., & Hulin, C. L. (1969). *The measurement of satisfaction in work and retirement*. Chicago: Rand-McNally.

Smith, R. L., & Hopkins, A. H. (1979). Public employee attitudes toward unions. *Industrial and Labor Relations Review, 32*, 484–495.

Smither, R. D. (1988). *The psychology of work and human performance*. New York: Harper & Row.

Spencer, D. G. (1986). Employee voice and employee retention. *Academy of Management Journal, 29*, 488–502.

Spinrad, W. (1960). Correlates of trade union participation: A summary of the literature. *American Sociological Review, 25*, 237–244.

Stagner, R. (1954). Dual allegiance to union and management (A symposium). *Personnel Psychology, 7*, 41–66.

Stagner, R. (1956). *Psychology of industrial conflict*. New York: Wiley.

Stagner, R. (1981). Introduction. *International Review of Applied Psychology, 30*, 135.

Stagner, R., & Eflal, B. (1982). Internal union dynamics during a strike: A quasi-experimental study. *Journal of Applied Psychology, 67*, 37–44.

Starling, G. (1984). *The changing environment of business*. Boston: Kent Publishing Co.

Staw, B. M. (1977). *Two sides of commitment*. Paper presented at the National Meeting of the Academy of Management, Orlando, Florida.

Steele, E., Myles, W. R., & McIntyre, S. C. (1954). Unionism and personnel policies in the Southeast. *Industrial and Labor Relations Review, 8*, 253–264.

Steers, R. M. (1977). Antecedents and outcomes of organizational commitment. *Administrative Science Quarterly, 27*, 46–56.

Steers, R. M. (1984). *Introduction to organizational behavior* (2nd ed.). Glenview, IL: Scott, Foresman & Co.

Steers, R. M., & Rhodes, S. R. (1978). Major influences on employee attendance: A process model. *Journal of Applied Psychology, 63*, 391–407.

Stern, R. N. (1978). Methodological issues in quantitative strike analysis. *Industrial Relations, 17*, 32–42.

Stevens, J. M., Beyer, J. M., & Trice, H. M. (1978). Assessing personal, role, and organizational predictors of management commitment. *Academy of Management Journal, 21*, 380–396.

Stogdill, R. M., & Coons, A. E. (1957). *Leader behavior: Its discription and measurement*. Bureau of Business Research Monographs, 88, Ohio State University.

Stoner, C. R., & Arora, R. (1987). An investigation of the relationship between selected variables and the psychological health of strike participants. *Journal of Occupational Psychology, 60,* 61–71.

Strauss, G. (1977a). Union government in the U.S.: Research past and future *Industrial Relations, 16,* 215–242.

Strauss, G. (1977b). Bridging the gap between law and psychology: A first but difficult step. *Contemporary Psychology, 22,* 833–834.

Strauss, G. (1979). Can social psychology contribute to industrial relations? In G. M. Stephenson & C. J. Brotherton (Eds.), *Industrial relations: A social psychological approach.* Chichester: Wiley.

Strauss, G., & Sayles, L. R. (1953). Occupation and the selection of local union officers. *The American Journal of Sociology, 58,* 585–591.

Summers, T. P., Betton, J. H., & DeCotiis, T. A. (1986). Voting for and against unions: A decision model. *Academy of Management Review, 11,* 643–655.

Swann, J. P. (1983). The decertification of a union: The rules of the game. *Personnel Administrator, 28(1),* 47–51.

Szilagyi, A. D., & Wallace, M. J. (1983). *Organizational behavior and performance* (3rd ed.). Glenview, IL: Scott, Foresman & Co.

Tagliacozzo, D. L., & Seidman, J. (1956). A typology of rank and file union members. *Amerian Journal of Sociology, 61,* 546–553.

Tannenbaum, A. S., & Kahn, R. L. (1958). *Participation in local unions.* Evanston, IL: Row, Peterson.

Tannenbaum, F. (1952). *A philosophy of labor.* New York: Alfred Knopf.

Taylor, F. W. (1911). *Scientific management.* New York: Harper & Row.

Tetrick, L. E. (1989). Paper presented at the Canadian Psychological Association, Halifax.

Tetrick, L. E., Thacker, J. W., & Fields, M. W. (1989). Evidence for the stability of the four dimensions of the Commitment to the Union Scale. *Journal of Applied Psychology, 74,* 819–822.

Thacker, J. W., & Rosen, H. (1986). Dynamics of employee reactance to company and union dual allegiance revisited and expanded. *Relations Industrielles, 41,* 128–144.

Thacker, J. W., Fields, M. W., & Barclay, L. A. (1990). Union commitment: An examination of antecedent and outcome factors. *Journal of Occupational Psychology, 63,* 33–48.

Thacker, J. W., Fields, M. W., & Tetrick, L. E. (1989). The factor structure of union commitment: An application of confirmatory factor analysis. *Journal of Applied Psychology, 74,* 228–232.

Thacker, J. W., Tetrick, L. E., Fields, M. W., & Rempel, D. (1991). Commitment to the union: A comparison of United States and Canadian workers. *Journal of Organizational Behavior, 12,* 63–71.

Thompson, C. W. (1987). Managing changes in clinical and administrative roles: Staying on top with a union. *Journal of Mental Health Administration, 14(2),* 32–36.

Thompson, D. E., & Borglum, R. P. (1973). A case study of employee attitudes and labor unrest. *Industrial and Labor Relations Review, 27,* 74–83.

Tossi, H. L., Rizzo, J. R., & Carroll, S. J. (1990). *Managing organizational behavior* (2nd ed.). NY: Harper & Row.

Towers, B. (1989). Running the gauntlet: British trade unions under Thatcher, 1979–1988. *Industrial and Labor Relations Review, 42,* 163–188.

Troy, L. (1986). The rise and fall of American trade unions: The labor movement from FDR to RR. In S. M. Lipset (Ed.), *Unions in transition* (pp. 3–38). San Francisco: ICS Press.

Turner, H. A. (1962). *Trade union growth, structure and policy*. London: Allen & Unwin.

Umstot, D. (1988). Understanding organizational behavior (2nd ed.). St. Paul, MN: West Publishing Co.

Van de Vall, M. (1970). *Labor organizations*. London: Cambridge University Press.

Van Maanen, J. V. (1977). Toward a theory of the career. In J. V. Van Maanen (Ed.), *Organizational careers: Some new perspectives* (pp. 161–179). New York: Wiley.

Van Maanen, J. V., & Schein, E. H. (1979). Toward a theory of organizational socialization. In B. M. Staw (Ed.), *Research in organizational behavior*, (Vol. 1), (pp. 209–264). Greenwich, CT: JAI Press.

von Haller-Gilmer, B. (1975). *Applied psychology: Adjustments in life and work* (2nd ed.). New York: McGraw-Hill.

von Haller Gilmer, B., & Deci, E. L. (1977). *Industrial and organizational psychology* (4th ed.). New York: McGraw-Hill.

Voos, P. B. (1983). Union organizing expenditures: Determinants and their implications for union growth. *Journal of Labor Research*, *8*, 19–30.

Vroom, V. H. (1964). *Work and motivation*. New York: Wiley.

Vroom, V., & Deci, E. L. (1971). The stability of post-decisional dissonance: A follow-up study of the job attitudes of business school graduates. *Organizational Behavior and Human Performance*, *6*, 36–49.

Walker, J. M., & Lawler, J. J. (1979). Dual unions and political processes in organizations. *Industrial Relations*, *13*, 32–43.

Walker, J. M., & Lawler, J. J. (1984). Representation elections in higher education: Occurrence and outcomes. *Journal of Labor Research*, *5*, 63–80.

Wanous, J. P. (1980). *Organizational entry: Recruitment, selection and socialization of newcomers*. Reading, MA: Addison-Wesley.

Warner, K. L., Chisholm, R. F., & Munzenrider, R. F. (1978). Motives for unionization among state social service employees. *Public Personnel Management*, *8*, 181–191.

Warner, M. (1975). Unions as complex organizations: Strategy, structure and the need for administrative innovation. *Industrial Relations/Relations Industrielles*, *30*, 43–59.

Warr, P. (1981). Psychological studies of union-management relations in the United Kingdom. *International Review of Applied Psychology*, *30*, 311–320.

Webb, S., & Webb, B. (1897). *Industrial democracy*. London: Longmans.

Weber, M. (1947). *Theory of social and economic organization*. Trans. A. M. Henderson & T. Parsons of Pt. I., *Wirtschaft und Gesellschaft*. New York: Oxford.

Weeks, J. L. (1985). The effect of unionization on safety in bituminous deep mines: Comment. *Journal of Labor Research*, *6*, 209–210.

Wertheimer, B. M., & Nelson, A. H. (1975). *Trade union women: A study of their participation in New York City locals*. New York: Praeger.

Wexley, K. N., & Yukl, G. A. (1984). *Organizational behavior and personnel psychology*. Homewood, IL: Richard D. Irwin.

White, B. (1988). *Hard bargains: My life on the line*. Toronto: McLelland and Stewart.

Whyte, W. F. (1944). Who goes union and why. *Personnel Journal*, *23*, 215–230.

Wickens, C. D. (1984). *Engineering psychology and human performance*. Columbus, OH: Charles E. Merrill.

Wilensky, H. (1960). Work, careers and social integration. *International Social Science Journal*, *12*, 543–560.

Wilson, G. D. (Ed.). (1973). *The psychology of conservatism*. New York: Academic Press.

Winch, G. (1980). Shop steward tenure and workplace organization. *Industrial Relations Journal*, *11*, 50–62.

Winch, G. (1983). The turnover of shop stewards. *Industrial Relations Journal*, *14*, 84–86.

Won, G. (1964/65). *Local union leadership orientation and union democracy*. Reprint series No. 72, School of Labor and Industrial Relations. Michigan State University.

Wood, S., & Pedler, M. (1978). On losing their virginity: The story of a strike at the Grosvenor Hotel, Sheffield. *Industrial Relations Journal, 9*, 15–37.

Work in America (1972). Report of a Special Task Force to the Secretary of Health, Education, and Welfare. Cambridge, MA: MIT Press.

Worrall, J. C., & Butler, R. J. (1983). Health conditions and job hazards: Union and nonunion jobs. *Journal of Labor Research, 4*, 339–347.

Yanish, D. L. (1985). Healthcare unions lose about 60% of decertification elections since '77. *Modern Healthcare, 15*, 60.

Youngblood, S. A., Mobley, W. H., & DeNisi, A. S. (1981). Attitudes, perceptions, and intentions to vote in a union certification election: An empirical investigation. In *Proceedings of the Thirty-fourth Annual Meeting of the Industrial Relations Research Association* (pp. 244–253). Madison, WI: Industrial Relations Research Association.

Youngblood, S. A., DeNisi, A., Molleston, J. L., & Mobley, W. (1984). The impact of work environment, instrumentality beliefs, perceived labor union image, and subjective norms on union voting intentions. *Academy of Management Journal, 27*, 576–590.

Zalesny, M. D. (1985). Comparison of economic and noneconomic factors in predicting faculty vote preference in a union representation election. *Journal of Applied Psychology, 70*, 243–256.

Author Index

Note: Italicized page numbers indicate an "et al." text citation.

Subject Index